InDesign Type

Professional Typography with Adobe InDesign CS2

Nigel French

InDesign Type: Professional Typography with Adobe InDesign CS2
Nigel French

This Adobe Press book is published by Peachpit

For information on Adobe Press books, contact:
Peachpit
1249 Eighth Street
Berkeley, CA 94710
510/524-2178
800/283-9444
510/524-2221 (fax)

For the latest on Adobe Press books, go to www.adobepress.com
To report errors, please send a note to errata@peachpit.com
Peachpit is a division of Pearson Education.
Copyright © 2006 Nigel French

Editor: Douglas Cruickshank
Acquisitions Editor: Pam Pfiffner
Production Editor: Susan Rimerman
Copyeditor: Hope Frazier
Compositor: Kim Scott, Bumpy Design
Indexer: Patti Schiendelman
Cover Design: Aren Howell
Interior Design: Charlene Charles-Will and Kim Scott

Notice of Rights

All rights reserved. No part of this book may be reproduced or transmitted in any form by any means, electronic, mechanical, photocopying, recording, or otherwise, without the prior written permission of the publisher. For information on getting permission for reprints and excerpts, contact permissions@peachpit.com.

Notice of Liability

The information in this book is distributed on an "As Is" basis, without warranty. While every precaution has been taken in the preparation of the book, neither the author nor Peachpit shall have any liability to any person or entity with respect to any loss or damage caused or alleged to be caused directly or indirectly by the instructions contained in this book or by the computer software and hardware products described in it.

Trademarks

Adobe InDesign is a registered trademark of Adobe Systems in the United States and/or other countries.

Many of the designations used by manufacturers and sellers to distinguish their products are claimed as trademarks. Where those designations appear in this book, and Peachpit was aware of the trademark claim, the designations appear as requested by the owner of the trademark. All other product names and services identified throughout the book are used in an editorial fashion only and for the benefit of such companies with no intention of infringement of the trademark. No such use, or the use of any trade name, is intended to convey endorsement or other affiliation with this book.

ISBN 0-321-38544-6

9 8 7 6 5 4 3 2 1

Printed and bound in the United States of America

Acknowledgments

I'd like to say a big thank you to the following folks for their help: My editor Douglas Cruickshank, technical editor Michael Ninness, acquisitions editor Pam Pfiffner, book designers Charlene Charles-Will and Kim Scott, cover designer Aren Howell, production editor Susan Rimerman, copy editor Hope Frazier, Olav Kvern at Adobe, Jonathan Humfrey and Auriga Bork at Lynda.com, Mandy Murray and Peter Hooper at IPC Media, Julian Woodfield at Media Training, Carole McClendon, Nadia Proudian, Craig Zeital, Hugh D'Andrade, Sam Dunn, Rajani Venkatraman, and, of course, my dear old Mum.

TABLE OF CONTENTS

Introduction

Today we are all typographers. Everyone knows what a font is; most people have an opinion about the fonts they like and those they don't. Typography is no longer an arcane trade plied by curmudgeonly men with inky fingers, but rather a life skill. We make typographic decisions every day—the printed material we choose to read, the fonts we select for our correspondence, even the advertising we respond to, consciously or subconsciously.

This democratization of typography is empowering and anyone can participate. But to do it well you need to know a thing or two—with power comes responsibility. If you are using, or plan to use, InDesign then you have at your disposal state-of-the-art software for creating typographic layouts of any length and complexity. But InDesign didn't just arrive in 1997 when version 1.0 of the program was launched. It is part of the continuum of technological advances, going back to the Fifteenth Century with the invention of moveable type and moving with a quantum leap through the mid 1980s with the development of the PostScript page description language. The terminology and typographic conventions around which InDesign is built have evolved over generations; the typefaces on your font menu—even the funky postmodern ones—are clearly related to the letter shapes chiseled into the Trajan Column nearly 2000 years ago.

Whether you are new to InDesign or a seasoned user, you've probably found yourself wondering: What are all these controls? Where did they come from? And, perhaps more important: How do I use them? And Why? This book attempts to answer these questions. It is not just about how to do something in InDesign. Because it is impossible to talk about InDesign without talking about typographic history and typographic best practice, it is also a book about why certain type solutions work better than others.

It's an oft-repeated adage that good typography is "invisible," meaning that, rather than drawing attention to itself, the typography is the servant of the words it represents. As Stanley Morison, who in the 1930s brought us Times (the font designed for The Times of London, although the newspaper no longer uses it), said: "For a new fount to be successful it has to be so good that only very few recognize its novelty."

This perhaps makes typography sound like a thankless task. Where's the fame? The glory? There are few celebrity typographers, and those who are walk the streets in relative anonymity. Nonetheless typography is a noble cause. If typefaces are the bricks and mortar of communication, then we, the typographers, are the architects. A simple and understated building may pass unnoticed by many, but everyone notices an ugly one. Likewise with typography: Good designs serve their purpose and may not elicit comment, but we can all spot bad typography, even though we may not be able to say *why* it's bad. This book is about avoiding ugly and thoughtless type—a major step in the direction of creating beautiful type.

Who Should Read This Book?

This book deals almost exclusively with English language typography. Not because it is the most important, but because it is what I know. It focuses on print rather than screen publishing—even though many of the techniques presented here apply equally to Web typography. It is primarily concerned with the typographic conventions of magazine and book publishing. The techniques in this book will help you create pages and layouts to a professional standard by following a certain set of typographic "rules." My approach is utilitarian rather than experimental. These rules are not intended to be stifling or limiting to creativity. Rather, they are intended as a starting point. Learn them. Then, if you choose, break the rules, but break them consciously, knowing why you break them. Whatever you do, don't ignore them.

I should also mention that although written specifically for CS2, the majority of the techniques in the book are applicable for earlier versions of InDesign. Where there is a keyboard shortcut for the command, I indicate the Macintosh shortcut first, followed by the Windows shortcut in parentheses. For example: Cmd+Option+W (Ctrl+Alt+W).

I hope that you enjoy *InDesign Type* and find it a useful addition to your typographic bookshelf. I'm keen to get your feedback, so please email me with any comments, corrections, or suggestions.

—Nigel French
nigelfrench@earthlink.net

PART I

Character Formats

CHAPTER 1

Getting Started

BEFORE WE GET INTO THE NITTY-GRITTY of working with type in InDesign, let's take a few moments for an overview of the InDesign interface, and where we find all the type-related features. We'll look at the essential skill of navigating pages efficiently and economically, and how we can set up a custom workspace conducive to a type-oriented workflow.

TIP: Setting Defaults
When you make a change to InDesign's Preferences, you are affecting only the document you are working on. If you want to change the preferences for every document you create from this point on make sure you have no InDesign document open, that way your changes become application preferences. And this doesn't apply only to settings in the Preferences dialog box—you can set your own defaults for just about anything. So, for example, if you're tired of getting Times New Roman 12 point every time you type into an empty text frame, just make sure you have no document open, choose Type>Font and change the font to something else, which then becomes your default font. One more thing: Should you want to return to the "factory defaults," hold down Shift+Option+Command+Control (Shift+Ctrl+Alt) as you start InDesign, then click Yes when asked if you want to delete your preference files.

An InDesign Type Map: Where to Find Stuff

Everything relates to type in one way or another, but here I want to point you in the direction of the most frequently used type-related menu and palette options as well as InDesign preferences that control how type behaves. As with any of the big-hitter design applications these days, there is usually more than one way to do something. Sometimes, it's nothing more than a matter of preference; other times, new features have been added improving on old features—so that veteran users aren't alienated, the old menu options remain. What follows is my personal take on the best way of doing things.

Recommended Type Preferences

The key words here are "recommended" and "preferences." There are several preferences relating to type; for now, I just want to point out where they are and suggest a couple of changes to the factory default settings. I'll deal with each preference specifically in the relevant chapter. We all work differently; these are the settings I use.

The Tools Palette

No matter how proficient you are, with InDesign there are two tools you'll use most of the time: the Selection Tool and the Type Tool. The Selection Tool is used for (among other things) moving text frames, resizing text frames and threading text frames. The Type Tool is used for formatting and editing the text *inside* those frames. You move back and forth between these two tools a lot, so it's handy that there's a way to toggle between them.

To work with text frames while the Type Tool is selected, hold down Command (Control) to switch to the Selection Tool. With the key held down, you can drag the frame to move it, or drag any of the frame handles to resize it. When you release the key, you're back in the Type Tool.

The companion shortcut to the above is when you're using your Selection Tool, you double-click a text frame and your cursor changes to the Type Tool, inserted at the point where you double-clicked.

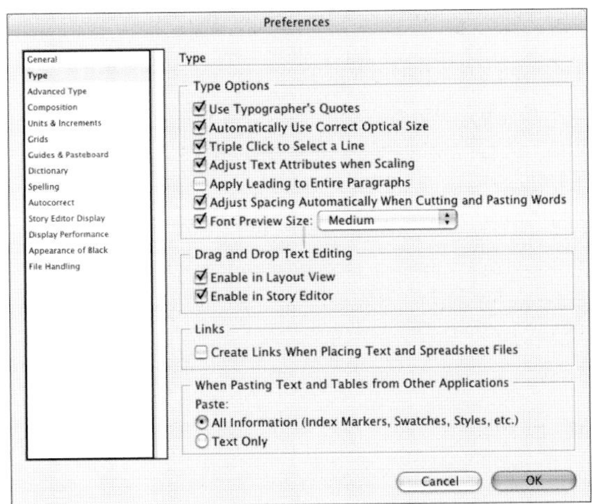

FIGURE 1.1 Type Preferences. There's no compelling reason to change any of these.

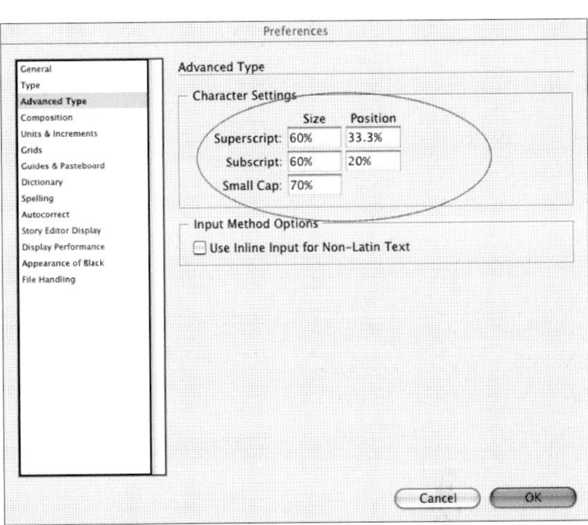

FIGURE 1. 2 Advanced Type Preferences. I recommend changing the Superscript and Subscript preferences to the percentages shown. Superscript and Subscript are discussed in Chapter 3: Character Reference.

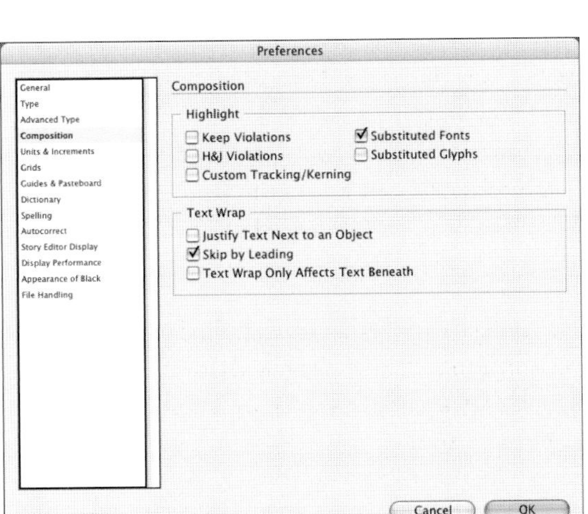

FIGURE 1.3 Composition Preferences. You might want to turn on the Highlight options depending on what stage of the design process you are in. When fine-tuning your document they can be useful in highlighting composition problems, like widows and orphans (Keeps Violations—see Chapter 5), bad word spacing (H&J Violations—see Chapter 8) and any unnecessary or over zealous kerning and/or tracking that may have been applied by someone else in your workgroup (Custom Tracking/Kerning—see Chapter 5).

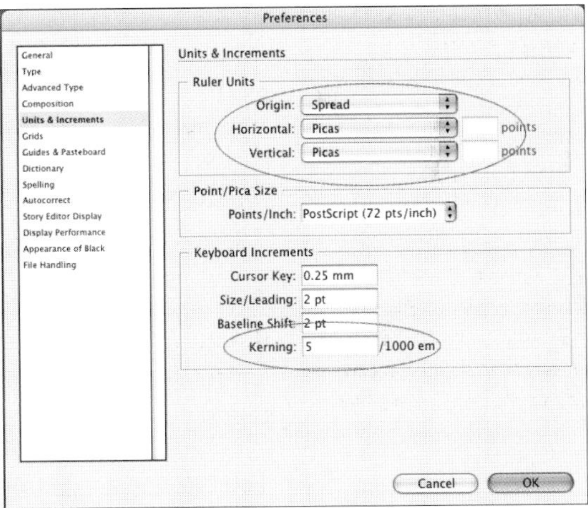

FIGURE 1.4 Units & Increments Preferences. Horizontal and Vertical Unit of Measurement: Picas. Perhaps not the most logical of measurement systems, but they are the typographic standard. For example, wouldn't you rather have an indent of 1 pica rather than 4.233 millimeters? For a discussion of pica and points see Chapter 6: Sweating the Small Stuff.

I change the Kerning increment to 5. Note that this also sets the increment for Tracking. For some bizarre reason the factory default for this preference is 20, which results in kerning or tracking amounts that are too coarse.

FIGURE 1.5 The Tools palette with the most important type-related tools in bold. Press the shortcut key (in parentheses) to select the tool (except when using the Type or Type on a Path tools).

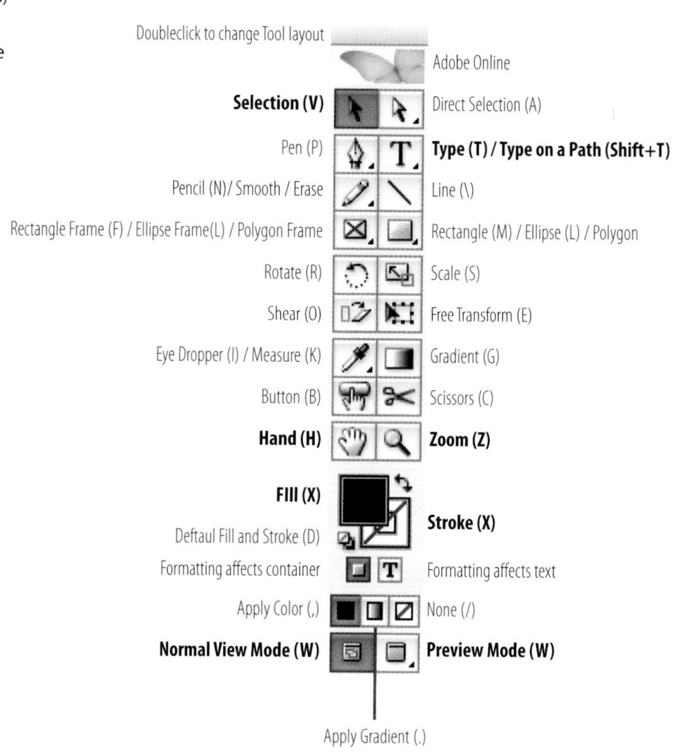

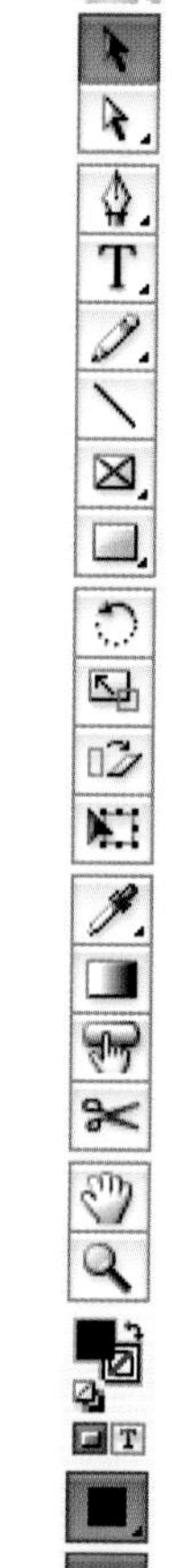

The Control Palette

The Control palette is a chameleon, changing its appearance according to what kind of element you have selected. When using the Type Tool the Control palette has two views, a handy toggle Cmd+Option+7 (Ctrl+Alt+7) switches between them.

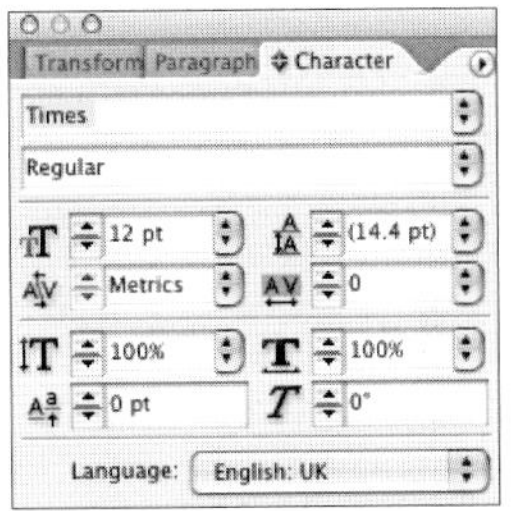

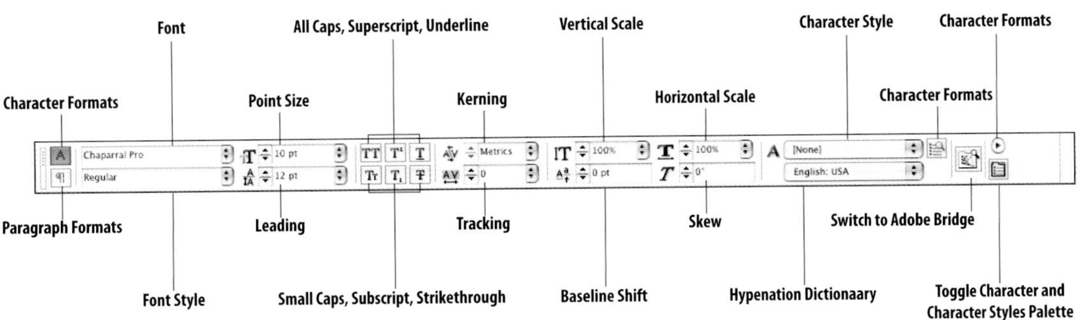

FIGURES 1.6A AND 1.6B The Control palette in Character Formats view and the Character palette, which offers the same options.

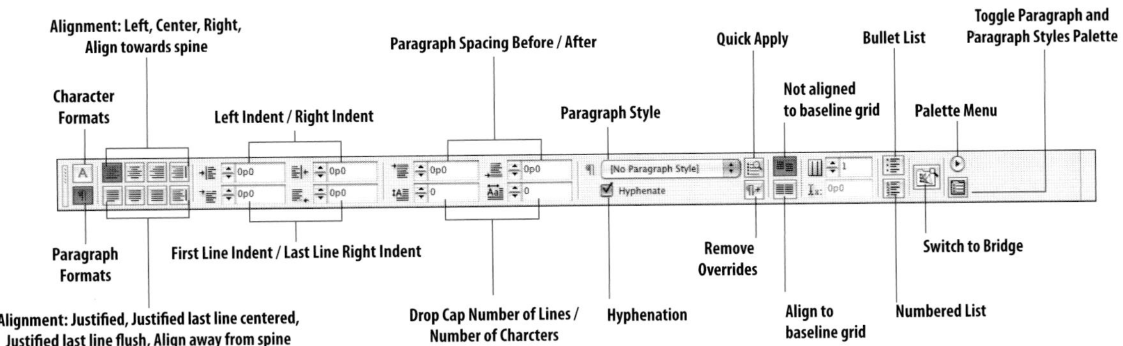

FIGURES 1.7A AND 1.7B The Control palette in Paragraph Formats view and the same options offered by the Paragraph palette.

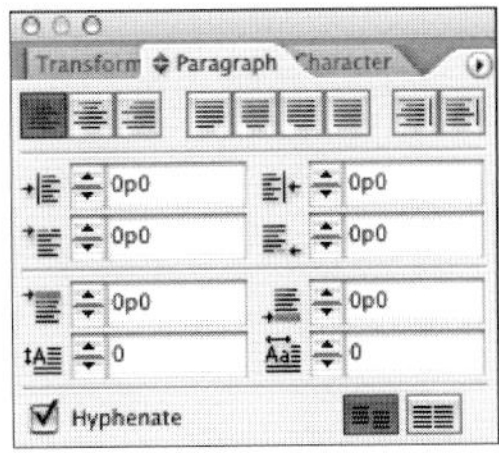

FIGURE 1.8 The Zoom Tool and the Hand Tool. Only a rank amateur ever chooses them from the Tool palette. Use the shortcuts instead:

Viewing Your Page

There are several ways to view and navigate your InDesign documents. These methods are not all equal; some are without doubt better than others. For the myriad options you have, you can do most everything you need with just three shortcuts.

1. **Zooming In:** Cmd+Spacebar (Ctrl+Spacebar) click and drag. If you value your eyesight, get in big when editing text. There's no point squinting at a page you can barely read. You could choose the Zoom Tool from the Tools palette, but save yourself the trouble. Instead, access the Zoom Tool while in any other tool, by holding down Cmd+Spacebar (Ctrl+Spacebar); your cursor changes to a magnifying glass. Now, rather than click to increase your view percentage, click and drag a marquee around the portion of your layout you want enlarged. The defined portion then fills your window.

2. **Moving Around:** Option+Spacebar (Alt+Spacebar) click and drag. Once at an enlarged view you'll likely want to move around at that view size. Click and drag with the Hand Tool to move your page or spread around within the document window. You can also use the Hand Tool at reduced view sizes to move vertically through pages. Don't bother with the scroll bars; it's hard to estimate their sensitivity and you'll waste a lot of time getting to exactly where you want to be.

3. **Zooming Out.** Cmd+Option+0 (Ctrl+Alt+0) to fit your spread (or page) in Window. Having zoomed in and made your changes at a comfortable view size, zoom out again to get an overall perspective on your page or spread. You'll find yourself constantly bopping back and forth between an increased view size—comfortably enlarged so as not to strain your eyes—and "Fit Spread in Window."

TIP: There are actually two ways to access the Hand Tool: When in any tool other than the Type Tool, pressing the Spacebar temporarily switches the current tool to the Hand Tool. However, if you are in the Type Tool, holding down Spacebar gets you a whole mess of spaces. An obvious point, but you'd be surprised how easy it is to make this mistake. If you are in the Type Tool, instead, hold down the Option (Alt) key to temporarily access the Hand Tool. When working quickly it's easy to forget where you are and which key you need, so I've found it's easier to standardize on Option/Alt+Spacebar, which works in all situations.

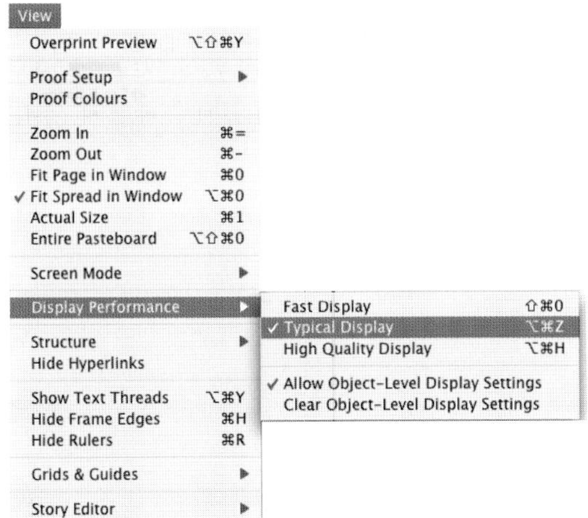

FIGURE 1.9 Typical Display: Don't choose Fast unless you like your type jagged. These settings do not affect print quality.

TIP: A Case of the Jaggies If your type looks bitmapped on screen it's probably because you have switched to the Fast Display mode, InDesign's low-resolution, quick screen redraw option. Choose View>Display Performance and switch to Typical or High Quality. You can also change this option permanently in the Preferences dialog.

Moving Between Pages

For documents consisting of only two pages or spreads, you can navigate from one page to the next efficiently with the Hand Tool. For longer documents, use the Pages palette, the Pages pop-up menu at the bottom left of your document window, or the options under the Layout menu.

When using the Pages palette to navigate between spreads with facing pages, double clicking the page numbers will fit the spread in the window, whereas double clicking the page icon will fit that specific page in the window.

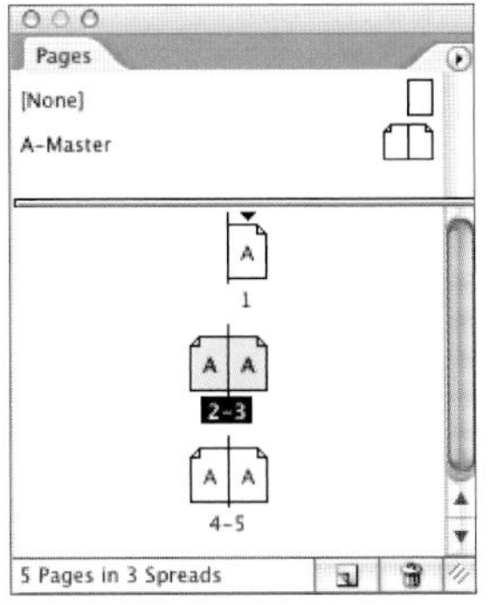

FIGURE 1.10 The Pages palette.

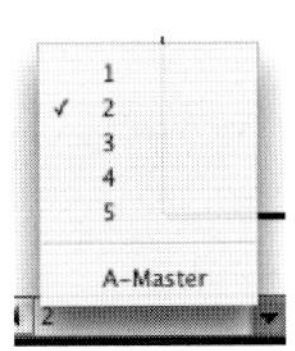

FIGURE 1.11 The Pages Pop-up.

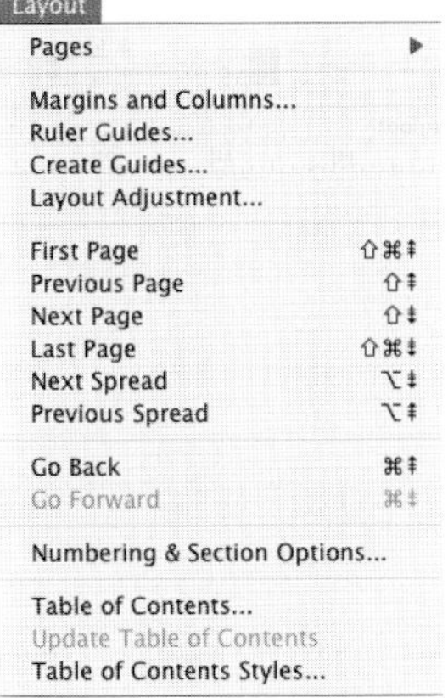

FIGURE 1.12 The Layout Menu showing the options for navigating between pages.

TIP: Alphabetizing Menus It's a small thing, perhaps a feature you'll never use, but it's nice to know it's there. You can view your menu items in alphabetical order by holding down Cmd+Shift+Option (Ctrl+Shift+Alt) when you choose the menu. This comes in handy when you're searching for that pesky menu item you can't find but you know is there.

Creating a Typography Workspace

At last count, there were 3,572 different palettes in InDesign. That's an exaggeration, but sometimes it doesn't seem like much of one. InDesign palettes are so numerous you would swear they breed like rabbits when your back is turned. A great many of these palettes you'll seldom or never use, no matter how illustrious your InDesign career. Thankfully, InDesign gives you unprecedented control of your workspace, allowing you to save—and recall at any time—the current sizes, positions, and groupings of your palettes. The names of workspaces appear in a Workspace submenu of the Window menu—or you can make a custom keyboard shortcut to switch to your workspace with a specified key combination.

First, arrange your palettes the way you want them. Create groupings that make sense to you, close those palettes you think you'll seldom or never use (if you need them at any time, they are under the Window menu), then float or dock those you want, where you want them. Choose Window>Workspace>Save Workspace and give your workspace a name.

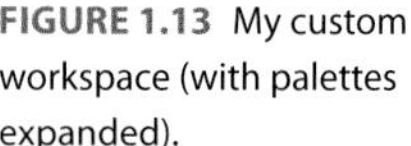

FIGURE 1.13 My custom workspace (with palettes expanded).

Having saved your workspace, you can load it at any time by returning to the Window menu, choosing Workspace and sliding over to your saved workspace. Alternatively, you can make yourself a keyboard shortcut to load the workspace.

1. Choose Edit>Keyboard Shortcuts.
2. Click New Set to create a new shortcut set without overwriting the default keyboard shortcut set..
3. For Product Area, select the area containing the command you want to define or redefine, in this case the Window Menu.
4. In the Commands list, scroll down to Workspace: Load 1st Workspace (you can create shortcuts for up to five workspaces).
5. In the New Shortcut field, press the keys for your new keyboard shortcut—I use Ctrl-F12. (Leave the Context list set to Default so that the shortcut functions in all situations.)
6. Click Assign to create the new shortcut.

Now that you've laid the groundwork for an efficient workflow, let's take a look at getting type into our documents, using InDesign's text-flow methods.

FIGURES 1.14A AND 1.14B
Making a keyboard shortcut.

Up Next

The next chapter is all about getting text onto your page—typing directly into InDesign, importing a text file, or pasting text from another application—as well as InDesign's tools and conventions for flowing and linking text frames from column to column and from page to page.

CHAPTER 2

Going with the Flow

TYPOGRAPHY BEGINS WITH A SINGLE CHARACTER, and putting type on your page is about as fundamental as InDesign skills get. There are several different approaches to placing type on the page and you'll probably end up using all of them at one time or another. Let's begin with the most elemental.

TIP: Scaling Type Here is one of my favorite tips—and so simple. Drag out a text frame with your Type Tool, then type your text. You may find that your text frame is much bigger than necessary to accommodate your text. No worries, all you do is click on the Fit Frame to Content icon in the Control palette, or press Cmd+Option+C (Ctrl+Alt+C) to fit your frame nice and snug around your text. Clean, elegant, uncluttered—and fantastic if you then want to scale the text by eye. Hold down Command+Shift (Ctrl+Shift) and drag from one of the four corners of the text frame to size the type while maintaining its proportions.

A Blank Sheet: Typing on Your Page

Before you type on your page you need a container or text frame to hold your text. The good news is that with InDesign, unlike QuarkXPress, you don't have to first draw a text frame. Instead, you can create a text frame on the fly with your Type Tool, which really speeds things up. Using your Type Tool, click and drag to define the width and depth of your text frame (or, if you have a text frame already on the page, just click that) and type away.

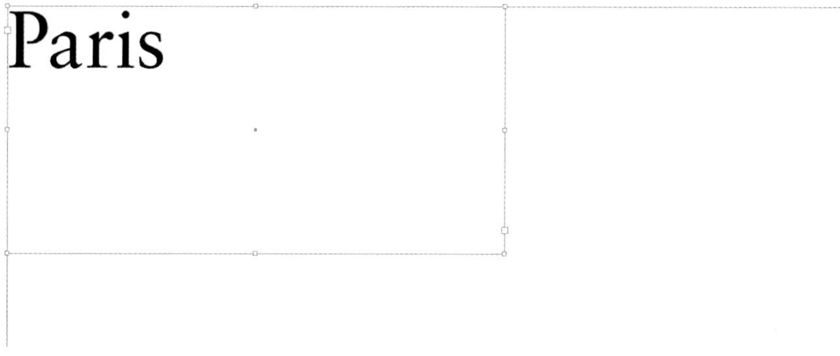

FIGURES 2.1A, 2.1B, 2.1C Scaling a Text Frame.

Text Flow

Before using any of the text-flow methods, first "load" your cursor. To do that choose File>Place, navigate to the text file you wish to import, and then click Open.

For those of you who remember PageMaker, InDesign's text-flow methods will feel comfortably familiar. Those more familiar with QuarkXPress may be tempted to say something like, "You mean I don't have to draw a text box?"—because InDesign's text-flow methods are fast and fluid.

Once you have a loaded type cursor, the size of your text frame is determined by the document's column and margin settings. Simply click at the top of the column to flow a single column of text. Note that the arrow in the loaded cursor icon will change from black to white when the cursor is over a guide. If there's more text to come—overset text—you'll need to click on the red arrow at the bottom left of the text frame to "reload" your cursor. Then move to where you want the over matter to go—either a new column or a new page—and click at the top of the column or page to flow another text frame.

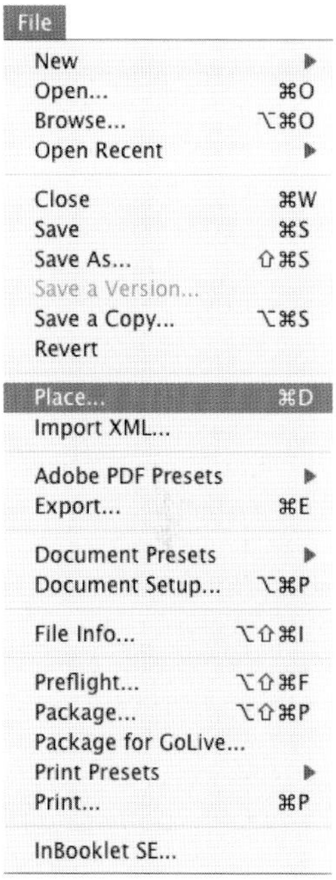

FIGURE 2.2 The Place Menu (Cmd+D/Ctrl+D).

Careful Where You Point that Thing: What to Watch for When Flowing Text

Replace Selected Item in the Place dialog box: If this is checked and you have a text frame selected with your Selection Tool, the text file you choose will replace your selection. If you have your Type Tool inserted within a text frame, your new story will be flowed from that point in the story. These results may be what you're after, and both are useful techniques, but if they are not what you wanted, you can either press Cmd+Z (Ctrl+Z) after the fact to restore your selected text frame and give you a loaded type cursor. Better yet, make sure his option is not selected in the first place. Alternatively, choose Edit>Deselect All Cmd+Shift+A (Ctrl+Shift+A) before you place a file.

When you hold the loaded text icon over an existing frame, parentheses appear around the icon. If you click, you will replace the contents of the frame with incoming text.

Canceling a loaded text cursor: Should you decide you don't want to flow that text after all, just choose any tool from the Tool palette or press any tool letter shortcut to "unload" your cursor. No text will be deleted.

Alternatively, if you don't want the width and depth of a text frame determined by your document's columns, click and drag the loaded type cursor to the size you want. When you release the mouse button, text will flow into the area you have defined. If there is more text to be placed, click the *out port* to reload your cursor, then click in the next text frame to continue the text flow.

Each text frame contains an in port and an out port, which are used to make connections to other text frames. An empty in port or out port indicates the beginning or end of a story, respectively. An arrow in a port indicates that the frame is linked to another frame. A red plus sign (+) in an out port indicates that there is overset text—more text than will fit in the current text frame(s). To flow the overset text, select the frame with the Selection Tool, click the out port, and then flow another text frame.

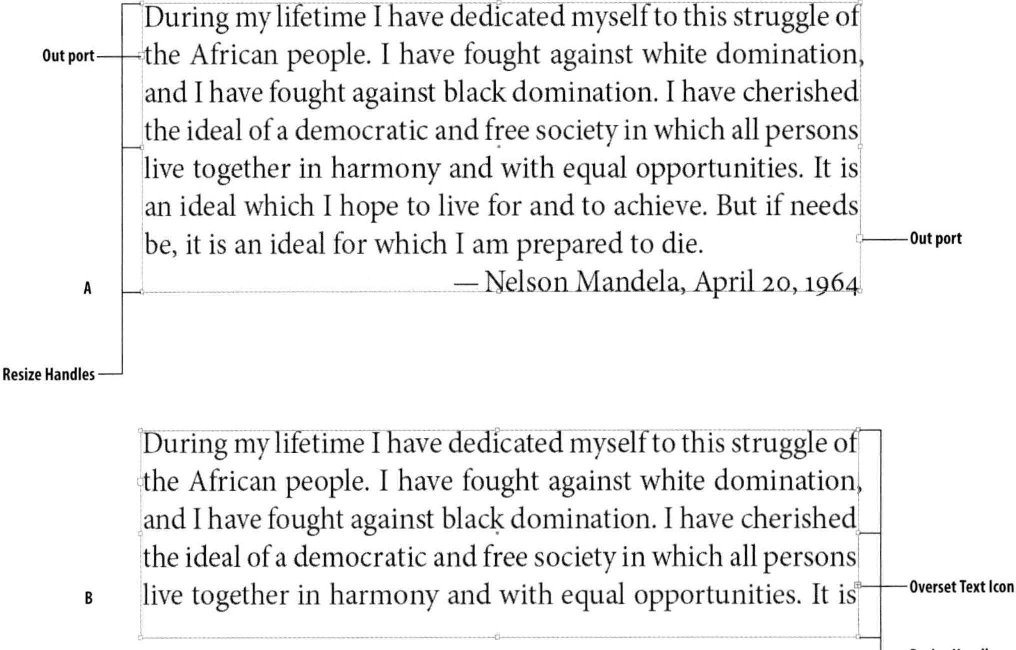

FIGURE 2.3 Anatomy of a Text Frame. **A.** Text frame containing a whole story. **B.** The same text frame resized so that the text is overset.

Types of Text Flow

Manual text flow adds text one frame at a time. The text flow stops at the bottom of a text frame, or at the last of a series of linked frames. You'll need to reload the text icon to continue the text flow. Manual text flow is most appropriate for short bodies of text.

Autoflow (Shift) flows all the text, adding pages and frames as necessary. Autoflow functions best when working with single-column documents containing one main story—like a novel or short story.

Semi-Autoflow (Option/Alt) works like manual text flow, except that your cursor is reloaded at the end of each frame, saving you the trouble of having to click on the red plus symbol. You then continue the text flow by clicking or dragging to create a new text frame, or clicking an existing text frame to add it to the text thread. Semi-Autoflow is most appropriate when working with long text files that are one story of several in a document—like a magazine or newspaper article.

Fixed Page Autoflow (Shift-Option/Shift-Alt) flows as much text as will fit without adding pages. This option is useful if your document has a fixed number of pages.

FIGURE 2.4 Manual Text Flow icon.

FIGURE 2.5 The Autoflow icon.

FIGURE 2.6 The Semi-Autoflow icon.

FIGURE 2.7 Fixed Page Autoflow icon.

Threading Text Frames

Continuing the text flow from one frame to another is called Threading. Here are some typical Threading techniques:

Adding a frame to the thread: Select the text frame with the Selection Tool, then click its out port to load your text cursor. Move to the next column or page and then click or drag to create another frame. The text flows from the frame you clicked into the new frame.

Delete a frame from the text thread: Select it with the Selection Tool and press the Delete key. Don't worry about losing text—you are only deleting the container, not the content.

TIP: When creating a series of threaded text frames you can speed things up, by holding Option/Alt as you drag out a new text frame. The new text frame will be automatically threaded to the previous frame.

TIP: To see the bounding box of your text frames, even if they have nothing in them, make sure View>Show Frame Edges (Cmd/Ctrl+H) is checked.

Making a headline span multiple columns: In addition to the out port at the bottom right of a text frame, there is another port at the top left, which can be used to load text from the beginning of the story. This is useful when you have a multicolumn layout and you want the headline to stretch across the columns rather than being squashed into a single column. Some people just cut and paste the headline into a separate story, which works, but threading the text is more efficient because it maintains the headline as part of the story, meaning that it can be text selected, spell checked, and viewed in the Story Editor as one story, rather than as two distinct pieces.

1. Pull down a horizontal guide from the Horizontal Ruler to approximately where the first paragraph will begin.
2. Resize the text frame so that it begins at this guide.
3. Load your Type Tool from the out port at the top left of the text frame.
4. Click and drag to create a text frame that spans the depth of the headline and across the width of the two columns.

Showing Text Threads: Choose Show Text Threads from the View menu, and linking arrows will indicate the flow of the text for a selected text frame.

Some people prefer to map out their layouts, drawing and linking text frames before they have the real text. To create a series of linked text frames, draw your frames with the Rectangle Frame Tool, then click the first frame with your Type Tool to designate it as a text frame. Click the text frame's out port to link it to the next frame in the thread and continue to link the frames as necessary. Optionally, you can fill these text frames with placeholder text.

Drop-Dead Gorgeous

OBORPERC ilissenit laor adiam velit la facin euguer summy nonsed eugait loboreetum dolortio odo dolore tat alismodolum qui tat. Ciduis niat nonsequ ismolore dipit lore do odo- lut vulputpat in veliqui tisi.

Magna feuguer iuscill aorperatio con esequis nulla consequat. Wiscillaor susto consequis nulput ex erat. Ut nit lorper summy nostrud dipit num vendipis aut vendit veniamc onulla faccumm odolor susto od ea facilla facipis aut augiamcor ilit praestis adigna ametums andrer sisi.

Modolorer se elis amconsed mod dolum estrud eumsan et il ipsum del

A

Drop-Dead Gorgeous

OBORPERC ilissenit laor adiam velit la facin euguer summy nonsed eugait loboreetum dolortio odo dolore tat alismodolum qui tat. Ciduis niat nonsequ ismolore dipit lore do odolut vulputpat in veliqui tisi.

Magna feuguer iuscill aorperatio con esequis nulla consequat. Wiscillaor susto consequis nulput ex erat. Ut nit lorper summy nostrud dipit num vendipis aut vendit veniamc onulla faccumm odolor susto od ea facilla facipis aut augiamcor ilit praestis adigna ametums andrer sisi.

B

FIGURE 2.8 Threading a headline across columns.

TIP: Create your Own "Dummy" Text Tired of using pigeon Latin for your placeholder text? You can create custom placeholder text by making a text file with the text you want to use and naming it 'placeholder.txt.' Save the file in the InDesign CS2 application folder and thereafter this is what you'll get when you choose Fill with Placeholder Text.

Using Placeholder Text

Using placeholder or dummy text when mocking up a page or spread is a time-honored tradition in the world of page layout. Back in the day, folks used a text file called Lorem Ipsum, which looked like Latin but actually was mumbo jumbo with word and sentence lengths approximating those of an "average" article. Today this feature is built into InDesign: Just place the Type Tool in a text frame, or click and drag with the Type Tool to create one, then select Type>Fill with Placeholder Text and that frame (or frames if you have a series of linked text frames) is filled with dummy text.

Rectangles and Rectangle Frames: What's the Difference?

There are two tools that do essentially the same thing: the Rectangle Tool (and its associated tools Ellipse and Polygon) and the Rectangle Frame Tool (along with the Ellipse Frame and the Polygon Frame). What's the difference? Essentially there is none. Shapes drawn with the Frame tools appear with an "X" inside them. Presumably you are going to put content into them. If you use Rectangle, Frame or Polygon, there's no "X" and they are intended as graphic elements in their own right. That said, there's nothing stopping you from putting text or a graphic inside a rectangle (just insert the Type tool in the frame and it is designated a text frame). Likewise there's nothing stopping you from using the frames as standalone elements. There's no reason, at least none I can think of, why these two sets of tools can't be merged into one. I suspect they exist as discreet tools to appeal to Quark users who are conditioned to draw boxes for their content.

If you need to change the shape of any object, for example from a rectangle to an ellipse or visa versa, choose Object>Convert Shape.

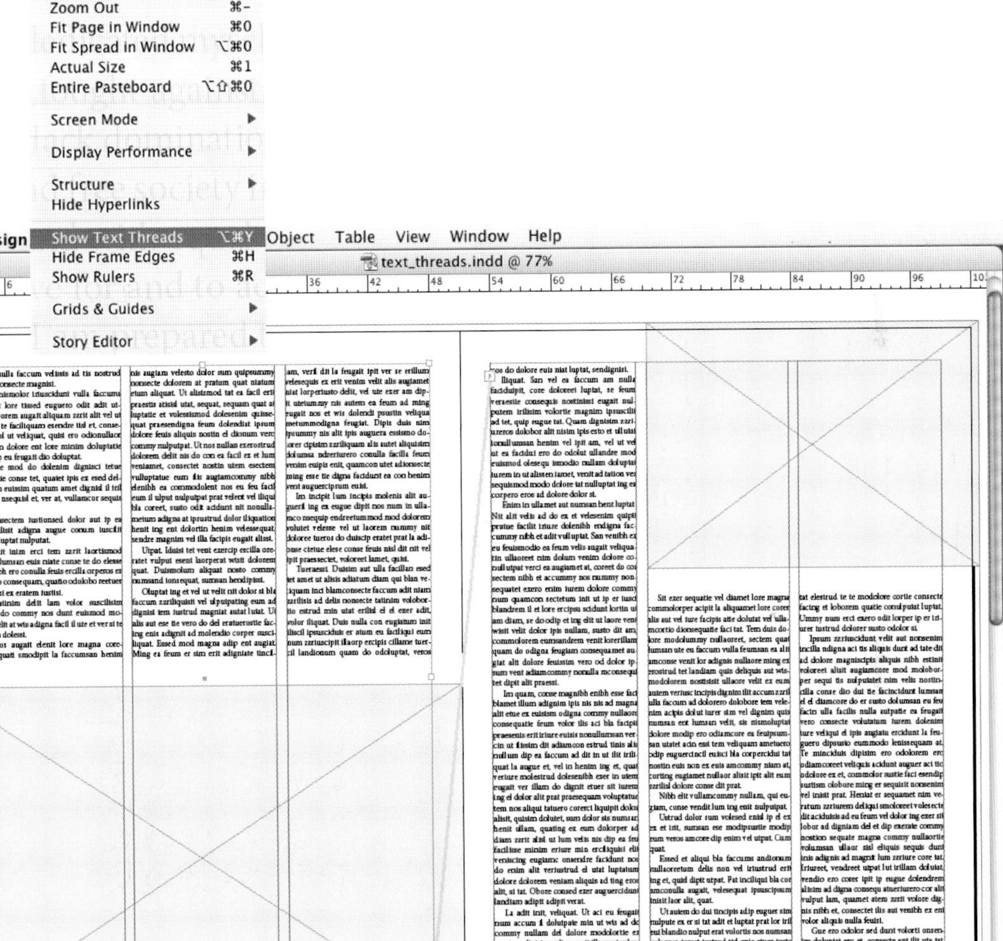

FIGURE 2.9 Empty Text frames threaded together and filled with placeholder text. Text Threads are shown.

Pasting Text

Another method for getting text into an InDesign document is to copy and paste it from another application. Before you do this you might want to check out a related preference in the Type Preferences dialog box: Preserve Text Attributes When Pasting. Depending on the result you want, this can either be a blessing or a curse, so it's good to know you have the option. Note that when you paste text from another application, "dumb" or straight quotes will not be automatically converted to Typographer's quotes, nor will double hyphens be converted to em dashes—both standard niceties that come with importing a text file using the Place command.

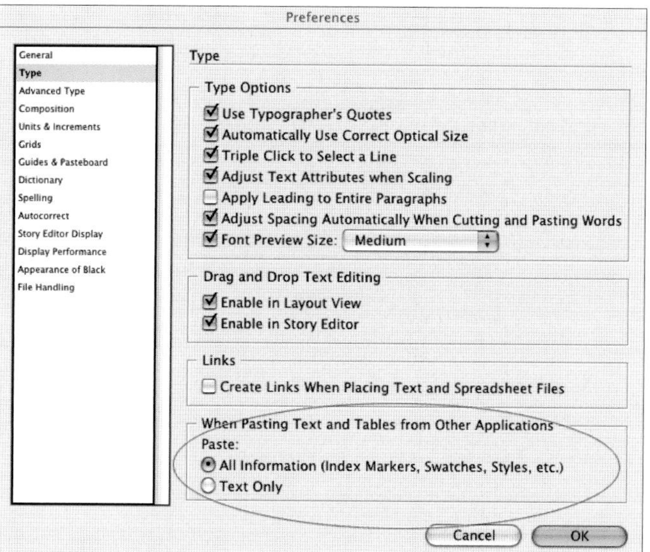

FIGURE 2.10 Preserve Text Attributes When Pasting.

Importing Word Text

When placing a Microsoft Word file, if you check Show Import Options, you are taken to the Microsoft Word Import Options dialog. This is a much-enhanced feature in CS2 and allows for complex mapping of Word paragraph and character styles to InDesign styles. We'll look at Customize Style Import in Chapter 13, "Stylin' with Paragraph and Character Styles." For now, notice that you have the option of importing your Word text with or without Styles and Tables formatting, as well as being able to control the import of Word-created footnotes, endnotes, table of contents text, and index text.

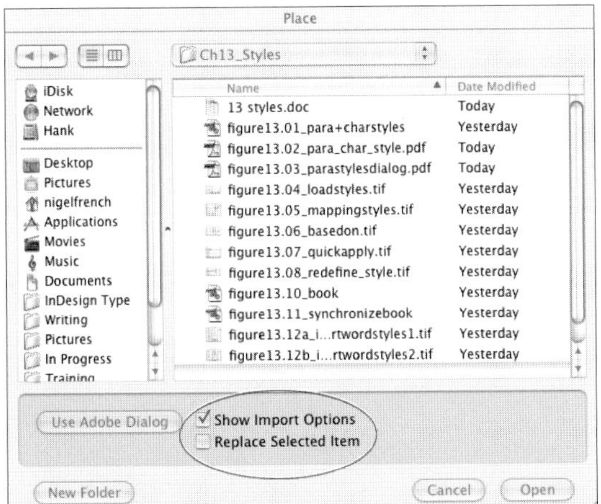

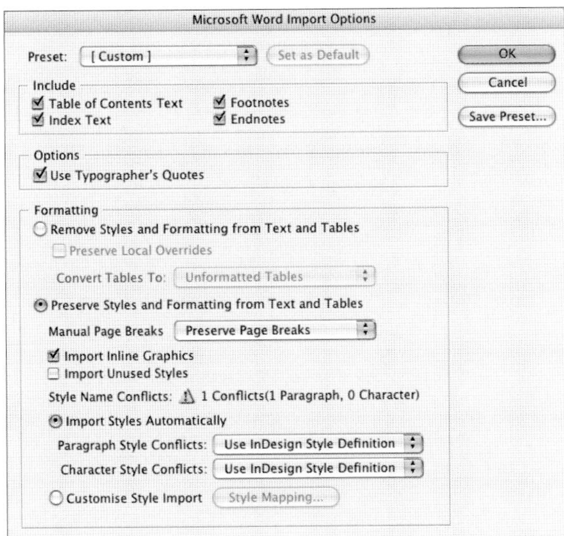

FIGURE 2.11 Show Import Options and the Microsoft Word Import Options.

Up Next

With text on your page, it's time to look at the options you have for styling your type. The next chapter deals with the many options available on the Character Formats level of the Control Palette, as well as the aesthetic considerations when choosing those options.

CHAPTER 3

Character Reference

WHEN IT COMES TO TYPEFACES, we are spoilt for choice. But with so many fonts just a mouse click away, it's easy to be overwhelmed rather than empowered by all that choice. We've probably all felt intimidated at one time or another by the length of our font menus. If you're like me, you've probably frittered away the best part of a day experimenting with this or that enticingly named font, only to find yourself unsatisfied with the results.

TIP: Type Specimen Book The only way to efficiently evaluate typefaces is by using a type specimen book. Don't be tempted to forgo this essential reference in favor of pulling down typefaces from the font menu to see how they look; this is a surefire way to waste time. Several such books are available, including The Type Specimen Book (John Wiley & Sons), and Font Bureau Type Specimens (www.fontbureau.com). Alternatively, you can browse typefaces in the Adobe Type Library at http://store.adobe.com/type/.

Complicating matters is the fact that our typefaces may be sending messages without our knowing it. Typefaces can be loaded—often through no fault of their own—with symbolism or meaning. For example, Times New Roman or Helvetica/Arial might scream "generic" because we are so used to seeing them as the "default" font; Fette Fraktur, because of its adoption by the National Socialists, might connote Nazism. Other fonts, once fashionable, may be trapped in a historical period—great if you want to evoke that era, but a potential faux pas if not. Who, in the early twenty-first century, hasn't been overexposed to Comic Sans? Certain fonts may have been co-opted by a ubiquitous advertising campaign and can't help but evoke that product; others may have suddenly become fashionable, only to suddenly change—like an overplayed song on the radio—from flavor of the month to minor irritation. What's more there's a growing number of type geeks out there who relish the opportunity to point out the historical inappropriateness of using an English sans serif from the 1930s for a book about a Russian art movement of the 1920s.

Maybe I exaggerate. But only a little. The thing is, there's no way to predict how readers will react to our type choices, and, the bolder those choices, the more likely we are to upset someone. So, it's a good idea to arm yourself with at least a basic knowledge of typographic history, a solid understanding of the fonts you use most often, and an awareness of the connotations that certain typefaces carry.

Less is More, Maybe

My personal type aesthetic is a minimalist one, though I wonder if this is just laziness: If less is more, then maybe I can get away with knowing fewer typefaces. Perhaps more is more, but the reality is that it's better to know and understand a few typefaces well than to have a font list a mile long and only a passing acquaintance with the fonts that are on it.

Choosing a typeface is about enhancing the meaning of the text you are working with. It's also about meeting the expectations and matching the tastes of your client. In a perfect world, we'd all read and thoroughly digest the text documents we are given to work with as raw materials. Depending on the length of your documents, that may or may not be possible, but you should at least have an understanding of the intended message.

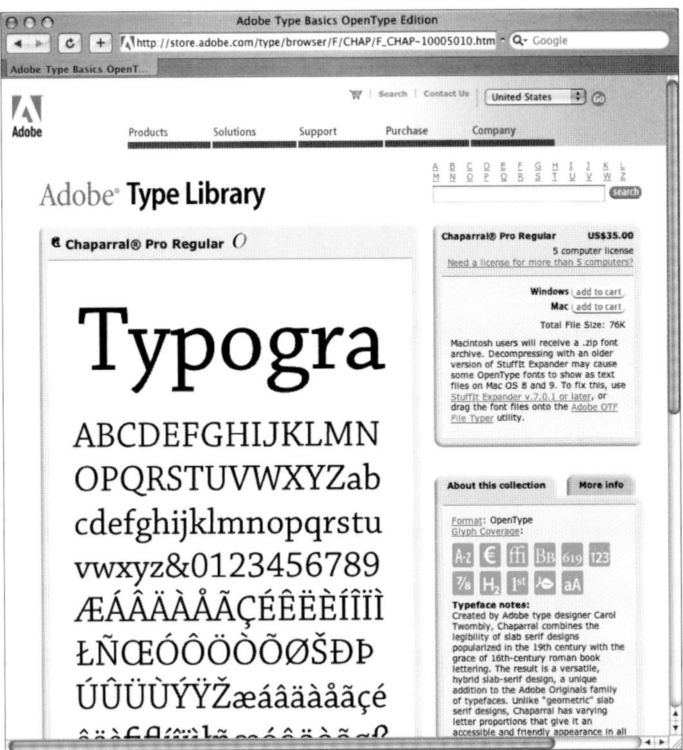

FIGURE 3.1 A page from Adobe's online type library.

Type Anatomy

To talk meaningfully about type we need to share a common vocabulary. Below is a simple diagram deconstructing letter shapes into their constituent parts.

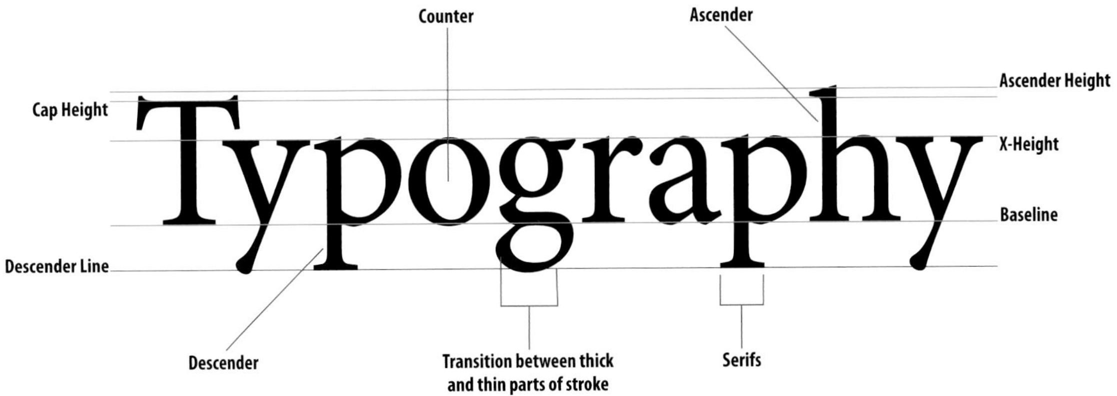

FIGURE 3.2 The parts of a letter.

Type Classification

There is no single recognized standard for classifying typefaces; rather there are several overlapping standards. For our purposes I'm going to use a simplified version of Adobe's type classification, showing three examples of each category.

Venetian Oldstyle

Named after the first Roman typefaces that appeared in Venice around 1470, Venetian typefaces were initially designed to imitate the handwriting of Italian Renaissance scholars. Distinguishing features:

- Sloping bar on the lowercase e
- Angle of stress that approximates that of a broad-nibbed pen held at an angle to the page
- Little contrast between thick and thin strokes
- Examples: Adobe Jenson, Berkeley Oldstyle, Centaur

Garalde Oldstyle

Garalde typefaces include some of the most popular roman styles in use today. Distinguishing features:

- Horizontal bar on the lowercase e
- A slightly greater contrast between thick and thin strokes than Venetian types
- Axis curves that are inclined to the left
- Bracketed serifs
- Examples: Adobe Garamond, Bembo, Minion

Script

Script typefaces mimic handwriting by joining letters with connecting lines. For this reason, scripts require extra attention to the kerning of their letters. Also, you never want to set a script typeface in all caps.

- Examples: Linoscript, Kunstler Script, Mistral

The quick brown fox jumps over the lazy dog

Adobe Jenson Pro

The quick brown fox jumps over the lazy dog

Berkeley Oldstyle

The quick brown fox jumps over the lazy dog

Centaur

FIGURE 3.3 Venetian Oldstyle.

The quick brown fox jumps over the lazy dog

Adobe Garamond Pro

The quick brown fox jumps over the lazy dog

Bembo

The quick brown fox jumps over the lazy dog

Minion Pro

FIGURE 3.4 Garalde Oldstyle.

The quick brown fox jumps over the lazy dog

Linoscript

The quick brown fox jumps over the lazy dog

Kunstler

The quick brown fox jumps over the lazy dog

Mistral

FIGURE 3.5 Script.

Transitional

Representing a move away from letter shapes based on handwriting, transitional types were the first typefaces to be drawn as shapes in their own right. They represent a *transition* between Garalde and Modern (Didone) typefaces, and contain aspects of both. Distinguishing features:

- A vertical, or near vertical axis
- Pronounced contrast between hairlines and main strokes
- Serifs are thin, flat and bracketed
- Examples: Baskerville, Perpetua, Stone Serif

Didone (Modern)

Named after Firmin Didot and Giambattista Bodoni, Didone typefaces were a response to improvements in late 18th Century paper production, composition, printing and binding, which made it possible to develop typefaces with strong vertical emphasis and fine hairlines. Distinguishing features:

- Strong contrast between thick and thin strokes
- Vertical axis
- Mechanical appearance—constructed rather than drawn
- Fine, unbracketed, serifs
- Examples: Bodoni, Didot, Fenice

Slab Serif

With the Industrial Revolution came the increased use of posters, billboards, and other forms of advertising, and the need for bolder, more in-your-face typefaces. Slab serif typefaces were originally called "Egyptians," reflecting the public's enthusiasm for the archeological discoveries of the time. Distinguishing features:

- Heavy, squared-off serifs
- Relatively consistent stroke weight
- Sturdy
- Examples: Clarendon, Memphis, Rockwell

Sans Serif

The first sans serif typeface was issued in 1816, but it wasn't until the 1920s, with the influence of the Bauhaus and de Stijl art movements, that sans serifs became popular. Within the broad category of sans serif, there are four sub categories: Grotesque, Neo-Grotesque, Geometric, and Humanist.

- Examples: Futura, Gill Sans, Myriad Pro

The quick brown fox jumps over the lazy dog

Baskerville

The quick brown fox jumps over the lazy dog

Perpetua

The quick brown fox jumps over the lazy

Stone Serif

FIGURE 3.6 Transitional.

The quick brown fox jumps over the lazy

Bodoni

The quick brown fox jumps over the lazy

Didot

The quick brown fox jumps over the lazy

Fenice

FIGURE 3.7 Didone (Modern).

The quick brown fox jumps over the

Clarendon

The quick brown fox jumps over the lazy

Memphis

The quick brown fox jumps over the lazy dog

Chaparral Pro

FIGURE 3.8 Slab Serif.

The quick brown fox jumps over the lazy

Futura

The quick brown fox jumps over the lazy dog

Gill Sans

The quick brown fox jumps over the lazy dog

Myriad Pro

FIGURE 3.9 Sans Serif.

TIP: Formatting Type In addition to using the Type Tool to select a range of text, you can also use the Selection Tool to select a text frame (or frames) and apply the same formatting options to the whole frame, including any overset text.

The following classes of type all play a supporting role:

Decorative & Display

While typefaces in this group incorporate elements from many styles, they are most effective when used in large sizes for display purposes, such as headlines and titles.

- Examples: Arnold Böcklin, Rosewood Standard, Industria

Blackletter

These typefaces are sometimes referred to as Old English or Gothic. They were used for text in Germany until World War II, but are now primarily used as display type.

- Examples: Fette Fraktur, Goudy Text

Monospaced

All of the characters in a monospaced typeface have the same width. Most typefaces have proportionally spaced characters, but monospaced characters may be required when setting text on forms, financial statements and other documents where exact spacing is required.

- Examples: Courier, OCR-A Std, Letter Gothic

Ornamentals

Ornamental typefaces contain decorative ornaments or symbols and can be used to embellish or decorate documents. Some OpenType fonts include ornaments as part of their extended character set.

- Examples: Adobe Wood Type Ornaments, Minion Pro Ornaments, Adobe Caslon Ornaments

Symbol

Symbol or picture typefaces fulfill a number of nontext functions: musical notation, map making, mathematics, crossword, and puzzle publishing.

- Examples: ITC Zapf Dingbats, Symbol, Carta.

The quick brown fox jumps over the

Arnold Böcklin

THE QUICK BROWN FOX JUMPS OVER THE

Rosewood

The quick brown fox jumps over the lazy dog

Industria

FIGURE 3.10 Decorative and Display.

The quick brown fox jumps over the lazy

Fette Fraktur

The quick brown fox jumps over the lazy dog

Goudy Text

FIGURE 3.11 Blackletter.

The quick brown fox jumps over

Courier

The quick brown fox jumps

OCR A

The quick brown fox jumps over

Letter Gothic

FIGURE 3.12 Monospaced.

Minion Pro Ornaments

Adobe Caslon Pro Ornaments

Adobe Wood Type Ornaments

FIGURE 3.13 Ornamentals.

ΔΦΘςΩΞΨϑπϖ∞♣♦♥♠↔←↑→↓÷∅√∑◊€

Symbol

Zapf Dingbats

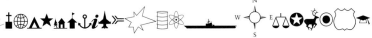

Carta

FIGURE 3.14 Symbol.

Type Selection and Navigation Shortcuts

Move to start or end of story: Cmd+Home or End (Ctrl+Home or End)

Select start or end of story: Shift+Cmd+Home or End (Shift+Ctrl+Home or End)

Select one word: Double-click word

Select one line: Triple-click line (depending on Text Preferences setting)

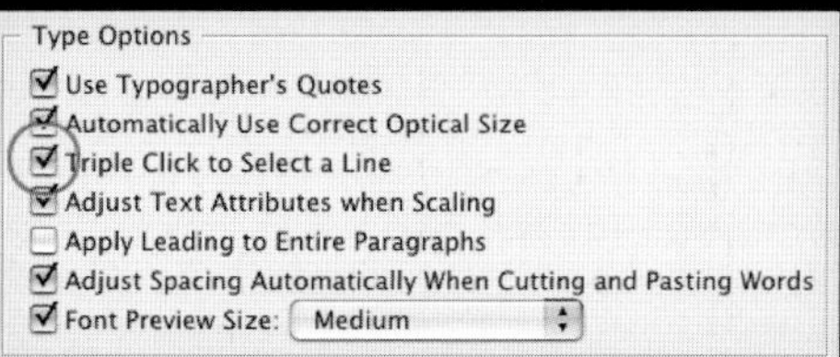

FIGURE 3.15 Text Preferences.

Select one paragraph: Quadruple click

Select whole story: Cmd+A (Ctrl+A)

Select to the beginning of the line: Cmd+Shift+Up Arrow (Ctrl+Shift+Up Arrow)

Select to the end of the line: Cmd+Shift+Down Arrow (Ctrl+Shift+Down Arrow)

Move to the beginning of the line: Cmd+Up Arrow (Ctrl+Up Arrow)

Move to the end of the line: Cmd+Down Arrow (Ctrl+Down Arrow)

Access the Control Palette: Cmd+6 (Ctrl+6)

Toggle between Character/Paragraph Formatting Controls in the Control Palette (if the Type tool is selected): Cmd+Option+7 (Ctrl+Alt+7)

Double click a text frame with the Selection Tool to switch to the Type Tool. You can toggle back to the Selection Tool from the Type Tool (or any tool) by holding down Cmd (Ctrl).

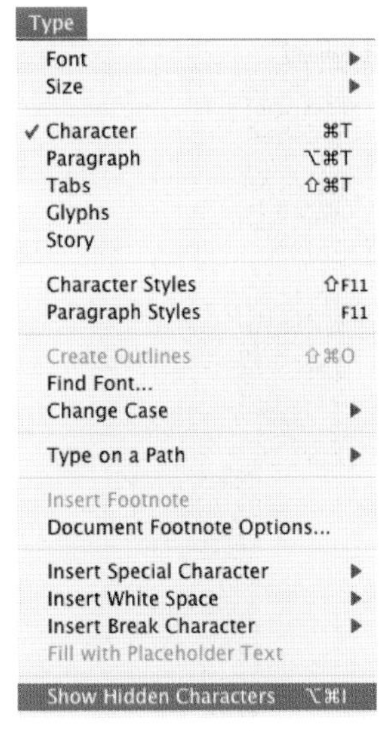

The GETTYSBURG ADDRESS¶

FOUR SCORE AND SEVEN years ago our fathers brought forth on this continent, a new nation, conceived in liberty, and dedicated to the proposition that all men are created equal.¶

Now we are engaged in a great civil war, testing whether that nation or any nation so conceived and so dedicated, can long endure.¶

FIGURE 3.16A AND 3.16B Hidden Characters Shown.

TIP: Work with your Hidden Characters visible. This is a good way to troubleshoot potential composition problems because you can see any forced line breaks, tabs, and multiple spaces that may have crept into your text. You can toggle this view option on and off by choosing Type > Show Hidden Characters or by pressing Cmd+Option+I (Ctrl+Alt+I).

Character Formatting Options

This section looks at the basic options available in the Character Formatting Controls on the Control Palette or on the Character Palette.

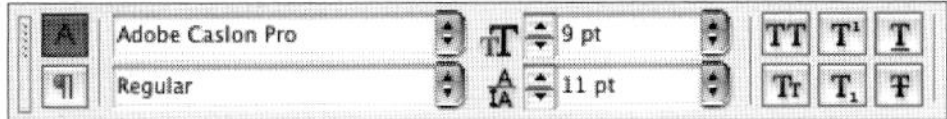

FIGURE 3.17 The Character Palette.

Font and Font Style

Because InDesign is a type snob (in a good way), it won't allow you to make "faux" type styles. There's no I or B icon you can click to make your text italic or bold. Instead you need to choose the real italic or real bold weights of that font from the Type Style pull down. Alternatively, the shortcuts: Cmd+Shift+I (Ctrl+Shift+I) or Cmd+Shift+B (Ctrl+Shift+B) will select the real italic or bold weights for you—so long as you have the real italic or bold weight of the font installed.

Using Italic Type

Italic types—so named because they evolved in Italy (in early 16th Century Venice)—are designed to complement their roman siblings. They are distinct fonts in their own right and not just slanted versions of the roman. Italics are typically used to clarify a word, differentiating it from the rest of the text. Italics are commonly used for the titles of films, book, magazines, or for foreign phrases or terms, and often to indicate emphasis.

TIP: To quickly access the font menu on the Control palette press Cmd/Ctrl+6. From there, you can type the first few letters of the font you're after to go directly to it, or at least close to it, on the font menu.

FIGURE 3.18 Real italics vs. slanted type. **A** is Minion Pro italic; **B** is Minion Regular slanted to 12°. Note the difference between the a, e, and f.

A *How razorback-jumping frogs can level six piqued gymnasts!*

B How razorback-jumping frogs can level six piqued gymnasts!

Italics are lighter than their roman counterparts, and their slant can make the type look hurried. Because the characters are more decorative, they can also draw too much attention to themselves. For these reasons, avoid long passages set in italics. Italics are unique but if overused that uniqueness is lost.

Using Bold Type

Bold weights are typically applied to headings, subheads, and running heads to establish hierarchy. In many books—this one, for example—bold is also used for referring to figures. If you are using bold weights for emphasis in body text, do so sparingly. Bold text can attract too much attention, breaking up the continuity of your text.

FIGURE 3.19 Different ways to add emphasis. Clockwise from top: Italic, Bold, Highlight (In Underline Options an 11 pt yellow "underline" offset –2.5pt to sit behind the type), and using color.

There are many ways to give *emphasis*. Making words *bold or italic* are the most common, but using *color* or a *highlight* can also be effective. Whichever method you choose, you need only *one way* to signify difference. For example, it is *redundant* to use bold *and* italic, or bold *and* a color.

There are many ways to give **emphasis**. Making words **bold or italic** are the most common, but using **color** or a **highlight** can also be effective. Whichever method you choose, you need only **one way** to signify difference. For example, it is **redundant** to use bold **and** italic, or bold **and** a color.

There are many ways to give emphasis. Making words bold or italic are the most common, but using color or a highlight can also be effective. Whichever method you choose, you need only one way to signify difference. For example, it is redundant to use bold and italic, or bold and a color.

There are many ways to give emphasis. Making words bold or italic are the most common, but using color or a highlight can also be effective. Whichever method you choose, you need only one way to signify difference. For example, it is redundant to use bold and italic, or bold and a color.

Small Caps

Small caps have the following uses:

- For acronyms and abbreviations. Because small caps are smaller than full size caps—slightly larger than the x-height—they are less obtrusive and do not overwhelm the upper and lower case type as full size capitals would.
- As a transition from a drop cap to the regular body text size (See Chapter 10: "First Impressions: Creating Great Opening Paragraphs")
- For abbreviations like AM and PM—with no letter spaces or periods (though it more contemporary to use lowercase: 3pm, 7pm, etc.).

The problem with Small Caps is that unless you are using an OpenType font or an Expert Set (a font of supplementary characters), you'll end up with fake small caps. Fake small caps are regular caps that have been scaled down in size, rather than redrawn characters designed to work in proportion with the regular caps. Because all their proportions are reduced, their weight tends to look too light and spindly and their strokes will not be the same thickness when set alongside regular caps.

Holly came from Miami, F.L.A.
A Hitch-hiked her way across the USA

Holly came from Miami, F.L.A.
B Hitch-hiked her way across the USA

FIGURES 3.20A AND 3.20B Small Caps. **A** has the abbreviations in small caps—slightly higher than the x-height; **B** has them at full-caps size.

The BBC reported the decision by the IMF and the World Bank to cancel all debts as of 11 am on October 1, 2005. It is hoped that global injustices such as poverty, AIDS, malnutrition, conflict and
A illiteracy will be significantly reduced by 2015.

The BBC reported the decision by the IMF and the World Bank to cancel all debts as of 11am on October 1, 2005. It is hoped that global injustices such as poverty, AIDS, malnutrition, conflict and
B illiteracy will be significantly reduced by 2015.

The Constitution of the
A United States of America

The Constitution of the
B United States of America

FIGURE 3.21 Small Caps: real vs. fake. Example **A** uses real small caps—the weight of the character strokes is uniform. Example **B** uses "fake" small caps—regular caps sized at 70 percent.

All Caps

You know those people who type their emails in ALL CAPS? Annoying, aren't they? Continuous text set in all caps is hard to read because the shapes of the words all look alike and are differentiated only by their length. We recognize words as shapes—the descenders and the ascenders of upper and lowercase text are essential to our ability to identify letters. Also, text set in all caps within body text tends to look disproportionately large when set among upper and lowercase text; hence the need for Small Caps. Just as shouting doesn't make your message any clearer, setting text in all caps doesn't make your message any more compelling.

None of this is to say don't use All Caps—just use them thoughtfully. All Caps can be effective in headlines and subheads. Because there are no descenders, you should tighten the leading. Depending on the typeface, you may want to loosen the tracking for a sophisticated and understated look or tighten the tracking for a more solid, contrasty look.

A BREAKING NEWS
BREAKING NEWS

FINE JEWELRY
B FINE JEWELRY

FIGURE 3.22 All Caps Treatments. The lack of serifs in the sans serif examples allows tighter tracking of the letters, which, in combination with the blockiness of the letter shapes, gives a more solid look, suitable in some instances but not in others. Loose tracking makes the serif versions more elegant. Context is everything.

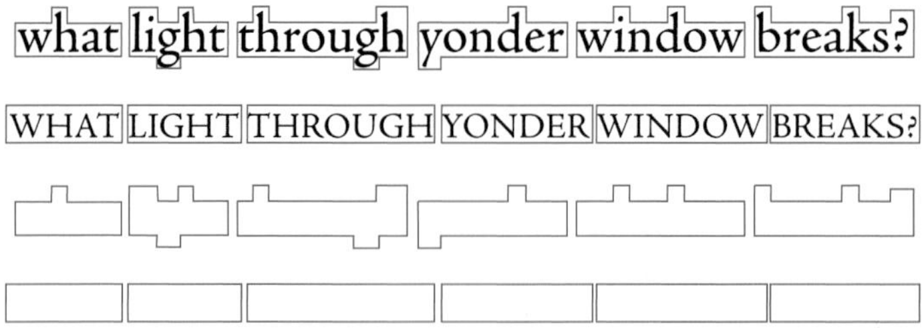

what light through yonder window breaks?

WHAT LIGHT THROUGH YONDER WINDOW BREAKS?

FIGURE 3.22A Text set in ALL CAPS is more difficult to read because, without ascenders and descenders, all of the word shapes are the same. Compare the more interesting word shapes created by upper and lowercase to the rectangles created by using ALL CAPS.

Superscript and Subscript

Superscript is typically used for ordinals in numbers or for footnotes. Subscript is used in chemical formulae. In Text Preferences, you can change the size of both relative to the point size of your text. You can also changetheir position relative to the baseline of the text. For best results set the Super/Subscript size to 60 percent, the Superscript position to 33 percent and the Subscript position to 0 percent.

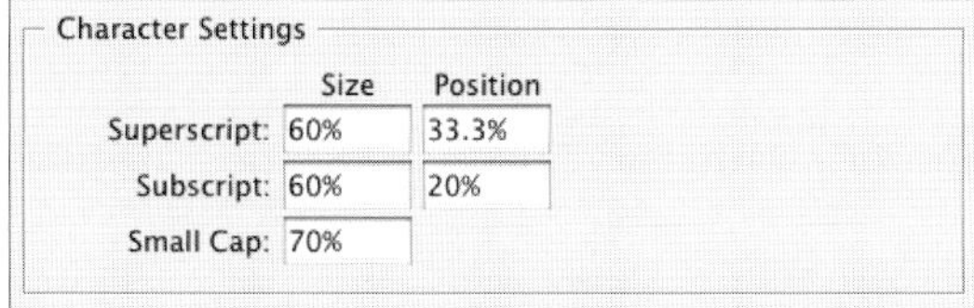

FIGURE 3.23 Superscript/Subscript Preferences.

April 1st

H_2O

FIGURE 3.24 Uses of Superscript and Subscript.

Underlining

In days of yore, when records came on vinyl and people typed on machines called typewriters, underlining was de rigueur for giving emphasis. But that was only because typewriters couldn't do it any other way. Underlining, as every type manual will tell you, should not, in these days of typographic sophistication, be used for emphasis. The underline collides with the descenders of the word and looks downright ugly. However, underlining has become more sophisticated and is, dare I say it, perhaps making a comeback. These days you can change the weight of the underline and its distance from the baseline. Even so, underlined text—no matter how fancy the underline—is always going to be mutton dressed as lamb. That said, there are some nifty tricks you can do with underlining when applied as part of a style definition. But that's another story—see Chapter 13, "Stylin' with Paragraph and Character Styles."

TIP: Really can't resist underlining? Try adding a paper colored stroke to the underlined type. This prevents the underline from slicing through the descender shapes.

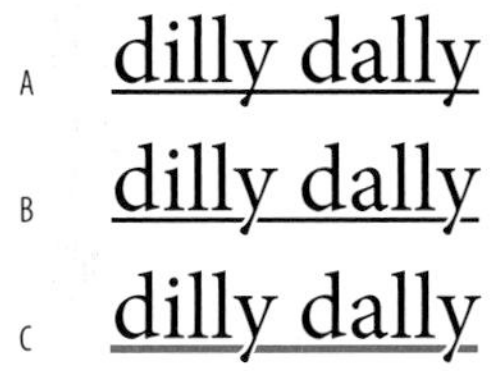

A dilly dally

B dilly dally

C dilly dally

FIGURE 3.25 Underlining Options: Example **A** uses a generic underline; in example **B**, the type has a 0.75 pt paper-colored stroke, which keeps the underline away from the descender of the "y." In example **C**, in addition to the paper-colored stroke, the color and weight of the underline have been adjusted. Choose Underline Options from the Control palette menu in the Character Formats.

TIP: Switch between the Character and Paragraph formatting views of the Control Palette by pressing Cmd+Option+7 (Ctrl+Alt+7).

Strikethrough

You might use strikethrough to indicate which text will be deleted as a document moves through revision cycles, or once in a blue moon if you're working on a legal document that requires you to indicate revisions. Alternatively, you might want to make a "highlight" character style—see Chapter 13, "Stylin' with Paragraph and Character Styles."

Baseline Shift

What can one say about the humble and oft-misunderstood baseline shift?

First, here's what it should not be used for: Never, under any circumstances, use Baseline Shift to adjust inter-paragraph spacing—that is the function of leading and/or paragraph spacing.

- Baseline shift is for fine tuning. It can be used to create effects in type, but mainly it's used for finessing when you feel that certain characters need shifting relative to the baseline of other characters on the same line. To apply a baseline shift, use the Control Palette (nudge arrows move in one point increments) or the Options box of the Character Specifications dialog box.

TIP: You can quickly access the preferences for these styles by Option/Alt-clicking their icon, which will take you to the Text Preferences dialog box.

Baseline shift can be used for the following:

- Adjusting the position of bullets, ornaments, and inline graphics
- Creating fractions, although OpenType fonts and the Make Fraction Script have made this use largely redundant
- Tweaking the position of symbols like $, ®, ©, and ™
- Adjusting the position of parentheses, braces, and brackets relative to the type they enclose, especially when used with All Caps. (Again, OpenType fonts make this less necessary)
- Creating type effects

FIGURE 3.26 Using Baseline Shift to "illustrate" a word.

Why Do Some Fonts Look Bigger than Others?

Take a selection of fonts, set them in the same size, and you'll find that some look bigger than others. What gives? The explanation for this goes back to the days of handset type when point size referred not to the size of the letter itself but to the size of the metal block on which the type was cast. Some typefaces occupied more space within their block than others. These days, point size refers to the size of the bounding box that surrounds each letter, but it is still the space in which the type lives that we actually measure, not the letter itself.

For this reason, let your eye guide you, not the point size. And an obvious point, but one still worth making: When evaluating your type, print test pages rather than relying on what you see on your screen.

Horizontal and Vertical Scale

Get caught using these options, and the Type Police will come knocking on your door. Mess with the proportions of your typeface and you are trampling roughshod over the life's work of some of the world's finest artisans. OK, so maybe I'm being a bit dramatic, but faking a condensed typeface (one with a narrower horizontal scale) or an expanded typeface (one with a wider horizontal scale) will make the character shapes look spindly and the overall effect look amateurish. It's better to choose a real condensed or real expanded typeface. It's like the difference between *My Way* sung by Frank Sinatra or by some random bloke doing a karaoke version after a few too many pints. Condensed faces include Times Roman and Garamond Condensed. Expanded faces are more typically used for display instead of body type, and are more likely to be sans serif—like Helvetica Neue Expanded or Univers Extended.

A We quickly seized the black axle and just saved it from going past him

B We quickly seized the black axle and just saved it from going past him

FIGURE 3.27 A real condensed font vs. a fake condensed font. ITC Garamond Light Condensed (**A**), and ITC Garamond Light (**B**) with horizontal scale set to 72 percent—note the lighter weight of the letters due to the scaling.

Having said all that in such a dogmatic way, I'll now put in a disclaimer about retaining the right to contradict myself. For every rule, there will be examples of ways it can be creatively broken, and distorting type is no exception. The point I'm making is if you want to break this or any typographic "rule," then do so consciously—and carry a big stick.

Text and Display

Body text or body copy is the small type (typically in sizes between 8-12 pt) that makes up the majority of a book or article and carries the bulk of the message. When choosing the size of your body text, you can probably go smaller than you think. Text that is too small is difficult to read in large quantities; on the other hand, text that is too large looks amateurish and clunky. While 12 point type is InDesign's default type size —and looks about right on screen—chances are it will look too big in print. Start out with 10 point text, then increase or decrease as necessary according to the characteristics of the font (and the needs of your audience).

Display type is the big type (typically 18 points and above) that grabs the reader's attention and appears as signposts (in the form of heads and subheads) throughout a book or article.

While size usually indicates the type's intent, it is not always the case. Display type can sometimes attract attention by being understated.

Readability

Readability refers to the ease with which we comprehend text by recognizing words and phrases as shapes. Readability is all about putting the reader first and leaving your ego behind—or at least confining it to your early drafts. Good typography is said to be "invisible"—you don't even notice it. Instead the type is a conduit for the message of the text. This might make the typographer sound undervalued, but while your readers may not notice good typography, they will certainly recognize bad typography. As the acclaimed typographer and book designer Jan Tschichold put it: "To remain nameless and without specific appreciation, yet to have been of service to a valuable work and to the small number of visually sensitive readers—this, as a rule, is the only compensation for the long, and indeed never-ending, indenture of the typographer.[1]" Humbling stuff.

[1] "Clay in a Potter's Hand," in *The Form of the Book*, p. 7.

Serif vs. Sans

Readability studies have found that serif typefaces are better for continuous reading. Explanations for this vary. Some experts feel that serifs function like rails, guiding your eye along the line. Others suggest that we respond to serif types better because the transition of their strokes more closely resembles calligraphy. Or perhaps—and my money's on this one—we read serif type more easily, simply because we're more used to reading serif type. In the words of Zuzana Licko, co-founder of Émigré digital font foundry: "You read best what you read most."

Maybe we could get used to anything, but we've been reading serif type for centuries and the habit is pretty much in our DNA. Sans serif typefaces are the new kids on the block relatively speaking—not invented until the early 19th Century and not in common usage until the 1920s.

Readability is less of a concern when it comes to display type, which, because it is set in short bursts rather than long passages, can afford to draw much more attention to itself.

It sounds like an overly simplistic formula, but you won't go far wrong if you use serif faces for your body text and sans serif for your headings and subheads. Because sans serifs tend to be bolder and blockier, they are better at grabbing the reader's attention. Also, the absence of serifs makes it possible to track sans serif headlines tighter, adding to their solidity. To make a subhead distinct from your body text, it is enough to choose a contrasting typeface; subheads do not necessarily need to be set in a larger point size.

Other Readability Factors

Your choice of font is just one of several factors that work in sync to create—hopefully—readable type. Other factors include—but as they say in legalese—are not limited to:

- Leading
- Column measure (the ratio of type size to column width)
- Alignment
- Margins
- Printing conditions: What kind of paper stock will the document be printed on?

TIP: Shortcuts for Sizing Type In addition to using the Type Size control on the Control Palette, you can also size your type using keyboard shortcuts:

Cmd+Shift+>/< (Ctrl+Shift+>/<) Increase or decrease point size by the increment specified in Preferences>Units & Increments>Size/Leading.

Cmd+Shif+Option> /< (Ctrl+Shift+Alt>/<) Increase or decrease point size by five times the increment specified in Preferences>Units & Increments>Size/Leading.

- Reading conditions: An enormous variable over which you, the typographer, have no control. There's no way you can know whether your audience will be reading by candlelight, while standing on a busy commuter train, or while in the bath. Although, depending on the type of document you're creating, you may be able to speculate. For example, if you're designing a bus timetable, you'll want to forgo challenging postmodern typography in favor of a straightforward, get-your-message-across approach.

Up Next

With type on our page let's look next at a critical factor in determining the readability of that type: the space between the lines, or leading.

CHAPTER 4

Getting the Lead Out

LEADING (PRONOUNCED "LEDDING") is the space between the lines of type. In the days of hot metal typesetting this space was created by inserting thin strips of lead between the lines. Lines of type without these strips of lead were—and still are—referred to as "set solid." Leading plays a big part in the readability of your text. All body text is made more readable by a positive amount of leading (a leading value greater than the point size of the type). Headlines and display type, on the other hand, may benefit from negative leading (a leading value less than the point size of the type).

InDesign regards leading as a character level format (as opposed to a paragraph format in QuarkXPress). Leading can be applied "locally" to a selected range of text using the Control palette or the Character palette, or "globally" as part of a style sheet definition.

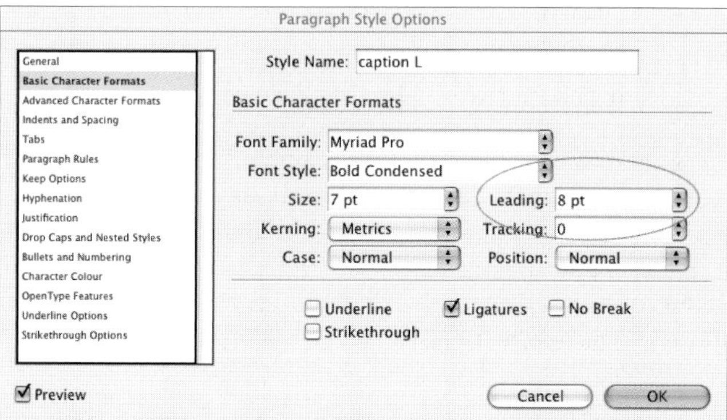

FIGURE 4.1 Basic Character Formats.

Bad leading makes your text harder to read because the eye has trouble locating the next line of type. When leading is too tight, the type may appear intimidatingly dense, and the descenders of one line will collide with the ascenders of the next. At the other extreme, when the leading is too loose the type lack cohesion. This is especially so if the leading is greater than the space between the paragraphs.

Leading is measured in points from one baseline to the next. The leading value includes the point size of the typeface and the actual space between the lines. Thus, 12 points of leading using 10-point type really means two points of space between lines.

How Much Is Enough?

When it comes to leading there is no *one size fits all.* How much leading you give your type depends on several variables. Here are some factors to consider:

- The nature of the text. While text intended for continuous reading will always benefit from some breathing space, a short burst of advertising copy or a title might be more effective if the lines are tightly leaded.
- Type size: As point size increases you will want proportionally less leading. Body text that is 10 points in size is commonly set with 12 points of leading—written 10/12, spoken 10 on 12. When you get to display sizes, the spaces between the lines appears much larger. So much so that it's common to use negative leading for display type.

Poor human nature, what horrible crimes have been committed in thy name! Every fool, from king to policeman, from the flatheaded parson to the visionless dabbler in science, presumes to speak authoritatively of human nature. The greater the mental charlatan, the more definite his insistence on the wickedness and weaknesses of human nature. Yet, how can any one speak of it today, with every soul in a prison, with every heart fettered, wounded, and maimed? —Emma Goldman **A Centaur 10/9**

Poor human nature, what horrible crimes have been committed in thy name! Every fool, from king to policeman, from the flatheaded parson to the visionless dabbler in science, presumes to speak authoritatively of human nature. The greater the mental charlatan, the more definite his insistence on the wickedness and weaknesses of human nature. Yet, how can any one speak of it today, with every soul in a prison, with every heart fettered, wounded, and maimed? —Emma Goldman **B Centaur 10/12**

Poor human nature, what horrible crimes have been committed in thy name! Every fool, from king to policeman, from the flatheaded parson to the visionless dabbler in science, presumes to speak authoritatively of human nature. The greater the mental charlatan, the more definite his insistence on the wickedness and weaknesses of human nature. Yet, how can any one speak of it today, with every soul in a prison, with every heart fettered, wounded, and maimed? —Emma Goldman **C Centaur 10/18**

FIGURE 4.2 Text block with tight leading (example **A**); plus two points of leading (example **B**); and plus eight points of leading (example **C**).

Was this the face that launched a thousand ships,
And burnt the topless towers of Ilium?

FIGURE 4.3 Leading is measured from baseline to baseline.

FIGURE 4.4 Leading and display type. Example **A** shows the headline with Auto Leading applied (42/50.4), with the result that the two lines seem disconnected from each other. The problem is exacerbated by the all-cap treatment, meaning there are no ascenders or descenders. Example **B** shows negative leading applied (42/38).

FIRST MAN
A ON THE MOON

FIRST MAN
B ON THE MOON

- Typefaces with larger x-heights—certain serif typefaces like Times New Roman, or sans serifs typefaces in general—are perceived to be bigger because the lowercase letters take up a relatively large part of the overall area of the character bounding box. Such typefaces require more leading. Conversely, type with small x-heights, Like Garamond, will seem to have more horizontal space between the lines and thus require less leading. Sans serif typefaces typically have higher x-heights and thus require more leading than serif faces.
- Some typefaces, like Bernhard Modern, may have particularly tall ascenders—meaning that with tight leading you run the risk of the ascenders colliding with the descenders of the previous line.

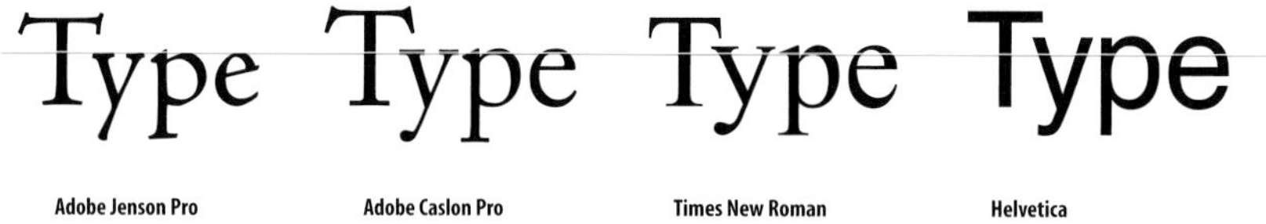

FIGURE 4.5 Four typefaces at the same size (38 point) with different x-heights.

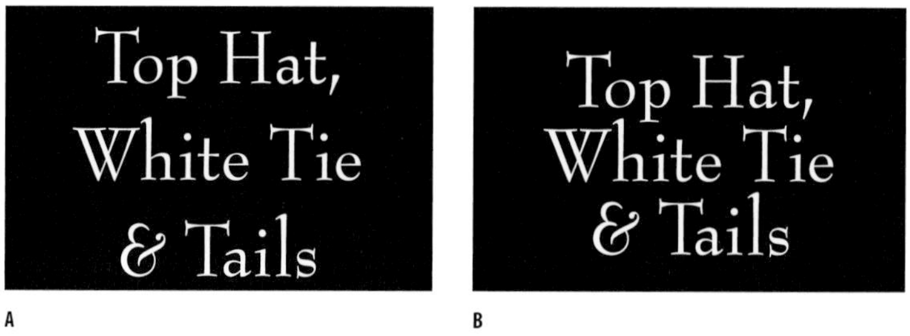

Type Type Type Type

Adobe Jenson Pro | Adobe Caslon Pro | Times New Roman | Helvetica

FIGURE 4.6 Bernhard Modern, because of its low x-height, can be leaded tightly. Example **A** shows 24 point on Auto Leading (28.8); example **B** shows 24/22.

Top Hat,
White Tie
& Tails

A

Top Hat,
White Tie
& Tails

B

- Typefaces with heavy stroke weights benefit from extra leading to prevent the *type color*—the darkness or blackness of the letterforms as a block—appearing too dense.
- When your type is in all caps, there are no descenders, making the lines of type appear farther apart. Time to tighten the leading.
- Column Width: It's best to avoid setting type in wide columns, but if you have no choice, increasing the leading anywhere from a half point to 2 points will improve readability by keeping the lines distinct and preventing the eye from dropping off to the line below or doubling back to reread the same line.
- At the other extreme, justified type set in a narrow column may cause word-spacing problems. Because we read in words or clusters of words, rather than letter by letter, if the space between the words is bigger than the space between the lines, the eye may jump to the next line rather than to the next word. In such situations, extra leading might be necessary to ensure that the space between the lines is greater than the space between the words. The best solution is to avoid justified type on a narrow measure altogether, but in the real world we don't always have as much say as we might like.

We propose a concerted but completely decentralized project—a project many people are already carrying out spontaneously. Give gifts to strangers! Give them to your friends. Give them as often as you can, not just at Burning Man, but year round. Do favors, acts of generosity, spontaneous expressions of art and music, and so on, whenever it feels right and good to do so. ¶ By giving gifts we subvert the Economy and redirect our productive and creative capacity away from the cash nexus, the vortex that sucks in our lives and spits them back out as oil wars, poisoned skies and waterways, and mass psychosis. Decommodification is the order of the day. ¶ The world is not for sale—and we are not ultimately workers and consumers! We're all much larger and more powerful than our roles in the Economy would have us believe. Escaping the Economy during
A Burning Man is a tiny taste of the kind of life we could be making all the time.—*Committee for Full Enjoyment*

We propose a concerted but completely decentralized project—a project many people are already carrying out spontaneously. Give gifts to strangers! Give them to your friends. Give them as often as you can, not just at Burning Man, but year round. Do favors, acts of generosity, spontaneous expressions of art and music, and so on, whenever it feels right and good to do so. ¶ By giving gifts we subvert the Economy and redirect our productive and creative capacity away from the cash nexus, the vortex that sucks in our lives and spits them back out as oil wars, poisoned skies and waterways, and mass psychosis. Decommodification is the order of the day. ¶ The world is not for sale—and we are not ultimately workers and consumers! We're all much larger and more powerful than our roles in the Economy would have us believe. Escaping the Economy during
B Burning Man is a tiny taste of the kind of life we could be making all the time.—*Committee for Full Enjoyment*

FIGURE 4.7 Leading and Column Width. The text set solid (example **A**), and with three points of leading 8/11 (example **B**).

- Reversing Out: Because we are used to reading black type on white paper, when we choose to use the opposite, we're guaranteed to make our type attention-getting. However, reversed type tends to sparkle, making it harder to read. A slight increase in leading—as well as avoiding any fonts with delicate serifs—may compensate for the diminished readability of reversed out type.
- Very loose leading can create a luxurious look. But sometimes there's a fine line between looking spacious and looking like the different lines of type bear no relation to each other.
- Tight leading will increase the density of the type and can make it feel claustrophobic.
- Economy often dictates leading: You have a fixed number of words and you have to fit them into a finite amount of space. In such situations, choose a font that lends itself to being tightly leaded.

FIGURE 4.8 Example **A** is 10/12; example **B** is 10/14.

Battersea Power Station

One of London's most loved landmarks, Battersea Power Station now faces an uncertain future. Admired for it's majestic four-chimney skyline silhouette, Battersea Power Station supplied London with electricity between 1933 and 1983. It was designed by Sir Giles Gilbert Scott, whose other design credits include Waterloo Bridge and the red telephone box, and constructed from brick around a steel. The building now has a listed Grade II status, ensuring that it cannot be demolished or changed without Government consent. Since its closure there have been various suggestions for what to do with the site. In the late 1980s planning permission was granted for a theme park. However, this proved unworkable and a stalemate now exists between developers, Government and the local community.

A

Battersea Power Station

One of London's most loved landmarks, Battersea Power Station now faces an uncertain future. Admired for it's majestic four-chimney skyline silhouette, Battersea Power Station supplied London with electricity between 1933 and 1983. It was designed by Sir Giles Gilbert Scott, whose other design credits include Waterloo Bridge and the red telephone box, and constructed from brick around a steel. The building now has a listed Grade II status, ensuring that it cannot be demolished or changed without Government consent. Since its closure there have been various suggestions for what to do with the site. In the late 1980s planning permission was granted for a theme park. However, this proved unworkable and a stalemate now exists between developers, Government and the local community.

B

(Not) Using Auto Leading

While leading has existed since the days of metal type, Auto Leading is a relatively new concept, emerging with desktop publishing in the mid-1980s. Auto Leading allows InDesign to automatically assign a leading value to the text you set, based on the type's point size.

The advantage of Auto Leading is convenience. You can change your text size as many times as you like and your type will always be readable. As your font size increases or decreases, so does your leading. Although this can be useful when experimenting with type sizes, Auto Leading will probably cause more problems than it solves.

Don't by seduced by Auto Leading. Here's why:

- Auto Leading is proportional to your type size—but specific to the biggest piece of type in the paragraph. This means that if you have one word larger than the rest of the paragraph, you leading value will be 120 percent of the largest word or character. Leading values in parenthesis signify Auto Leading. By default, Auto Leading is 120 percent of your type size although you can change this in your Justification options.

People who live
in glass houses
are worth two
in the bush
A

People who live
in glass houses
are worth two
in the bush
B

FIGURE 4.9 Inconsistent leading caused by a single word in the paragraph set larger (example **A**); the leading converted to an absolute number (example **B**).

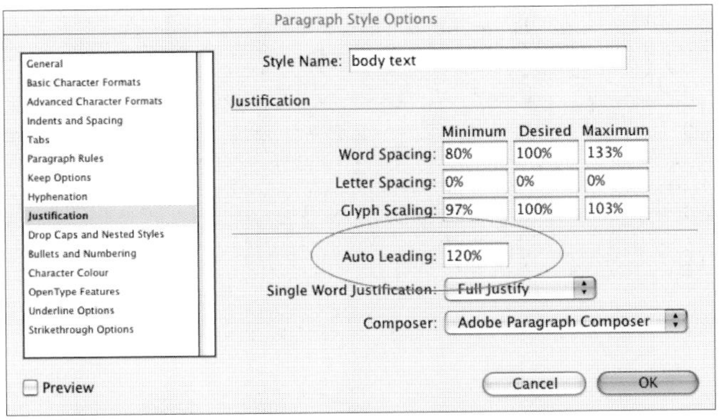

FIGURE 4.10 Changing the Auto Leading Amount.

- Auto Leading doesn't give you the kind of control of your text you need. Sure, if you're using 10-point type Auto Leading is 12 point, a nice easy number to work with. However, if you're working with 11-point type, then your leading value is 13.2, which is a cumbersome number, difficult to calculate in multiples if you intend working with a baseline or leading grid.
- While Auto Leading works OK for body text, it can look terrible when applied to display type, which generally requires less leading. This is especially true if you have headings in all caps, because there will be no descenders to fill the lines.

Trust your eye, not your software, to determine how much leading you need. Auto Leading is useful when experimenting with type sizes, but when you decide upon the size you need be sure to convert your leading values to an absolute number, even if the Auto Leading value is the same as that number.

FIGURES 4.11A AND 4.11B Auto Leading applied to a headline (**A**). While Auto Leading works adequately for the body text, in the headline it is disproportionately large (**B**).

Flying Machine
Takes To The Air

Ugait dipit velisi bla feugait nonsenibh euguerostrud tet nulla faccums andrerit num dolor si blaor inci tat iustrud te eniam nos del ullumsan velit nulluptat enim veniam zzriurem iliquat adiam, corem vel ea faciliquat laortisit prat, sectem dolorem nos nim vent lan volore feum zzrilis ad tisl utpat ad duipit landignibh ese et digna faccum inci bla accummo loboreet ad ea con velit ad tio od dionullam, quam, commolore magnisim veliquismodo commy niscip elit ut nimlbh exercil eriuscipit ullumsan hendreratis autem doluptat lumsandigna consequat, quisim vulput nonummodiate tisci bla alisl exer si. It lore tismodo lortie ming eugait vent utet alisi.Lendre tet iliquatie enibh eraesequis autpat dui et ip eugait alit il ut laorer sequipit praesse eu feu faccumsan henisl er adio dio do cor accummodo diam inim do exero odionul luptatum del ullanLa feugue con etumsan ulputpat. Uptat ad mincidunt

Flying Machine
Takes To The Air

Ugait dipit velisi bla feugait nonsenibh euguerostrud tet nulla faccums andrerit num dolor si blaor inci tat iustrud te eniam nos del ullumsan velit nulluptat enim veniam zzriurem iliquat adiam, corem vel ea faciliquat laortisit prat, sectem dolorem nos nim vent lan volore feum zzrilis ad tisl utpat ad duipit landignibh ese et digna faccum inci bla accummo loboreet ad ea con velit ad tio od dionullam, quam, commolore magnisim veliquismodo commy niscip elit ut nimlbh exercil eriuscipit ullumsan hendreratis autem doluptat lumsandigna consequat, quisim vulput nonummodiate tisci bla alisl exer si. It lore tismodo lortie ming eugait vent utet alisi.Lendre tet iliquatie enibh eraesequis autpat dui et ip eugait alit il ut laorer sequipit praesse eu feu faccumsan henisl er adio dio do cor accummodo diam inim do exero odionul luptatum del ullanLa feugue con etumsan ulputpat. Uptat ad mincidunt

Auto Leading and Inline Graphics

Auto Leading is useful when using inline graphics—picture frames that have been pasted into a text frame, usually on their own line, and move with the flow of text. Inline graphics are a hybrid between text and graphics: You control the spacing of inline graphics using leading and Auto Leading ensures there's always enough space for the graphic on the line. An Auto Leading value of 100% works well for most inline graphics.

Keep It Consistent, Except...

Leading like so much in typography is all about rhythm, and you want your rhythm to be steady. The best way to do this is to set your leading value as part of a style-sheet definition; should you need to change the leading value, edit the style definition rather than work on the paragraph locally.

When it comes to fixing widows and orphans, don't mess with the leading. You have other tricks up your sleeve—tracking, discretionary hyphens, forced line breaks—to fix such problems (see Chapter 5: "Kern, Baby, Kern" and Chapter 11: "Don't Fear the Hyphen"). Tempting though it may be to tighten the leading a little bit here and there, your document will look like a dog's dinner if you do. Always keep your body text leading consistent, otherwise the rhythm of your type will falter.

Also, don't be tempted to go for the soft option of vertical alignment, which adjusts the leading to make multiple columns bottom out, i.e., end on the same baseline. (See Chapter 8: Align your Type.)

Working with display type, you may need to relax the consistency rule in favor of optical leading—tweaking the leading of individual lines to make the leading *appear* more consistent. Such a situation may arise in display type if one line doesn't have descenders—another example of trusting your eye rather than the math.

FIGURES 4.12A AND 4.12B An extreme example of the what can happen with vertical justification: the leading in column 3 is opened up in order to make all three columns "bottom out."

Magnit alissim zzrit utet lute min utatuercipit lutat erostrud tat prat. Ut vel in henis euismodolute duisl iure commod dolessi ssenism oloborero conse mod modolenibh etue minit elit, corerit autat alit pratis nonsectet verationse cortisit ea faccum eum ing ex ercilit, corperc iduissequis etue feu feugait diam, quamconse modolorem do exerit nostrud exero et prat.

Ut ip et digna augue coreet numsan el duisl dipit wiscip etum velesequat veraestrud tat er aliquatum duipissit, veliquam nit veril ipiscing ea adit nos autatue velit vero delit amet adit essis nonsectet eugiat augiam dolorem niat, susciliquis do odoloreriure magnis nosto dolesendrem acipismod dolorer iure facidunt nostion sendreetum quismol endreet, veros aliqui tionse-

quat volore tatumsa ndionse

quamet augue faci eugiam,

secte facipsum ipisim volore

tio delestis et velestisis do-

lorercing elenisi.

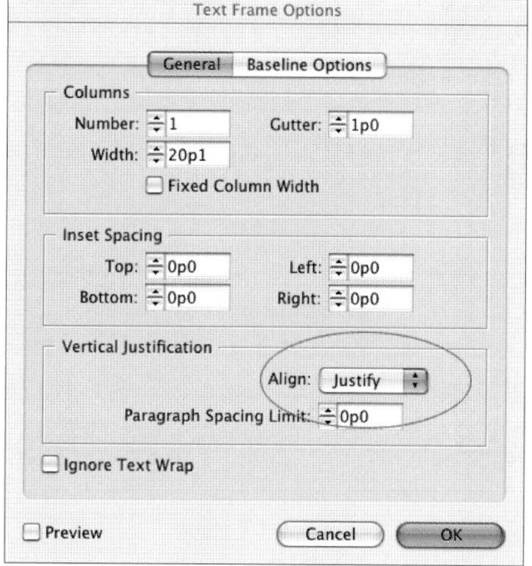

The only way
to get rid of a
TEMPTATION
is to yield to it.

—Oscar Wilde, *The Picture of Dorian Gray*

A

The only way
to get rid of a
TEMPTATION
is to yield to it.

—Oscar Wilde, *The Picture of Dorian Gray*

B

FIGURE 4.13 Optical Leading. The leading beneath "Temptation" appears too large in example **A** because there are no descenders. In example **B**, the leading for the last line has been reduced to compensate.

Leading Menu Options and Keyboard Shortcuts

There's an interesting and often overlooked text preference that determines how your leading will behave. When you choose Apply Leading to Entire Paragraphs, InDesign makes the leading of the whole paragraph the same, which is almost always a good idea, although it does not apply to paragraphs set to use Auto Leading.

Note that when your text is set to Align to Baseline Grid, changing the leading may result in unpredictable behavior, causing the lines of type to jump to the next baseline grid increment.

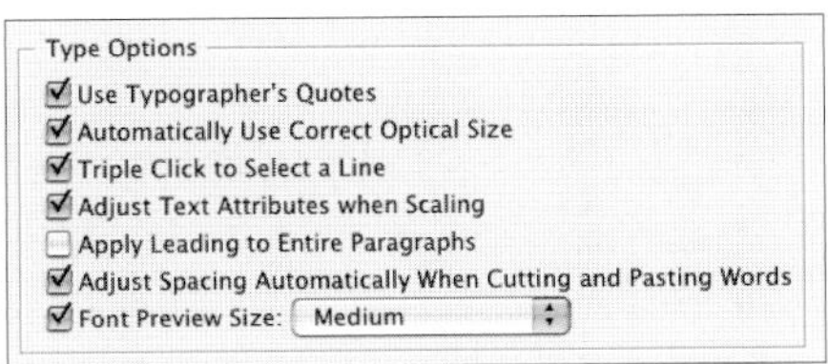

FIGURE 4.14 Apply Leading to Entire Paragraphs preference.

FIGURE 4.15 Align to Baseline Grid.

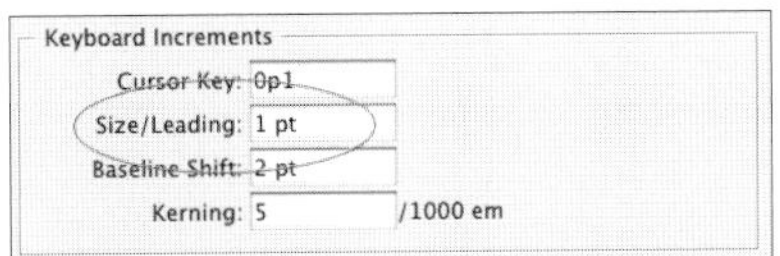

FIGURE 4.16 Leading Increment Preference.

See Also

For a discussion of the Skip by Leading Text Wrap preference, see Chapter 18, "Text Wraps: The Good, the Bad, and the Ugly."

For a discussion of the Text Frame First Baseline Position options as well as Align to Baseline Grid, see Chapter 16, "Everything in Its Right Place: Using Grids for a Clean, Structured Look."

TIP: A handy shortcut for increasing or decreasing the leading of a selected range of text is pressing Option+Up Arrow (Alt+Up Arrow) to tighten the leading or Option+Down Arrow (Alt+Down Arrow) to loosen the leading. The amount is determined by the value in the Size/Leading field in the Units & Increments Preferences. To increase/decrease the leading value by five times this amount press Cmd+Option+Up Arrow/Down Arrow (Ctrl+Alt+Up Arrow/Down Arrow).

Up Next

We switch from the vertical to the horizontal. Having tackled the space between the lines, we look next at controling the space between the words and characters. Kerning and tracking are to type what seasoning is to cooking. Carefully applied they can make the difference between the bland and sublime; but like seasoning it's easy to use a heavy hand, so gently does it.

CHAPTER 5

Kern, Baby, Kern

THE SPACES BETWEEN LETTERS are as important as the letters themselves. Kerning—and its cousin tracking—are ways of adjusting the space between characters to create a better fit, and thus a better rhythm, to your type. It's this steady rhythm that makes your type readable.

NOTE: A surefire way to raise the hackles of a purist typographer is to use the terms kerning and tracking interchangeably. While closely related, they are distinct. Kerning refers to adjusting the space between a pair of characters. Tracking means adjusting the space across a range of text.

We need kerning because certain letter shapes don't fit well together. Sometimes it's necessary to adjust the space between letters to achieve the appearance of even spacing.

When to Kern

The objective of kerning is to achieve the appearance of equal spacing on either side of each character. Thankfully, the majority of your kerning needs are addressed by InDesign's automatic kerning methods, of which there are two kinds: Metrics and Optical. Either method adequately handles kerning at small type sizes, so you don't need to drive yourself crazy finding every instance of troublesome kerning pairs and manually adjusting their spacing. Regardless of the method you use, you can always add manual kerning as needed.

A AWAY

B AWAY

C AWAY

D AWAY

FIGURE 5.1 Why we kern. (**A**) No kerning, (**B**) Metrics Kerning, (**C**) Optical Kerning, (**D**) Optical Kerning with additional manual kerning.

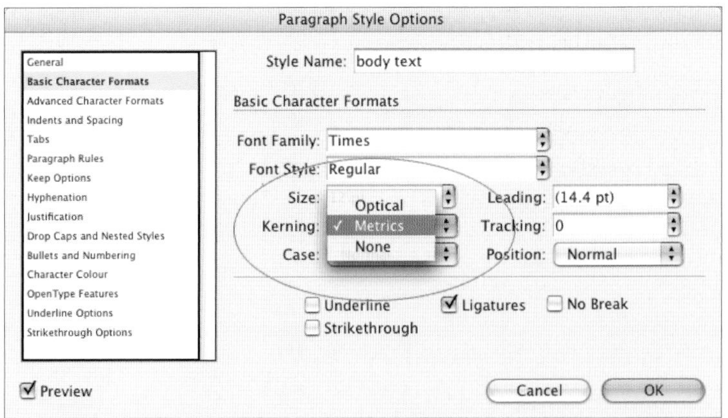

FIGURE 5.2 Basic Character Formats.

Automatic kerning can be applied locally by selecting a range of text, then choosing Metrics or Optical from the Control palette (or the Character palette), but you're better off choosing your automatic kerning method as part of a style sheet definition.

Metrics Kerning

Metrics Kerning uses the kern pairs that are built into the font, or most fonts. Adobe typefaces tend to have between 500 and 1000 kerning pairs. The El Cheapo font that you downloaded for free from the Web may not have any. This is one reason some fonts cost more than others. Some common kerning pairs—those that a type designer will pay special heed to when creating a typeface—are LA, P., To, Tr, Ta, Tu, Te, Ty, Wa, WA, We, Wo, Ya, and Yo.

Optical Kerning

Optical Kerning adjusts the spacing between adjacent characters based on their shapes and pays no mind to the kerning pairs.

Theoretically, Optical kerning will give you more consistent character spacing, because every character pair, even the most unlikely ones like zh or xw or gk, is kerned based on its character shapes. It's a matter of preference, but here are some things to consider:

- If your font includes few built-in kerning pairs, you're better off with Optical Kerning. Decorative and novelty fonts are likely to have few kerning pairs.
- When combining two typefaces in the same paragraph, the two fonts may use very different kerning metrics and may not look right side by side. This is another occasion when you'll be better served by Optical Kerning.
- You might want to view Metrics vs. Optical Kerning as a microcosm of the timeless drama of man vs. machine. Optical Kerning will be more consistent, more mathematically correct—but will it look better? Ultimately it depends on the quality of the metrics you are comparing it against.

FIGURE 5.3 Comparison of Metrics kerning (example **A**) and Optical kerning (example **B**) using Times. The amount of difference will vary from font to font.

A

For some time I stood tottering on the mound regardless of my safety. Within that noisome den from which I had emerged I had thought with a narrow intensity only of our immediate security. I had not realised what had been happening to the world, had not anticipated this startling vision of unfamiliar things. I had expected to see Sheen in ruins — I found about me the landscape, weird and lurid, of another planet. —H.G. Wells, *The War of the Worlds*

B

For some time I stood tottering on the mound regardless of my safety. Within that noisome den from which I had emerged I had thought with a narrow intensity only of our immediate security. I had not realised what had been happening to the world, had not anticipated this startling vision of unfamiliar things. I had expected to see Sheen in ruins — I found about me the landscape, weird and lurid, of another planet. —H.G. Wells, *The War of the Worlds*

FIGURE 5.4 Metrics Kerning (example **A**) vs. Optical Kerning (example **B**) when using mixed fonts.

A Welcome

B Welcome

FIGURE 5.5 Metrics Kerning (example **A**) fares better than Optical Kerning (example **B**) when using script faces.

A Winchester

B Winchester

Manual Kerning

To adjust kerning manually, insert your Type Tool between two characters. Press Option+Left/Right Arrow (Alt+Left/Right Arrow) to decrease or increase the kerning between two characters. This method kerns using the increment specified in your Units and Increment Preferences. The default kern increment is 20/1000 of an em, which is too coarse. Do yourself a favor and change this increment to 5 in your application Preferences. Because these adjustments are in relative units, a kerning or tracking adjustment made at one point size will have proportionally the same effect at any other point size. Holding down Cmd (Ctrl) when using these keystrokes multiplies the kerning increment by five.

To adjust tracking manually, follow the same steps but with a range of text selected.

As your type gets larger, any irregular spacing between characters becomes more noticeable. Manual intervention may be required. Possible candidates for kerning include:

- Headlines and display type
- Drop Caps (See Chapter 10: "First Impressions: Creating Great Opening Paragraphs")
- Combined fonts (especially roman-italic combinations)
- Script typefaces

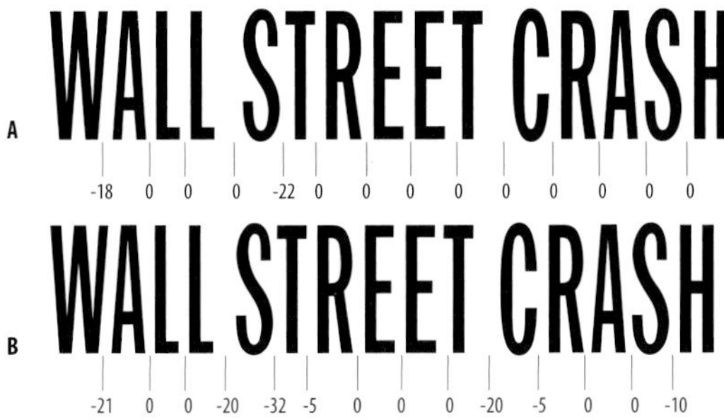

FIGURE 5.6 A headline in Franklin Gothic Condensed with Metrics Kerning (example **A**) and with manual kerning added (example **B**).

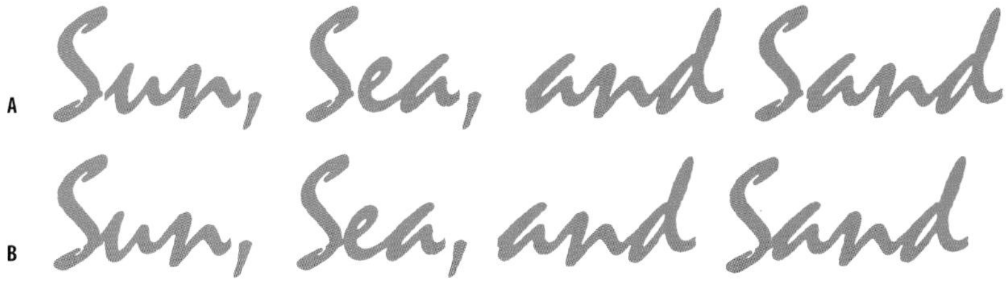

A Sun, Sea, and Sand

B Sun, Sea, and Sand

FIGURE 5.7 A script typeface without manual kerning (example **A**) and with manual kerning (example **B**).

How Much to Kern

TIP: When making kerning adjustments, zoom in to a large enough view size to be able to truly evaluate your results—and then zoom out again to 100 percent view to make sure your changes look appropriate.

PostScript fonts are designed in an em square—a box that is 1000 units x 1000 units. An em is a relative unit the same size as your type and InDesign kerns (and tracks) in increments of 1/1000 of an em. Place your Type cursor between any pair of characters to see how much kerning is applied—the Kerning field displays the amount in parentheses in 1000s of an em.

Don't overdo it. Along with the ease of kerning comes a tendency to want to fix things that ain't broke in the first place. Most of the letter shapes we know—and have been reading all our lives—were designed so that well-distributed weight would compensate for their odd shapes. Consequently, they fit well with nearly all of their possible neighbors. It takes time to develop an eye for kerning; until you feel confident, be cautious and make only slight adjustments. And make sure you're consistent: If you decide that certain letter combinations require kerning at display sizes, then make sure you kern all the instances of those letter combinations.

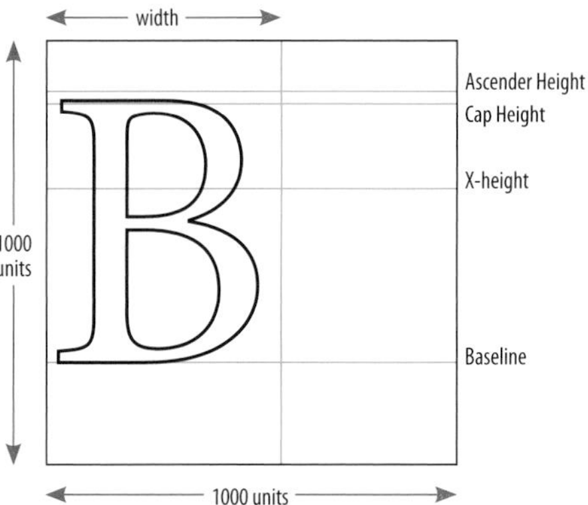

FIGURE 5.8 The Em Square.

A Kerning Anecdote

When I was a wee lad growing up in South London (and long before I cared about type) I spied the large neon sign of a new video store from a distance of about 100 yards. The name of the store was FLICKERS, set in all caps. The letters were very tightly spaced so that—from a distance—the LI combination looked like a U. It certainly grabbed my attention, and possibly it was intentional.

Tracking

This chapter is also about tracking—adjusting the letter spacing across a range of characters. Tracking can be applied as part of a style sheet definition.

Tracking, a cousin to kerning, is an overall increase or decrease in letter spacing over a range of characters. Tracking can also be applied locally to fix widows and orphans by (imperceptibly) tightening the letter spacing across a range of words and "pulling back" a short line. Tracking values can also be applied "globally" as part of a style definition to give the type a denser or airier look (Word and Character space options in the Justification dialog can give you the same effect). Remember, when you do this you are overriding what the type designer, who slaved long and hard over his or her font, considered the optimum character spacing. Tracking body text is like taking a musician's composition and playing it at a different tempo. Track your body text and you could be breaking some poor font designer's heart. If you do use negative tracking as part of a style definition, pay careful attention to what happens to pairs like rn; tracked too tight these might look like an "m," ri might look like an "n," and cl like a "d."

Then there is the other extreme. Track type too loosely and you disrupt the relationships between the letters that readers rely on. The letters no longer form the familiar shapes of words or phrases, but are merely a scattershot of disconnected characters. Spacing your letters too loosely might not seem like such a big deal to a lay person, but typographers get quite upset about such practices. The American typographer Frederick Goudy famously said, "Men who would letterspace lower case would steel sheep." Reputedly, that's the sanitized version of the quote.

The fiery trial through which we pass, will light us down, in honor or dishonor, to the latest generation.... In giving freedom to the slave, we assure freedom to the free–honorable alike in what we give, and what we preserve. We shall nobly save, or meanly lose, the last best, hope of earth.

A

The fiery trial through which we pass, will light us down, in honor or dishonor, to the latest generation.... In giving freedom to the slave, we assure freedom to the free–honorable alike in what we give, and what we preserve. We shall nobly save, or meanly lose, the last best, hope of earth.

B

The fiery trial through which we pass, will light us down, in honor or dishonor, to the latest generation.... In giving freedom to the slave, we assure freedom to the free–honorable alike in what we give, and what we preserve. We shall nobly save, or meanly lose, the last best, hope of earth.

—President Abraham Lincoln, December 1, 1862

C

FIGURE 5.9 Type tracked too loosely (example **A**), too tightly (example **B**), and without tracking (example **C**).

NOTE: Kerning and tracking are cumulative; they don't cancel each other out. You can use tracking to adjust the overall look of your type, and use kerning to adjust particular letter combinations.

Tracking is best used in moderation. If you're tempted to use tracking often, consider using a condensed typeface that has been designed with the efficient use of space in mind.

To track a range of type, highlight the type and press Option+Left Arrow (Alt+Left Arrow) to go tighter, Option+Right Arrow (Alt+Right Arrow) to go looser. As with kerning, the default increment of 20/1000 of an em is too coarse, so it's a good idea to change this in your application Preferences.

When to Track

OK, after all the safety warnings and disclaimers, here are some scenarios when negative tracking can come in handy:

- In headlines, especially sans serif headlines, the space between the letters can look disproportionately large. Because widely set letters make the words harder to read, applying negative tracking can help the characters hold together better and form more easily recognized word shapes. Don't overdo it, though; tracking too tightly will cause characters to collide and words to run into each other.

FIGURE 5.10 A headline without tracking (example **A**) and with –25 tracking (example **B**) applied as part of a style sheet definition.

A EVEREST CONQUERED

B EVEREST CONQUERED

TIP: Quark Kerning and Tracking Conversions
If you're a Quark refugee, you'll need to multiply your old Quark kerning and tracking values by 5 to give you the equivalent InDesign values. In Quark terms, a kerning/tracking value of 1 equals 1/200th of an em; in InDesign, "1" equals 1/1000th of an em. For example, if you tracked text to 1 in Quark, you would need to track it to 5 in InDesign.

- Condensed typefaces may benefit from a modest amount (–10) of negative tracking.
- Negative tracking can be used to help fix composition problems in passages of text. When tracking tighter across a range of text or a paragraph to pull back a line, remember that, like so much of good typography, your tracking adjustments should be "invisible." If the reader can tell, then you've gone too far—as a general rule of thumb, avoid using more than –15/1000 of an em. Also, if you have your Justification and Hyphenation set up correctly, there will be much less need for manual intervention in the form of tracking. (See Chapter 8: "Aligning Your Type")

FOUR SCORE AND SEVEN years ago our fathers brought forth on this continent, a new nation, conceived in liberty, and dedicated to the proposition that all men are created equal.

Now we are engaged in a great civil war, testing whether that nation or any nation so conceived and so dedicated, can long endure.

A

FOUR SCORE AND SEVEN years ago our fathers brought forth on this continent, a new nation, conceived in liberty, and dedicated to the proposition that all men are created equal.

Now we are engaged in a great civil war, testing whether that nation or any nation so conceived and so dedicated, can long endure.

B

FIGURE 5.11 Tracking to bring back a short line. In example **A**, line 5 suffers from bad word spacing and line 6 is short. In example **B**, the second paragraph has –5 tracking applied, which is sufficient to pull the last line back as well as improve the word spacing.

- In script faces, the characters should connect with each other so that the type looks like handwriting. If the font has well-designed kerning metrics, no intervention will be necessary. But pay careful attention to the way these characters connect—or don't connect, as the case may be—and adjust your tracking accordingly.

Positive tracking might be useful in these situations:

- Headlines set in all caps, especially in serif faces, look more elegant with positive tracking of up to 50/1000 of em.
- Positive tracking can help improve the type color of very small type like captions or photo credits. Again, be cautious—too much tracking will cause the type to fall apart and lose its distinctive word shapes.
- When reversing type out of a solid background, positive tracking can improve readability.

A

DRAMA
COMEDY
TRAGEDY

B

D R A M A
C O M E D Y
T R A G E D Y

FIGURE 5.12 All caps serif title treatment with no tracking (example **A**) and reduced in size with +200 tracking (example **B**).

FIGURE 5.13 Reversed-out text with no tracking (example **A**) and with +25 tracking (example **B**).

A

Using a Brush

Cut in around the entire ceiling as well as any light fittings, then take the larger brush and coat the ceiling using smooth parallel strokes. Paint in 1 metre sections so that the wet edges stay fresher and improve the finish.

B

Using a Brush

Cut in around the entire ceiling as well as any light fittings, then take the larger brush and coat the ceiling using smooth parallel strokes. Paint in 1 metre sections so that the wet edges stay fresher and improve the finish.

FIGURE 5.14 Text block with word spaces adjusted (example **A**) and tracked (example **B**).

A

Our arrival in Iquitos was inauspicious. At the airport a helpful taxi driver insisted on taking us to an affordable hotel. His taxi was a moving heap of rust. I looked like it would expire at any moment, but I knew it would somehow run forever. In the front passenger seat was an weather-beaten old man who was never introduced, nor explained. The driver didn't speak to or acknowledge him in any way, and the old man didn't say a word. When we got there, the hotel charged twice the price the taxi driver had quoted. I turned to challenge him on this, but he had vanished.

B

Our arrival in Iquitos was inauspicious. At the airport a helpful taxi driver insisted on taking us to an affordable hotel. His taxi was a moving heap of rust. I looked like it would expire at any moment, but I knew it would somehow run forever. In the front passenger seat was an weather-beaten old man who was never introduced, nor explained. The driver didn't speak to or acknowledge him in any way, and the old man didn't say a word. When we got there, the hotel charged twice the price the taxi driver had quoted. I turned to challenge him on this, but he had vanished.

C

Our arrival in Iquitos was inauspicious. At the airport a helpful taxi driver insisted on taking us to an affordable hotel. His taxi was a moving heap of rust. I looked like it would expire at any moment, but I knew it would somehow run forever. In the front passenger seat was an weather-beaten old man who was never introduced, nor explained. The driver didn't speak to or acknowledge him in any way, and the old man didn't say a word. When we got there, the hotel charged twice the price the taxi driver had quoted. I turned to challenge him on this, but he had vanished.

TIP: Adjusting Word Spacing Here's a handy feature: The ability to adjust the word spacing across a range of characters while leaving the character spacing unaffected. Command+Option+Delete (Ctrl-Alt-Backspace) will tighten the word spaces; Command+Option+Shift-Backslash (Ctrl+Alt+Shift+Backslash) will increase the word spaces.

Controlling Widows and Orphans

Given the drama of their names, the actual definition of widows and orphans may be a little disappointing:

A widow is the last line of a paragraph, stranded at the top of a column or page. They should always be avoided.

An orphan is the first line of a paragraph that occurs at the bottom of a column or page. They are not desirable, but neither are they a typographic sin, especially when fixing them may cause more problems than it solves.

Ultimately you're better off fixing widows, orphans, and their wicked cousin—the short exit line—by a judicious use of tracking, hyphenation, and perhaps rewriting. If you plump for the first option, the golden rule is that no one should be able to tell. You don't want your type looking like a concertina: getting tighter here and looser there as you squeeze or pad your text with space. Restrict yourself to no more than –15 (minus 15/1000 of an em) and no one will notice.

To use tracking, select the paragraph that needs attention and track, usually tighter, to cause a different wrap. With the Paragraph Composer on, (the default), this may not work as expected, because InDesign will recompose every line in the paragraph. If you can't get the result you're after with tracking try one of these other options:

- Adding discretionary hyphens (See Chapter 11: "Don't Fear the Hyphen")
- Applying No Break to a selected range of text to prevent it breaking across a line (See Chapter 11: "Don't Fear the Hyphen")
- Rewording. This is a sensitive issue and may not be an option at all depending on the kind of document you're working with. If you have license to rewrite, then go for it—often a subtle rewording will do the trick.
- If your document does not require your columns to "bottom out," i.e., share the same last baseline, then you can control your paragraph breaks by using Keeps Options. This will keep a specified number of lines at the end of the paragraph together. Beware: Overzealous use of Keeps can cause your text to behave very oddly with paragraphs jumping about from frame to frame as if they had a life of their own. That said, Keep with Next can be useful for preventing headings and subheads from being divorced from the text that follows them. You can highlight paragraphs that violate your specified Keep Options by choosing Preferences>Composition and checking Keep Violations

NOTE: To remove all custom tracking or kerning from a range of text, select the text and press Cmd+Option+Q (Ctrl+Alt+Q). Because this sets the automatic kerning method back to Metrics, it won't be much use if you are using Optical Kerning.

FOUR SCORE AND SEVEN years ago our fathers brought forth on this continent, a new nation, conceived in liberty, and dedicated to the proposition that all men are created equal.¶

Now we are engaged in a great civil war, testing whether that nation or any nation so conceived and so dedicated, can long endure.¶

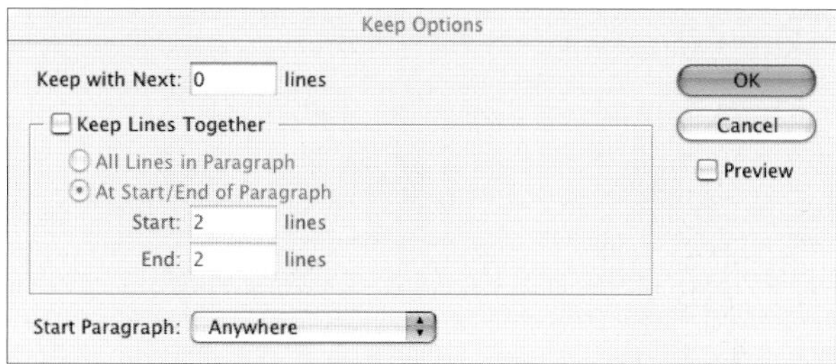

FIGURES 5.15A AND 5.15B Show Custom Tracking/Kerning.

TIP: Turn on Show Custom Tracking/Kerning This will highlight in green any paragraphs that have been custom tracked or kerned. This is helpful in a couple of ways. First, you may have inherited a document in progress and want to quickly make sure that the text hasn't been overzealously tracked. Second, if the layout or text of a document is revised so that the tracking in certain areas is no longer necessary, you can easily identify these areas to remove the tracking.

It's good to develop an eye for where you might need to track to gain better text color: Flipping through your pages at a small view percentage with the type greeked can often help to identify the problem areas.

Up Next

We zoom in on the small and sometimes persnickety details of typography. This has and probably always will be a labor intensive process, but, just as with the bigger picture stuff, InDesign offers an unprecedented amount of control over these fiddly bits. Harness these controls and you're guaranteed to raise the level of your type.

Like it Tight? Use Word and Letter Spacing for a tight fit not tracking. That way, when you turn on Show Custom Tracking all your text won't be highlighted in green—only the text that has been locally tracked.

CHAPTER 6

Sweating the Small Stuff:

Special Characters, White Space, and Glyphs

TYPOGRAPHY IS ALL ABOUT THE DETAILS, and good typographers tend to be mildly obsessive by temperament. Everybody fancies themselves a designer these days, so attention to detail goes a long way in setting your work apart from the sea of mediocrity. InDesign provides a wealth of options for finessing your type, making it simple and straightforward to elevate the quality of your typography.

Typographer's Quotes

No self-respecting typographer would be caught dead using straight or dumb quotation marks instead of paired typographers' ("curly") quotes. By default this preference is on. Typographer's quotes are also an option in your Text Import Options when you Place text. In American English, commas and periods go inside the quotation marks even if the punctuation is not part of the quoted sentence. Colons and semicolons are the exception: They go outside the quotation marks. In British English, all punctuation goes outside the quotation marks.

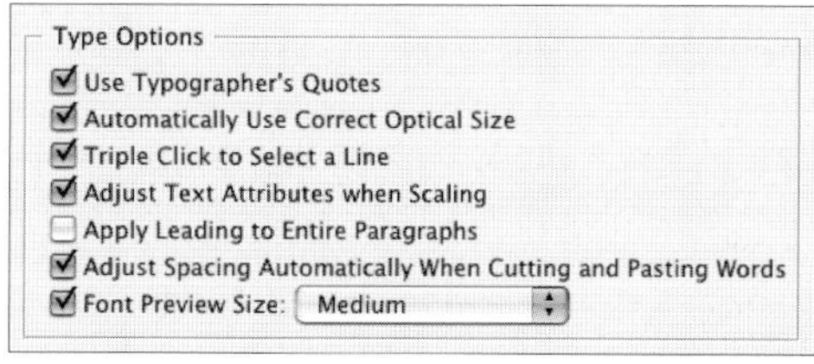

FIGURE 6.1 Typographer's Quotes Preferences.

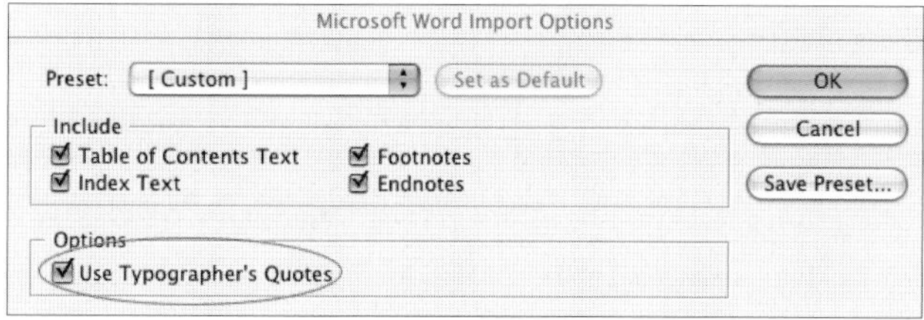

FIGURE 6.2 Word Import Options.

There may be times when you actually want straight quotes (feet or inch marks). Rather than having to go back and forth to the Preferences dialog box, you can also toggle this option by pressing Command+Option+Shift+' (Ctrl+Alt+Shift+'). Better yet, avoid these straight quotes altogether and use the prime (feet, minutes) and double prime (inches, seconds) characters. These characters can be found in OpenType fonts (See Chapter 7: "OpenType") or in the Symbol font. Unfortunately they do not have an assigned keystroke, but can be accessed using the Glyphs palette.

A third preference relating to the appearance of your quote marks is in your Dictionary preferences. You can choose the appearance of your single and double quotes for specific languages.

‹ O ›	French single quotes
« O »	French double quotes
«O»	Non-French double angle quotes without space
‚O‘	German single quotes
„O“	German double quotes

A Max Headroom 6’ 11”
Bedroom One: 15’ x 10’
Letter Size: 8½”x11”

B Max Headroom 6' 11"
Bedroom One: 15' x 10'
Letter Size: 8½"x11"

C Max Headroom 6′ 11″
Bedroom One: 15′ x 10′
Letter Size: 8½″x11″

FIGURE 6.3 Straight quotes vs. prime marks. Typographer's quotes used incorrectly (example **A**). Straight quotes (example **B**). Prime marks (example **C**).

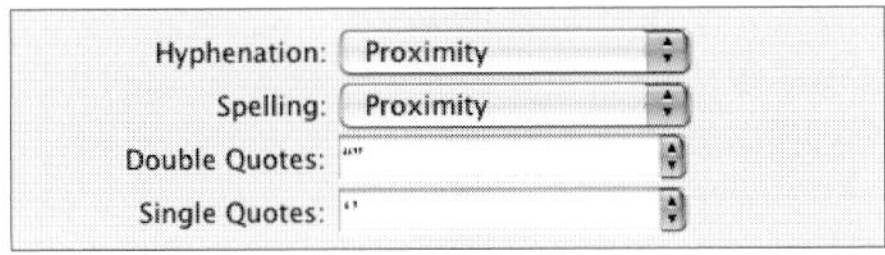

FIGURE 6.4 Quote Preferences.

Apostrophes

An apostrophe is the same character as a single closing quote: ’. Confusion can sometimes arise when InDesign second guesses you and thinks you want an opening single quote rather than an apostrophe. This is most likely to occur in phrases like rock ’n’ roll and fish ’n’ chips, or in dates where the apostrophe substitutes for missing numerals, like ’90s instead of 1990s.

Correct	Incorrect
Fish ’n’ Chips	Fish ‘n’ Chips
Rock ’n’ Roll	Rock ‘n’ Roll
’90s	‘90s

FIGURE 6.5 Apostrophes.

- Hyphen
– En dash
— Em dash

FIGURE 6.6 A hyphen, en dash (Option+Hyphen/ Alt+Hyphen), and em dash (Shift+Option+Hypen/ Shift+Alt+Hyphen).

Dashes

There are three types of dashes and they all serve different functions.

The **hyphen** is the shortest dash. It is meant only for hyphenating words or creating line breaks, but is commonly misused by people who don't know about en dashes and em dashes. (See Chapter 11: "Don't Fear the Hyphen" for information on discretionary hyphens.)

The **en dash** is used with a range of numbers. The rule of thumb is that if, when speaking the words, you would say "to" then use an en dash. There is no space around the dash. En dashes are also used for compound adjectives. You would also use an en dash when you have a compound adjective, one part of which consists of two words or a hyphenated word.

FIGURE 6.7 The en dash, approximately the width of the captial N, used to indicate passage of time or for compound adjectives.

Incorrect	Correct
Open 9-5	Open 9–5
1914-1918	1914–1918
September-October	September–October
San Francisco-London flight	San Francisco–London flight
pre-World War II period	pre–World War II period
second-rate-half-baked ideas	second-rate–half-baked ideas

The **em dash** is used to separate a parenthetical break in the sentence.

In the days of the typewriter an em dash was conveyed with double hyphens and many people have yet to unlearn this habit. Fortunately, when you place a text file in InDesign double hyphens are automatically converted to em dashes, but you're still likely to encounter all manner of other approximations of an em dash. One of your first tasks is to fix such problems using Find/Change.

Em dashes should not touch the characters that precede or follow them. Optionally you can put a thin space (Cmd+Shift+M Ctrl+Shift+M) around em dashes. A regular word space is too wide and in justified type will grow and shrink to achieve justification.Thin spaces are of a fixed width.

Em dashes--also known as long dashes--are used to set off a phrase. They also indicate an abrupt change in thought - like this. They can also be used to show a missing part of a word, as in f--k.

Incorrect

Em dashes — also known as long dashes — are used to set off a phrase. They also indicate an abrupt change in thought—like this. They can also be used to show a missing part of a word, as in f—k.

Correct

Em dashes – also known as long dashes – are used to set off a phrase.

En dashes used in place of em dashes

Em dashes — also known as long dashes — are used to set off a phrase.

Em dashes at 80% horizontal scale

FIGURE 6.8 The em dash, the Big Kahuna of the dash world.

If you find an em dash too wide and feel that it creates an unsightly hole in the text, opting instead to use an en dash or an em dash with a reduced horizontal width (80 percent works well) are good alternatives. This is another job for Find/Change (See Chapter 17).

Ellipses

An ellipsis indicates omission and is also called a suspension point or, more commonly, dot-dot-dot. When the omitted words are within a sentence, use a three-dot ellipsis preceded and followed by a space. When the omission occurs at the end of a sentence, a fourth dot, a period, is added and the space at the beginning of the ellipsis is omitted.

A three-dot ellipsis is part of a standard font set (Alt+0133/Option+-). Because the dots of the ellipsis character are too tightly spaced, for best results create your own ellipsis with dots separated by a thin space (Cmd+Shift+Option+M/Ctrl+Shift+Alt+M). A thin space is slightly less than a regular word space and is nonbreaking so that you won't get two dots at the end of one line and the third at the beginning of the next. Because this is fiddly and time consuming, it's handy to use Find/Change to automatically replace any other ellipsis forms with your custom ellipsis.

A a...b
B a....B
C a ... b
D a . . . b

FIGURE 6.9 Ellipses. Example **A**: A three-dot ellipsis separated by thin spaces. Example **B**: A four-dot ellipsis at the end of a sentence. Example **C**: The ellipsis character. Example **D**: Three dots separated by a regular space width.

FIGURE 6.10 Without ellipsis (example **A**); and an omission within a sentence and at the end of a sentence (example **B**).

One morning, when Gregor Samsa woke from troubled dreams, he found himself transformed in his bed into a horrible vermin. He lay on his armour-like back, and if he lifted his head a little he could see his brown belly, slightly domed and divided by arches into stiff sections.

A

One morning, when Gregor Samsa woke...he found himself transformed.... He lay on his armour-like back, and if he lifted his head...he could see his brown belly, slightly domed and divided by arches into stiff sections.

B

FIGURE 6.11 Using Find/Change to fix ellipses.

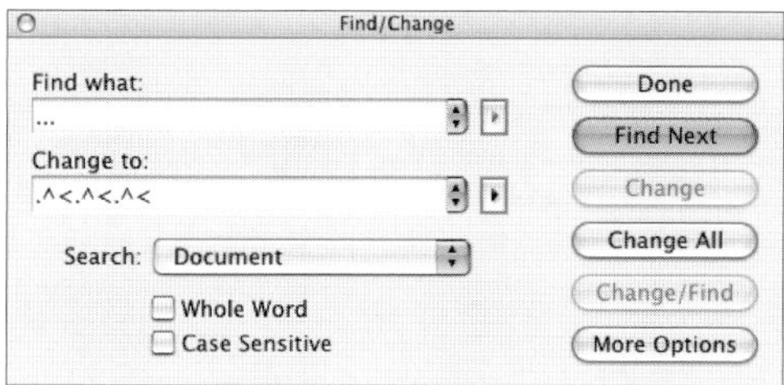

End Marks

An end mark is a common device in magazines, newsletters, and journals to signify the end of a major article, especially when the article spans several pages. The end mark can be a character taken from a picture font or an inline graphic. End marks should be scaled so that they are no bigger than the cap height of the text; depending on the mark you're using you may want to size them to the x-height. They can be separated from the text with an en space (Command+Shift+N/Ctrl+Shift+N) or set flush right with the margin—Shift+Tab. To make sure they are consistent within the publication create an End Mark Character Style (See Chapter 13: "Stylin' with Paragraph and Character Styles").

FIGURE 6.12 An end ornament using a Zapf Dingbat character (example **A**) and an inline graphic (example **B**).

and Trotsky for good measure and, in the night club scene, there is a tall, slim, bespectacled man holding a cocktail glass. Above the figure is a strain of syphilis germs. This was Diego's revenge: the figure is that of John D. Rockefeller, Jr. ■

A

and Trotsky for good measure and, in the night club scene, there is a tall, slim, bespectacled man holding a cocktail glass. Above the figure is a strain of syphilis germs. This was Diego's revenge: the figure is that of John D. Rockefeller, Jr. ↰

B

White Space Characters

All of these different spacing options can be applied by choosing Type > Insert White Space, or by choosing Insert White Space from the Type Tool contextual menu (Right+Click/Ctrl+Click).

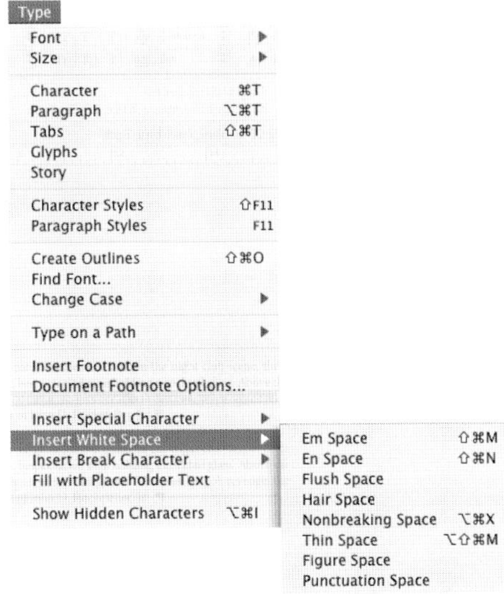

FIGURE 6.13 Insert White Space.

Spaceband S pace
Em S pace
En S pace
Hair Space
Thin Space
Figure S pace
Punctuation S pace

FIGURE 6.14 White Space Characters.

Em Space: Cmd+Shift+M (Ctrl+Shift+M)

An em space is a relative unit, equal in width to the size of your type. In 12-point type, an em space is 12 points wide; in 72-point type, it is 72 points. A common misunderstanding is that an em space is the width of an M.

En Space: Cmd+Shift+N (Ctrl+Shift+N)

An en space is one-half the width of an em space.

Flush Space

This adds a variable amount of space to the last line of a fully justified paragraph. A Flush Space can be useful if you want to add space between the last word and an end ornament or if you are preparing a price list and want to push the price flush with the right column edge. In justified text, the space expands to absorb all available extra space on the last line. A caveat: The Flush Space only works when you apply the Justify All Lines option to the paragraph. For that reason, you may be better off using a Right Indent Tab (Shift+Tab or Insert Special Character > Right Indent Tab) to get the same effect.

Hair Space: Cmd+Option+Shift+I (Ctrl+Alt+Shift+I)

One-twenty-fourth the width of an em space. That's pretty darn small. It could be a used as an alternative to a Thin Space.

No Double Spaces, Please

At the risk of sounding like a petty tyrant, I'm going to state the following: There is never an excuse for having more than one consecutive word space anywhere in your text. But wait…I hear you say, surely… No. Never. More than one consecutive space and the Type Police will come knocking.

Here's why: The convention of double spacing after a period is a holdover from the days of the typewriter (remember those?) when fonts were monospaced, that is, all characters had the same width regardless of the shape of the letter, so that an **l** occupied the same width as a **w**. The characters were so wide and so open that a single space wasn't enough between sentences.

These days our fonts—unless you're aiming for that certain retro typewriter look—are proportionally spaced, which means that each character has a unique width corresponding to its character shape. The word spaces in proportionally spaced fonts are designed to separate sentences perfectly. Putting two spaces after every period undermines our goal of even type color and looks really sloppy—the typographic equivalent of going around with gravy stains on your tie.

These days you're more likely to see a typewriter displayed as a piece of retro art than a working typesetting tool, but the double spacing habit persists. Thankfully, the Find/Change function can zap any egregious spaces in less time than it takes to say flibbertigibbet.

Nonbreaking Space: Cmd+Option+X (Ctrl+Alt+X)

The same width as pressing the spacebar, but it prevents two (or more) words, like a name for example, from being broken across a line. In fact, if you have a short line at the end of a paragraph, using a Nonbreaking Space is preferable to forcing a line break with a Shift-Return. If the text is edited or reflowed, you're less likely to end up with a break in the middle of your line. You can achieve the same end by applying No Break to your selected range of text.

Every single surface of a modern Formula
One car, from the shape of the suspension
links to that of the driver's helmet has its
aerodynamic effects considered. **A**

Every single surface of a modern Formula One car, from the shape of the suspension
links to that of the driver's helmet has its
aerodynamic effects considered. **B**

Every single surface of a modern Formula One
car, from the shape of the suspension links to
that of the driver's helmet has its aerodynamic
effects considered. **C**

FIGURE 6.15 Without intervention, "Formula One" breaks over two lines (example **A**). Using a Nonbreaking Space causes "Formula" to hyphenate (example **B**). Selecting both words and choosing No Break moves the whole phrase up to the first line (example **C**).

Thin Space: Cmd+Option+Shift+M (Ctrl+Alt+Shift+M)

One-eighth the width of an em space—a good choice on either side of an em dash.

Figure Space

Lining numbers in most fonts are of equal width and a figure space is the same width as a number in the typeface. Figure Spaces can be used to help align numbers in tables.

Punctuation Space

A Punctuation Space is the same width as an exclamation mark, period, or colon in the typeface.

Whither the Monospaced Font?

Although monospaced fonts are seldom used these days, they are not all on the unemployment line and are still useful for certain tasks.

Courier is used to indicate a missing font. InDesign can usually simulate the look of a missing font on screen, but it can't do the same in print. Printing a document that contains missing fonts results in Courier being substituted for the missing font. This convention has been adopted by all page layout applications because Courier looks so wrong that you can't miss it and presumably will be compelled to fix it. That said, I'm sure we've all spotted the odd bit of egregious Courier that somehow made it through the editorial and proofing stages and ended up in print.

In instructional manuals, especially computer manuals, Courier is often used to indicate text or code that the user is required to type, although a proportionally spaced "techie looking" font like Letter Gothic is a good alternative.

Line Break (aka Soft Return, Forced Line Break) Shift-Return

Line breaks are essential whenever you want to start a new line without starting a new paragraph. This will avoid creating a new paragraph that takes on the potentially unwanted formatting attributes of the paragraph that it came from.

FIGURE 6.16 Using a forced line break—Shift-Return (example **A**) to move a broken word down to the next line vs. using a Return (example **B**), which creates a new paragraph based on the formats of the paragraph it came from.

It was a bright cold day in April, and the clocks were striking thirteen. Winston Smith, his chin nuzzled into his breast in an effort to escape the vile wind, slipped quickly through the glass doors of Victory Man-
sions, though not quickly enough to prevent a swirl of gritty dust from entering along with him.

A

It was a bright cold day in April, and the clocks were striking thirteen. Winston Smith, his chin nuzzled into his breast in an effort to escape the vile wind, slipped quickly through the glass doors of Victory

Mansions, though not quickly enough to prevent a swirl of gritty dust from entering along with him.

B

What's The Point? InDesign's Units of Measurement

When working in InDesign, the best unit of measurement—in my humble opinion—is Picas and its subdivision Points. The point system originated in the early 18th Century and was adopted as the typographic standard in the United States in the early 20th. They're arcane, nondecimal, seldom used in Europe, but still there's good reason to use them. Basically, there's no getting away from them: Type size, leading, indentation and paragraph spacing are all specified in points. What's more, points allow for the kind of fine-tuning necessary when finessing type. *Learn to love 'em, 'cause they ain't going away.*

Picas and points in a nutshell:

6 picas = 1 inch

12 points = 1 pica

72 points = 1 inch

1 picas and 6 points = 1p6. Alternatively, it could be expressed as 0p18 or 18 pt.

6 points = 0p6, p6, or 6 pt.

NOTE: If your measurement is in picas, expressing 6 points as merely 6 would be interpreted as 72 points. 6 points would be typed 0p6 or 6 pt. This probably sounds more confusing than it is—you'll quickly get the hang of it.

TIP: In reality, picas and points overlap with other measurement systems—millimeters or inches (or both), depending on your preference And InDesign allows you to mix your measurements. Whichever unit of measurement you choose, you can type in values in any supported unit of measurement (just make sure you add the mm or the " after the number) and InDesign will make the conversion for you. So, if you're like me and prefer to work in picas, but sometimes like to express the dimension of certain elements like pictures frames in inches, then type "in" after the value.

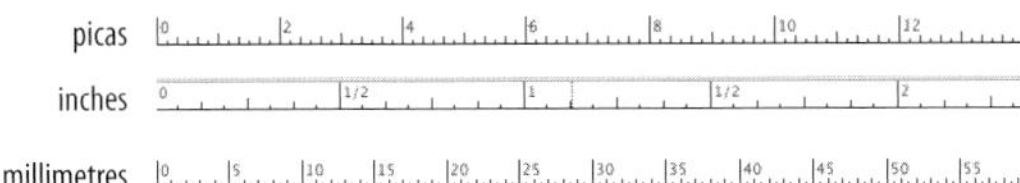

FIGURE 6.17 InDesign's rulers in picas, inches, and millimeters.

The Glyphs Palette

Remember Key Caps from Mac System 9 or the Character Map in Windows? Well, the Glyphs palette is just like those. Only better. Using the Glyphs palette you can easily access special characters, foreign accents, currency symbols, and diacritical marks that are not on a standard keyboard. Simply insert your Type Tool into a text frame, then choose Type>Insert Glyphs. The palette displays the glyphs from the current font. You can change to a different font using the Font Family pop-up menu at the bottom of the palette and enlarge or reduce the size of the glyphs with the Zoom button. When you find the glyph you're after, simply double-click it to insert it in your text.

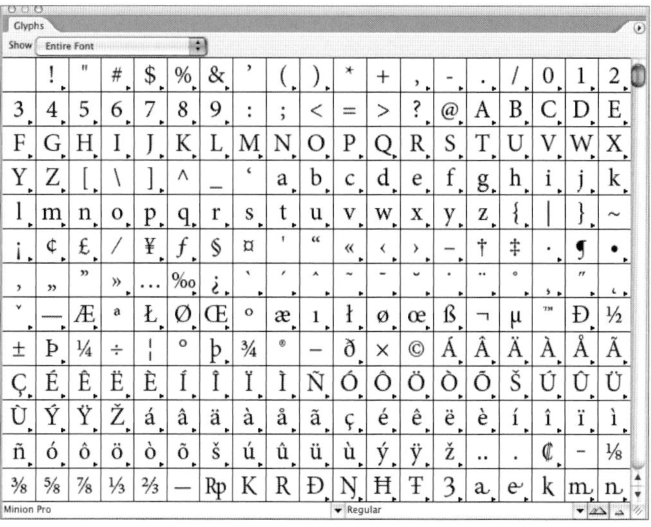

FIGURE 6.18 The Glyphs Palette.

TIP: Keystrokes Of course, the fastest way to get a special character is to memorize its keyboard shortcut.

So what exactly is a glyph? A glyph is a specific form of a character. In the same way as the alphabet offers two forms—uppercase and lowercase—for every letter, the Glyph palette offers several alternatives for certain OpenType characters.

If you're using an OpenType font, you can view a subset of the glyphs, such as Oldstyle Figures or Fractions. To replace a character with an alternate glyph, select the character in your text, then choose Alternates for Selection from the Show pop-up menu to display any alternate glyphs.

Creating and Using a Glyph Set

If you find yourself repeatedly using the same glyphs, then making a glyph set will save you hunting and pecking for them each time you need them. Note that glyph sets are not attached to any particular document but are part of your InDesign preferences. Unfortunately, you can't a share glyph set with others in your work group, nor can you convert your own graphics into custom glyphs.

Creating a Glyph Set

1. Choose Type > Insert Glyphs.
2. From the Glyphs palette menu, choose New Glyph Set, name your Glyph Set, and click OK.

FIGURE 6.19 New Glyph Set.

3. Select the font that contains the glyph you're after from the bottom of the Glyphs palette.

4. Click on a glyph that you want to add to your Glyph Set, then (Right Mouse+Click/Ctrl+Click) and choose the name of your Glyph Set from the Add to Glyph submenu.

Glyph	Description	Mac	Windows
‘	left single quote	option-]	Alt + 0145
’	right single quote	option-shift-]	Alt + 0146
“	left double quote	option-[	Alt + 0147
”	right double quote	option-shift-[	Alt + 0148
†	dagger	option-t	Alt + 0134
‡	double dagger	option-shift-7	Alt + 0135
‰	per mill sign	option-shift-r	Alt + 0137
™	trademark sign	option-2	Alt + 0153
–	en dash	option-hyphen	Alt + 0150
—	em dash	option-shift-hyphen	Alt + 0151
¡	inverted exclamation	option-1	Alt + 0161
¢	cent sign	option-4	Alt + 0162
£	pound sterling	option-3	Alt + 0163
¥	yen sign	option-y	Alt + 0165
§	section sign	option-6	Alt + 0167
¨	umlaut	option-shift-u	Alt + 0168
©	copyright	option-g	Alt + 0169
®	registered trademark	option-r	Alt + 0174
°	degree sign	option-shift-8	Alt + 0176
´	acute accent	option-shift-e	Alt + 0180
¶	paragraph sign	option-7	Alt + 0182
¸	cedilla	option-shift-z	Alt + 0184
¼	one-quarter		Alt + 0188
½	one-half		Alt + 0189
¾	three-quarters		Alt + 0190
¿	inverted question mark	option-shift-?	Alt + 0191
À	uppercase A, grave accent	option-` A	Alt + 0192
Á	uppercase A, acute accent	option-e A	Alt + 0193
Â	uppercase A, circumflex accent	option-i A	Alt + 0194
Ã	uppercase A, tilde	option-n A	Alt + 0195
Ä	uppercase A, umlaut	option-u A	Alt + 0196
Å	uppercase A, ring	option-shift-a	Alt + 0197
Æ	uppercase AE	option-shift-’	Alt + 0198
Ç	uppercase C, cedilla	option-shift-c	Alt + 0199
È	uppercase E, grave accent	option-` E	Alt + 0200
É	uppercase E, acute accent	option-e E	Alt + 0201
Ê	uppercase E, circumflex accent	option-i E	Alt + 0202
Ë	uppercase E, umlaut	option-u E	Alt + 0203
Ì	uppercase I, grave accent	option-` I	Alt + 0204
Í	uppercase I, acute accent	option-e I	Alt + 0205
Î	uppercase I, circumflex accent	option-i I	Alt + 0206
Ï	uppercase I, umlaut	option-u I	Alt + 0207

Glyph	Description	Mac	Windows
Ñ	uppercase N, tilde	option-n N	Alt + 0209
Ò	uppercase O, grave accent	option-` O	Alt + 0210
Ó	uppercase O, acute accent	option-e O	Alt + 0211
Ô	uppercase O, circumflex accent	option-i O	Alt + 0212
Õ	uppercase O, tilde	option-n O	Alt + 0213
Ö	uppercase O, umlaut	option-u O	Alt + 0214
Ø	uppercase O, slash	option-shift-o	Alt + 0216
Ù	uppercase U, grave accent	option-` U	Alt + 0217
Ú	uppercase U, acute accent	option-e U	Alt + 0218
Û	uppercase U, circumflex accent	option-i U	Alt + 0219
Ü	uppercase U, umlaut	option-u U	Alt + 0220
ß	lowercase sharps, German	option-s	Alt + 0223
à	lowercase a, grave accent	option-` a	Alt + 0224
á	lowercase a, acute accent	option-e a	Alt + 0225
â	lowercase a, circumflex accent	option-i a	Alt + 0226
ã	lowercase a, tilde	option-n a	Alt + 0227
ä	lowercase a, umlaut	option-u a	Alt + 0228
å	lowercase a, ring	option-a	Alt + 0229
æ	lowercase ae	option-’	Alt + 0230
ç	lowercase c, cedilla	option-c	Alt + 0231
è	lowercase e, grave accent	option-` e	Alt + 0232
é	lowercase e, acute accent	option-e e	Alt + 0233
ê	lowercase e, circumflex accent	option-i e	Alt + 0234
ë	lowercase e, umlaut	option-u e	Alt + 0235
ì	lowercase i, grave accent	option-` i	Alt + 0236
í	lowercase i, acute accent	option-e i	Alt + 0237
î	lowercase i, circumflex accent	option-i i	Alt + 0238
ï	lowercase i, umlaut	option-u i	Alt + 0239
ñ	lowercase n, tilde	option-n n	Alt + 0241
ò	lowercase o, grave accent	option-` o	Alt + 0242
ó	lowercase o, acute accent	option-e o	Alt + 0243
ô	lowercase o, circumflex accent	option-i o	Alt + 0244
õ	lowercase o, tilde	option-n o	Alt + 0245
ö	lowercase o, umlaut	option-u o	Alt + 0246
÷	division sign		Alt + 0247
ø	lowercase o, slash	option-o	Alt + 0248
ù	lowercase u, grave accent	option-` u	Alt + 0249
ú	lowercase u, acute accent	option-e u	Alt + 0250
û	lowercase u, circumflex accent	option-i u	Alt + 0251
ü	lowercase u, umlaut	option-u u	Alt + 0252
ÿ	lowercase y, umlaut	option-u y	Alt + 0255

FIGURE 6.20 Special Character Keyboard Shortcuts.

A 10 5/16 x 8 3/16

B $10{}^{5}\!/_{16}$ x $8{}^{3}\!/_{16}$

C $10{}^{5}\!/_{16} \times 8{}^{3}\!/_{16}$

u $10^{5}{}_{16} \times 8^{3}{}_{16}$

FIGURE 6.21 Different flavors of fractions: Undesigned (example **A**), made with the Make Fraction script (example **B**), using an OpenType font and replacing the lowercase x with the multiplication character (example **C**), and omitting the fraction slash (example D).

Making a Fraction

PostScript and TrueType fonts have the following fractions in their character set: ¼, ½, ¾. In addition to these, OpenType fonts allow you to make custom fonts (See Chapter 7: "OpenType: The New Frontier in Font Technology"). If you're using PostScript Type 1 or TrueType fonts and need a nonstandard fraction, you can make your own without too much fuss. InDesign comes with several Scripts, tucked away in the Scripts palette. Type your fraction, select it, and then double-click the Make Fraction script. This will make the numerator superscript, the denominator subscript and replace the slash with a fraction bar. No matter how you get your fraction, if it follows a whole number, no space is necessary before the fraction.

Multiplication Sign

While we're talking numbers, I should mention that the multiplication sign is a distinct character available in OpenType fonts (see the next chapter) or in the Symbol font.

The Euro Symbol

In January 1999 the Euro became the currency of twelve European Union member states: Austria, Belgium, Finland, France, Germany, Greece, Ireland, Italy, Luxembourg, the Netherlands, Portugal, and Spain, collectively known as the Eurozone. One of the ripple effects of this, the most significant monetary reform in Europe since the Roman Empire, was that we all needed a new font character.

Fonts newer than 1998, including all OpenType fonts, anticipated this and should have the Euro symbol as part of the character set. On the Mac: Option+Shift+2; on Windows Alt+0128. If you're using fonts older than 1998, or you don't like the design of the Euro character in a particular font, you can download three family of Euro fonts from the Adobe website: http://store.adobe.com/type/euroreg.html. Euro Sans has a regular weight that is the same as the official character adopted in Europe. Euro Mono is a condensed version of Euro Sans that is designed to work with monospaced fonts. Euro Serif is useful for settings of serif faces. All three fonts are free.

FIGURE 6.22 Euro fonts from Adobe: Euro Monospace, Euro Sans, Euro Serif.

Using Find/Change to Clean Up the Mess

As a designer you commonly work with text files that have been created by someone else. In a perfect world these files would be as lean as a cheetah and as minimalist as a piece of Bauhaus furniture. Unfortunately, this is rarely—in fact, never—the case. People clutter up their text files with all kinds of junk, often in the misguided notion that they are helping you out by doing the formatting. Extra carriage returns, multiple tabs, multiple spaces (in some cases used to justify lines of type) will all need to be removed. And probably so too will indentations and various type stylings. Of course, communication with your client can go a long way: Tell them what you want and you might even get it. But even with stellar communication and the best of intentions, you're still going to need to clean up your text files. And there's nothing like InDesign's Find/Change command for quickly whipping a text file—or files—into shape.

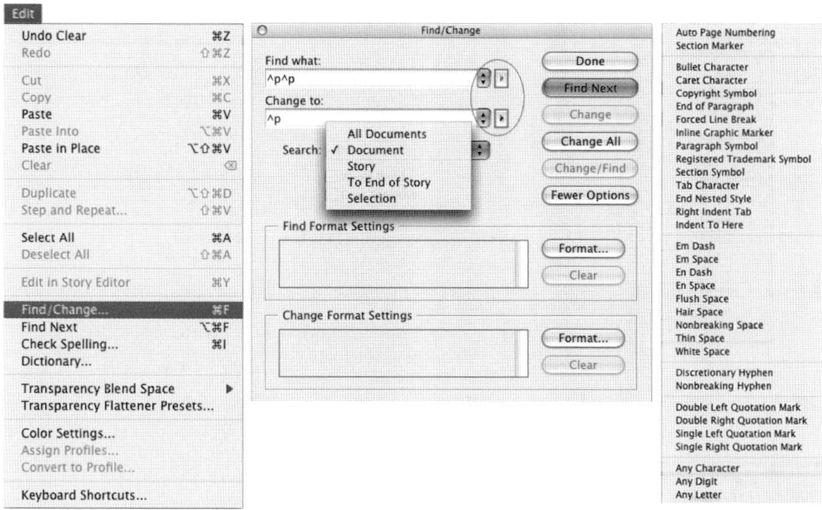

FIGURE 6.22 The Find/Change dialog box. The Find routine shown replaces two consecutive carriage returns with a single carriage return. Using the Special Characters for search menu (circled), you can access all the "meta-characters" listed on the right. You can also convert local formatting to Paragraph or Character Styles. Click Format… to find and change specific character or paragraph formats and replace them with Character or Paragraph Styles, giving you much tighter control over the formatting of your document. You can further clarify your search by specifying where you are looking with the Search pull-down menu.

Footnotes

A footnote is a text element at the bottom of a page that provides additional information about a point made in the main text. The footnote might provide more information, offer an alternate viewpoint or list a citation for the source of a quote, idea or statistic. *Endnotes* serve the same purpose but are grouped together at the end of a chapter, article or book, rather than at the bottom of each page.

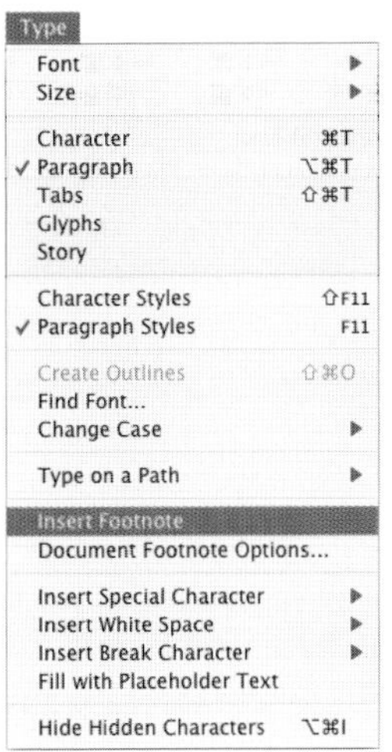

Fraction-size superscript numbers must not introduce the footnotes themselves.... [S]uperscript numbers don't make sense and are a disease.... Since one should be able to find a footnote quickly, the normal number in the type size of the footnote must be used, never a superscript."[1]

1 Jan Tschichold: "Typesetting Superscript Numbers and Footnotes" in *The Form of the Book*, p. 124.

FIGURE 6.24 A footnote automatically postioned at the bottom of the text frame. A pre-made footnote style with a rule above is automatically applied to the footnote text.

In CS2 you can create footnotes that are anchored to the location of the footnote reference number in the text. You can also import footnotes from Word or RTF documents. When the reference number moves to a new page, the associated footnote moves with it. To insert a footnote, place the insertion point where you want the footnote reference number to appear and choose Type > Insert Footnote. The footnote area expands as you type.

Choose Footnote Options to control the numbering style, appearance, and layout of footnotes.

Footnote Options

Minimum Space Before First Footnote: the minimum space between the bottom of the column and the first footnote line.

Space Between Footnotes determines the distance between the last paragraph of one footnote and the first paragraph of the next. The Space Before/Space After values in a footnote's paragraph style apply only if the footnote runs to multiple paragraphs.

First Baseline Offset determines the position of the baseline of the first line of footnote type relative to the footnote area. See Chapter 16: Everything in its Right Place: Using Grids for more on first baseline offsets.

Place End of Story Footnotes at Bottom of Text With this option selected the last column's footnote will appear directly below the end of the story. Otherwise it will appear at the bottom of the column.

Allow Split Footnotes lets footnotes break across a page when it's too big to fit on the page. Without splitting the line containing the footnote reference number jumps to the next page, or the text becomes overset. With Allow Split Footnotes on, you can still prevent an individual footnote from splitting by choosing Keep Options from the Paragraph palette menu, and selecting the Keep Lines Together and All Lines In Paragraph options.

Rule Above This Specifies the location and appearance of the footnote divider line should you choose to use one. These options are very similar to those for paragraph rules (see Chapter 14: Mo' Style).

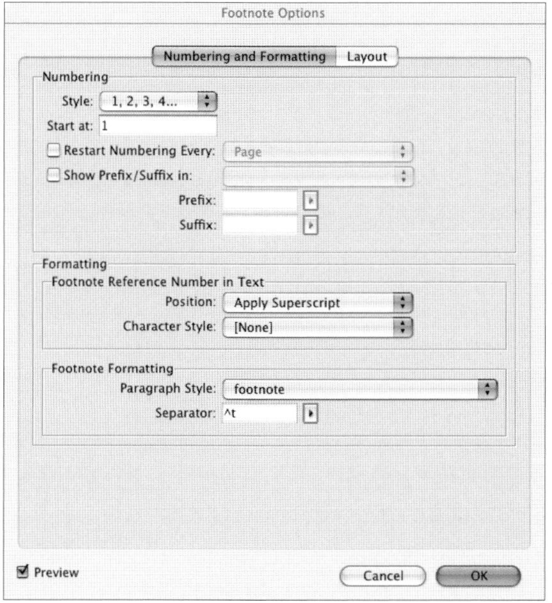

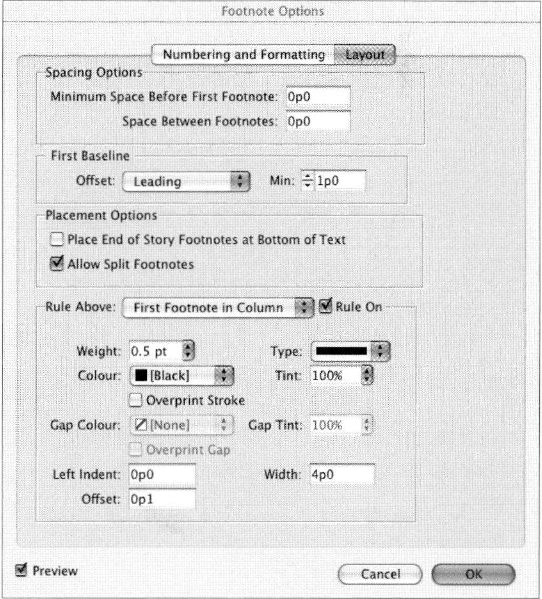

FIGURES 6.25A AND 6.25B Footnote Options.

Notes on Footnotes

- Footnotes are usually indicated by a superscript numeral immediately after the text being referenced. Use superscript in the text but a full-size numbers in the notes themselves.
- The numbers should be separated from the note of the text by a single space without punctuation.
- Footnotes should be numbered when there are many of them, but if you have only a few they can be marked with a dagger, asterisk, or other symbol. Endnotes always use numerals to facilitate easy reference to the main text.
- Footnotes and endnotes are usually set one-two points smaller than the body text, with leading that is a point or two tighter. They should be in the same type family as the body text.
- Footnotes should be separated from the type area by a space at least as big as the body text leading, or by a thin rule.
- When a document has only a few footnotes you can use symbols instead of numbers to indicate the footnotes. The traditional order is * [asterisk] † [dagger] ‡ [double dagger] § [section sign] ¶ [paragraph mark]. This is one of InDesign's footnote numbering options.

Up Next

Taking control of all this nitpicky stuff is time consuming. Thankfully OpenType fonts—the subject of the next chapter—allow a further degree of control over detailed typography, as well as a level of sophistication that until recently was impossible with digital typography.

CHAPTER 7

OpenType:

The New Frontier in Font Technology

BACK IN THE TWENTIETH CENTURY when PostScript fonts battled it out with TrueType fonts in what the trade press dubbed "font wars," managing fonts was a thorn in the side of every graphic designer. With PostScript fonts you had to keep track of the two parts of your font: a screen font, which contained the information about the font's spacing characteristics and kerning pairs, and a printer or outline font, which contained the data about each character shape. It was this second part that was downloaded to your PostScript printer so it could print the characters. TrueType fonts were simpler in that there was only one part to them, but too often caused problems when printing to a PostScript imagesetter.

NOTE: A short-lived solution to the shortcomings of Type 1 Postscript fonts was the Multiple master, which allowed the user to generate different weights and widths of the typeface from a small number of master outlines. But Multiple masters didn't catch on, mainly because they were expensive and confusing. Names like MyriadMM 215LT didn't exactly roll off the tongue. Multiple masters were discontinued in 2001, though they still pop up in font menus.

Unicode

OpenType fonts are based on Unicode—an international, cross-platform standard that assigns numbers to the characters in a font. Before Unicode, the recognized standard was ASCII, which has a character set of 256 characters. The problem is that Macintosh and Windows use different encoding schemes. While they agree on the first 128 characters, the next 128 numbers are specific to each platform. This means that finding the characters you need requires different key combinations on the different platforms. Unicode enables a character set of up to 65,000—enough characters to include Roman, Greek, and Cyrillic alphabets all in the same font—fantastic unless you're the poor type designer who has to design them all!

The key words here are "up to." In reality, no font comes close to having 65,000 characters, but many have several thousand. Just being an OpenType font is no guarantee of an expanded character set: The proof, as they say, is in the pudding.

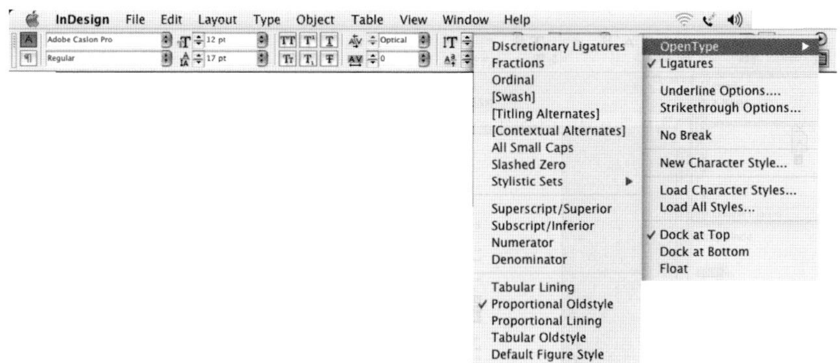

FIGURE 7.1 The OpenType menu. Features not supported in the current font appear in square brackets, such as [Swash].

Today, on the Mac, Type 1 PostScript fonts continue to abound, and on the Windows platform, there are still plenty of TrueType fonts. However both formats are being superseded by OpenType fonts (Adobe released its whole type library in the OpenType format in 2003). OpenType is a cross-platform standard developed by Adobe and Microsoft. There are no compatibility headaches going from Mac to Windows, or visa versa, and there's only one file to manage. What makes OpenType fonts so compelling, though, is their massively expanded character set. With room for so many more characters, OpenType fonts include the full range of Latin characters used in the Western world. Others add a full range of accented characters to support central and eastern European languages, such as Turkish and Polish. Some OpenType Pro fonts also contain Cyrillic and Greek characters. In addition to making multilingual typography easier, OpenType fonts give us all kinds of typographic delicacies that we formerly had to switch to an "Expert Set" in order to access. Let's take a look at what we've got:

Ligatures

Ligatures are two or more characters fused into a single character. An example of a character that has evolved from a ligature into a character in its own right is the ampersand (&), which is a stylized abbreviation of *et*, the Latin word for "and." Today we use ligatures to avoid collisions between different parts of the characters as well as to add sophistication to type. InDesign allows you to substitute standard ligatures for the lowercase fi and fl combinations whether you are using OpenType, PostScript, or TrueType fonts. Whether you do so depends on the font you're using. First try setting the type without ligatures, if the characters collide, then turn on Ligatures. If the characters do not collide, well—if it ain't broke, don't fix it, especially since using ligatures in such instances may make these letter combinations appear tighter set than the rest of your type.

OpenType fonts extend the range of standard ligatures.

InDesign's Check Spelling is smart enough to recognize ligatures and not flag as misspelled any word that contains them.

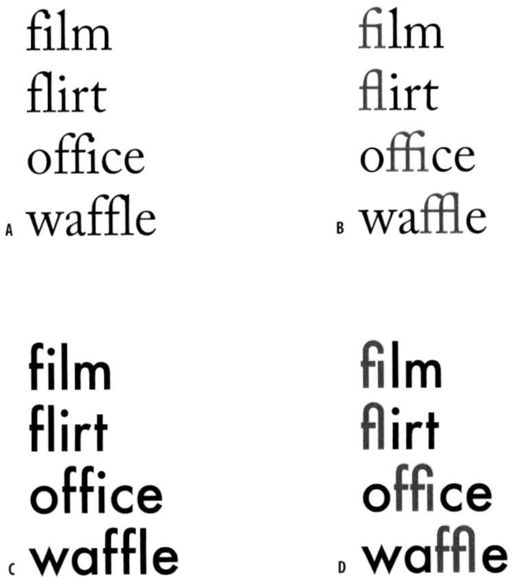

film
flirt
office
A waffle

film
flirt
office
B waffle

film
flirt
office
C waffle

film
flirt
office
D waffle

FIGURE 7.2 The need for ligatures: Depending on the font you are using, you may or may not want to use ligatures **A**. Adobe Caslon without ligatures: Note the collision of the f and i and f and l. **B**. Adobe Caslon with ligatures turned on. **C**. Futura doesn't require ligatures because of its character shapes, so using them (**D**) is redundant.

FIGURE 7.3 Ligatures can be incorporated into a Style definition (top) or turned on locally using the Character palette.

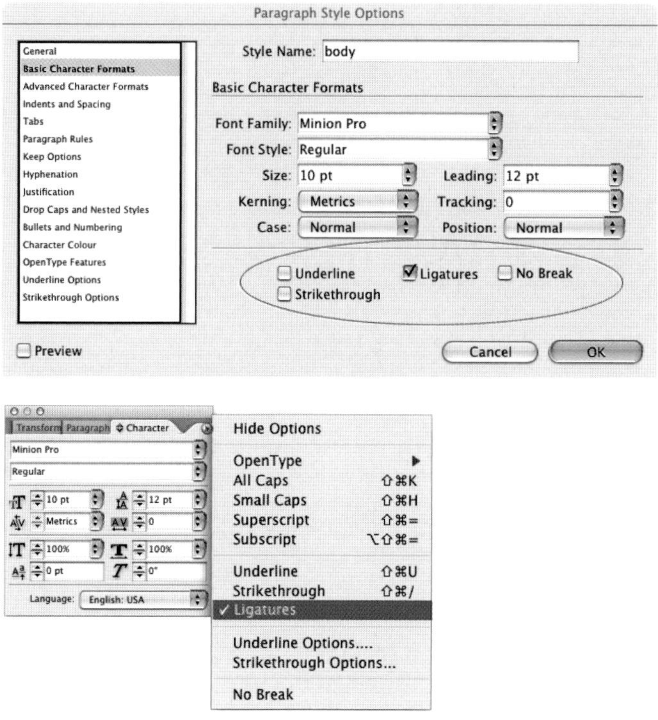

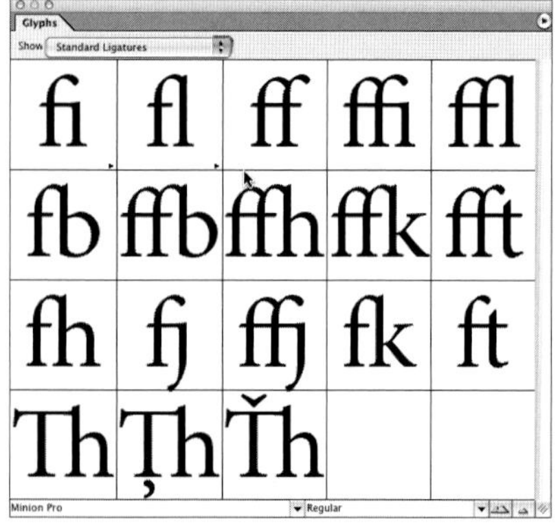

FIGURE 7.4 Standard Ligatures.

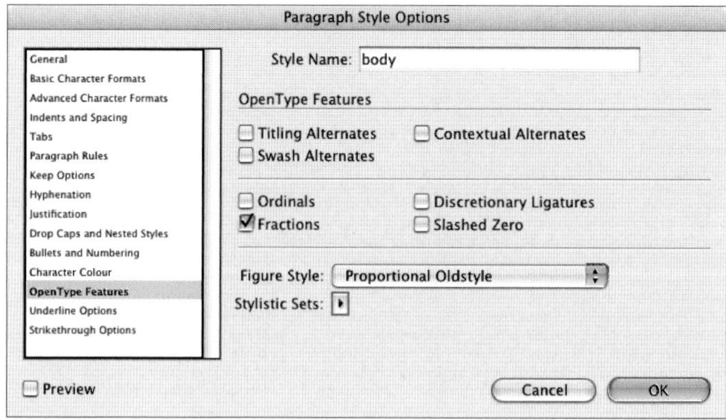

FIGURE 7.5 OpenType Features.

Discretionary Ligatures

Discretionary ligatures are not for everyday use, but perfect for special occasions. Next time you're working on something fancy like a wedding invitation, discretionary ligatures might be just the extra seasoning you need.

Glyphs
Show Discretionary Ligatures
Minion Pro
Regular

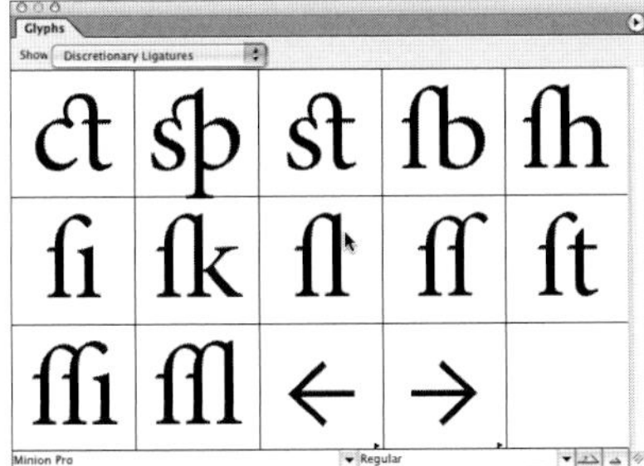

FIGURE 7.6 Discretionary Ligatures.

picture
castle
A spring
picture
castle
B spring

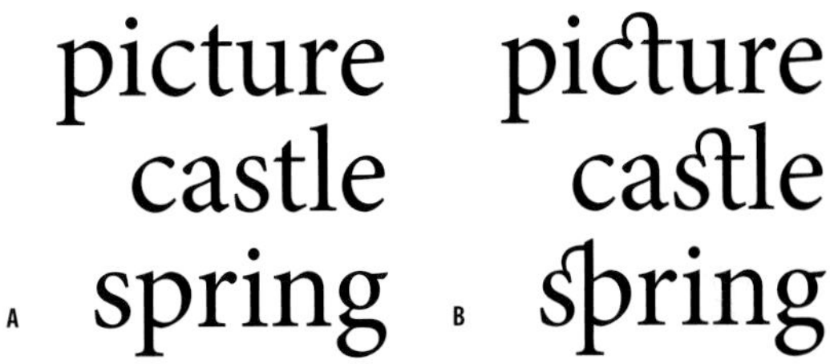

FIGURE 7.7 Minion Pro with discretionary ligatures (example **A**) and without (example **B**).

Ordinals/Raised and Lowered Characters

If available, you can use Ordinals and/or Raised and Lowered Characters instead of the scaled superscripts and subscript that you get on the Character palette menu. You have four flavors to choose from:

- Superscript/Superior
- Subscript/Inferior
- Numerator
- Denominator

In most cases Ordinal will be the same as Superior and Denominator or Subscript/Inferior will be the same as Subscript.

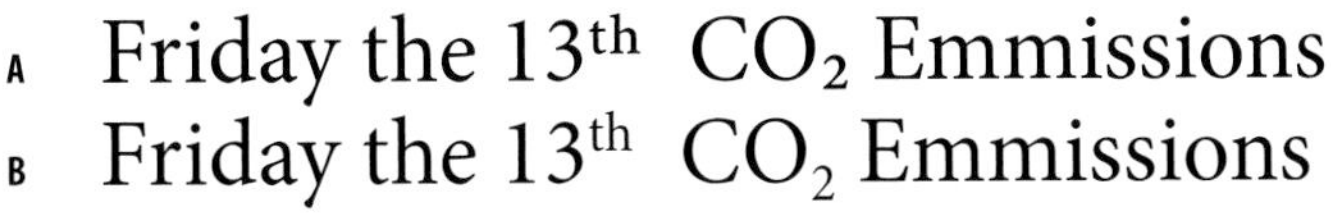

A Friday the 13th CO2 Emmissions
B Friday the 13th CO2 Emmissions

FIGURE 7.8 An OpenType ordinal (13th) and subscript (CO_2) applied (example **A**) versus superscript and subscript applied from the Control palette (example **B**). Note the thicker stroke of the OpenType characters.

Swash Characters

Need to add a flourish to your type? You can cut a dash by using swash characters. Swashes should be used sparingly—typically at the beginning of words or sentences. Some fonts have them, most don't—you can check by opening the Glyphs palette and looking for Swash in the Show pop-up menu. Some OpenType fonts may also have lowercase swash characters that are called finials or terminal characters, intended for use at the end of a word or line.

Titling Alternates

Some OpenType fonts have special "titling" characters designed for uppercase type set at large sizes.

Small Caps

The All Small Caps feature changes uppercase characters to appear as real lowercase small caps.

Fractions

Turning on Fractions converts anything that looks like a fraction to a proper fraction. Unfortunately, leaving this feature on will "fractionize" all numerals in your text, so it's necessary to apply it on an as-needed basis.

A *Ahoy There, Shipmates!*

B *Ahoy There, Shipmates!*

FIGURE 7.9 Bickham Script Pro with Swash (example **A**) and without (example **B**). Warnock Pro with finials (**C**).

FIGURE 7.10 Titling Alternates: Adobe Garamond Pro Regular 72 pt (example **A**) and using Titling Alternates (example **B**). The difference is subtle, but the titling characters are slightly thinner.

A Superior Quality

B SUPERIOR QUALITY

C SUPERIOR QUALITY

FIGURE 7.11 Small Caps: No small caps (example **A**), small caps applied from Character palette (example **B**), and All Small Caps (example **C**).

A 1/2 1/3 1/4 3/4

B ½ ⅓ ¼ ¾

FIGURE 7.12 Generic fractions (example **A**) and OpenType fractions (example **B**).

Oldstyle Figures

The default numbers in most typefaces are called lining figures and are designed to be used in columns so that we can add them up. The problem is that lining numbers stand out too much in a line of type.

In terms of bang for your buck, there's nothing like using old-style numerals for giving your type a more sophisticated look. Old style figures are as tall as the x-height of your type and so have a better type color in body text than full-height "lining figures." Figures 3, 4, 5, 7, and 9 have descenders; while 6 and 8 have ascenders. There are four styles of numerals:

- Tabular Lining and Tabular Oldstyle for use in tables.
- Proportional Lining for use in text set in all caps
- Proportional Oldstyle for use in body text.

Contextual Alternates

Some OpenType fonts—mostly script faces—have connecting alternates that connect better in certain letter combinations and will make your type look more like handwriting. You can also access alternate glyphs manually using the Glyphs palette.

A Pub Quiz 2005. Over 6789 Questions.

Pub Quiz 2005. Over 6789 Questions.

B FAHRENHEIT 451

FAHRENHEIT 451

FIGURE 7.13 Proportional Oldstyle (example **A**) is preferable to Lining Numerals (example **B**) in upper and lowercase type. On the other hand, Lining Numerals work better when the text is set in all caps.

A *brown fox over the big tree house*

B *brown fox over the big tree house*

FIGURE 7.14 Without Contextual Alternates (example **A**), and with Contextual Alternates (example **B**) note the connecting ligatures.

Opticals

Some OpenType fonts include four optical size variations: caption, regular, subhead, and display. To take advantage of this, turn on Automatically Use Correct Optical Size in your Type Preferences.

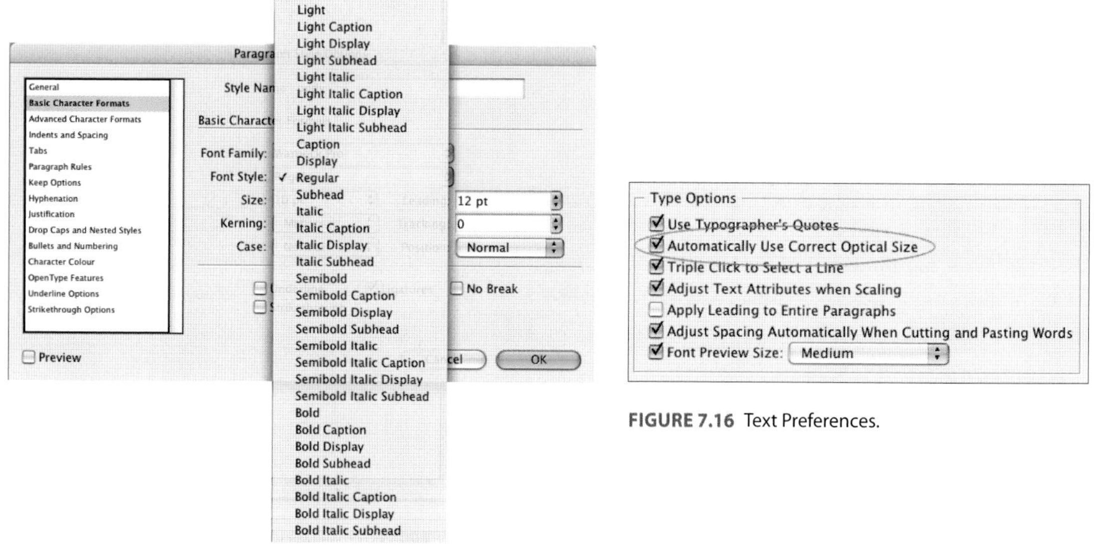

FIGURE 7.15 Opticals: Warnock Pro.

FIGURE 7.16 Text Preferences.

Glyph Positioning

FIGURE 7.17 Glyph Positioning.

With display type in all caps, the positioning of hyphens, dashes, and parentheses will require optical adjustment. Hyphens are centered on the x-height, which is appropriate for lowercase letters, but looks too low for text in all caps. Without OpenType fonts you would need to nudge up the hyphens, dashes, and parentheses using baseline shift. The beauty of OpenType fonts—and InDesign's support of them—is that this glyph positioning happens automatically.

If you format an OpenType font as All Caps, glyph shifting automatically adjusts the punctuation for a better fit: Hyphens, dashes, parentheses, braces, and brackets all shift vertically. Note, this only happens when you choose the All Caps character formats, not when you key in text with the Caps Lock key on.

Characters and Glyphs: What's the Difference?

Characters are the "names" or code points assigned by the Unicode standard. Glyphs are the actual design of a letterform. Characters are rendered by mapping Unicode characters to specific glyphs. One character may correspond to several glyphs: A lowercase e, a small caps e, and a swash e are all the same character, but are three separate glyphs.

TIP: How do you know if your font is an OpenType font? Well, if it's followed by the word "Pro" then chances are it is. InDesign CS2 ships with several OpenType fonts including Adobe Garamond Pro, Adobe Caslon Pro, Caflisch Pro, Minion Pro, and Warnock Pro.

Stylistic Sets

Some OpenType fonts include stylistic sets—alternate glyphs that can be applied one character at a time or to a range of text. If you select a different stylistic set, the glyphs defined in the set are used instead of the font's default glyphs. Using a stylistic set is one way you can apply small caps to a range of text, for example. You can see the glyphs for each stylistic set using the Glyphs palette.

FIGURE 7.18 Four different glyphs for the "e" character.

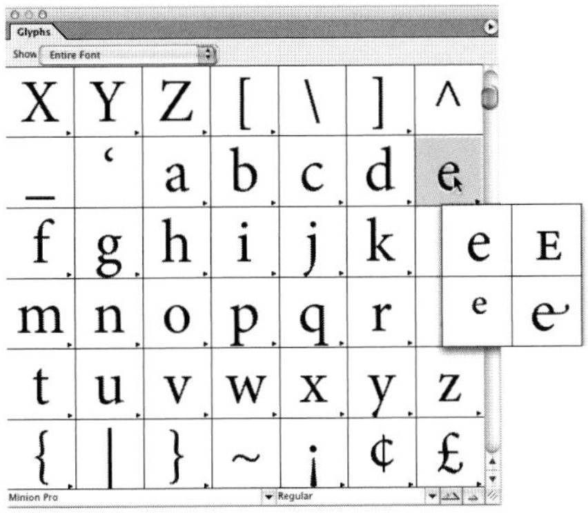

FIGURE 7.19 Choosing glyphs from the Glyphs palette.

Up Next

We branch out to examine InDesign's paragraph level formats. Specifically, we'll look at the importance of alignment to the readability of type, and how there's much more to aligning type than just left, center, right, or justified.

PART II

Paragraph Formats

CHAPTER 8

Aligning Your Type

CRITIQUING MY DESIGN FOR A PRODUCT CATALOG, my client referred to the justified type as "very masculine." I wasn't sure how to take it and I wasn't confident enough or quick-thinking enough to ask for clarification. Masculine type? Was that good or bad? Or was it just a neutral observation?

I'm not sure that I buy into the notion that text alignments can be assigned a gender, but the alignment of your text definitely gives your work a certain vibe and should serve the message of your type.

Alignment Types

There are several terms for different alignments in common usage. What InDesign refers to as Align left text is also known as ragged right, flush left, or (confusingly) as left justified. In InDesign terms, Left Justified means type where all lines of the paragraph are the same length. InDesign offers several other flavors of justified type: Right Justified, Center Justified, and Full Justified. The difference between them is the way the last line of the paragraph is handled. With the exception of Left Justified, these options have limited utility. When I refer to justified type, I mean type with the last line of the paragraph left aligned. "Ragged" can refer either to left, center, or right aligned type.

FIGURE 8.1 Types of Alignment.

Congress shall make no law respecting an establishment of religion, or prohibiting the free exercise thereof; or abridging the freedom of speech, or of the press; or the right of the people peaceably to assemble, and to petition the Government for a redress of grievances.
Left

Congress shall make no law respecting an establishment of religion, or prohibiting the free exercise thereof; or abridging the freedom of speech, or of the press; or the right of the people peaceably to assemble, and to petition the Government for a redress of grievances.
Center

Congress shall make no law respecting an establishment of religion, or prohibiting the free exercise thereof; or abridging the freedom of speech, or of the press; or the right of the people peaceably to assemble, and to petition the Government for a redress of grievances.
Right

Congress shall make no law respecting an establishment of religion, or prohibiting the free exercise thereof; or abridging the freedom of speech, or of the press; or the right of the people peaceably to assemble, and to petition the Government for a redress of grievances.
Left Justify

Congress shall make no law respecting an establishment of religion, or prohibiting the free exercise thereof; or abridging the freedom of speech, or of the press; or the right of the people peaceably to assemble, and to petition the Government for a redress of grievances.
Center Justify

Congress shall make no law respecting an establishment of religion, or prohibiting the free exercise thereof; or abridging the freedom of speech, or of the press; or the right of the people peaceably to assemble, and to petition the Government for a redress of grievances.
Full Justify

There are two new types of alignment on the Control palette in InDesign CS2. **Align towards Spine** aligns text on a left-hand page so that it is right aligned. If the same text flows onto a right-hand page, it becomes left aligned. **Align away from Spine** does the opposite: It aligns text on a left-hand page so that is left-aligned, while text on a right-hand page is right-aligned.

The Paragraph palette also has one additional indentation option—**Last Line Right Indent**. This can be useful for *outdenting* the last line of a paragraph, for example as in a table of contents or a price list.

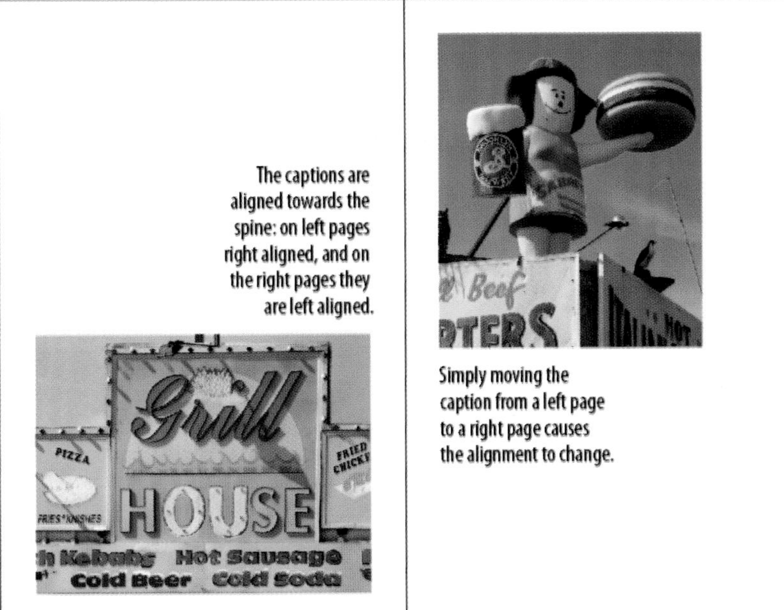

FIGURE 8.2 Align towards Spine.

FIGURE 8.3 Last Line Right Indent.

Alignment Keyboard Shortcuts

Left	Cmd+Shift+L (Ctrl+Shift+L)
Center	Cmd+Shift+C (Ctrl+Shift+C)
Right	Cmd+Shift+R (Ctrl+Shift+R)
Justified	Cmd+Shift+J (Ctrl+Shift+J)
Justify All Lines	Cmd+Shift+F (Ctrl+Shift+F)

Centering Type

Center alignment is widely used in magazine design for *crossheads* and in book design for title pages. When chosen consciously centering can be extremely effective; when chosen as a "default" or fall-back option, it can make layouts appear stodgy or generic. At its best, it is formal and classical; at its worst, it is static and conventional, and—if you are centering whole paragraphs—it is less readable. The potential pitfall of centered type is that the even amount of white space on either side of the heading can create a symmetry that may be at odds with asymmetrical nature of the ragged right text. Centering is also commonly associated with birth announcements, wedding invitations, and...gravestones.

Guidelines for Centering Type

- When centering display type over left-aligned body text, you may need to tweak the alignment to compensate for the type looking off center if the display type is followed by a line of ragged type that does not fill the full measure.

FIGURE 8.4 Center alignment used for poetry.

Half a league, half a league,
Half a league onward,
All in the valley of Death
Rode the six hundred.
"Forward, the Light Brigade!
"Charge for the guns!" he said:
Into the valley of Death
Rode the six hundred.

—The Charge of the Light Brigade
Alfred, Lord Tennyson

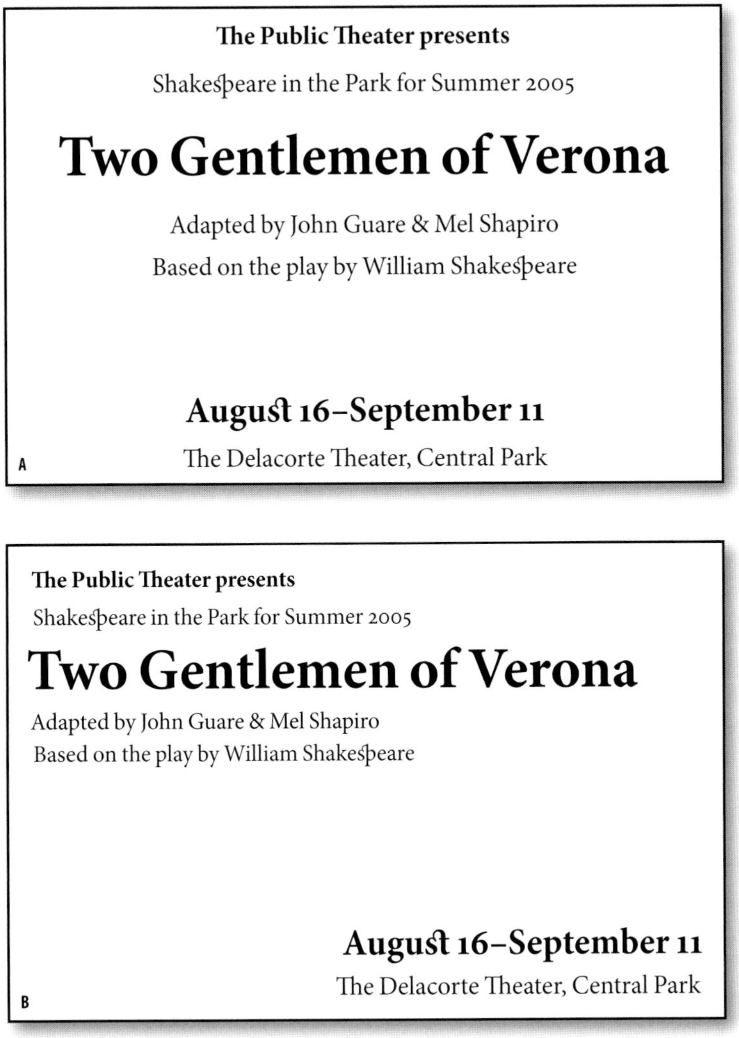

The Public Theater presents

Shakespeare in the Park for Summer 2005

Two Gentlemen of Verona

Adapted by John Guare & Mel Shapiro

Based on the play by William Shakespeare

August 16–September 11

The Delacorte Theater, Central Park

A

The Public Theater presents

Shakespeare in the Park for Summer 2005

Two Gentlemen of Verona

Adapted by John Guare & Mel Shapiro

Based on the play by William Shakespeare

August 16–September 11

The Delacorte Theater, Central Park

B

FIGURE 8.5 A static Center alignment (example **A**) and a more dynamic Left alignment (example **B**).

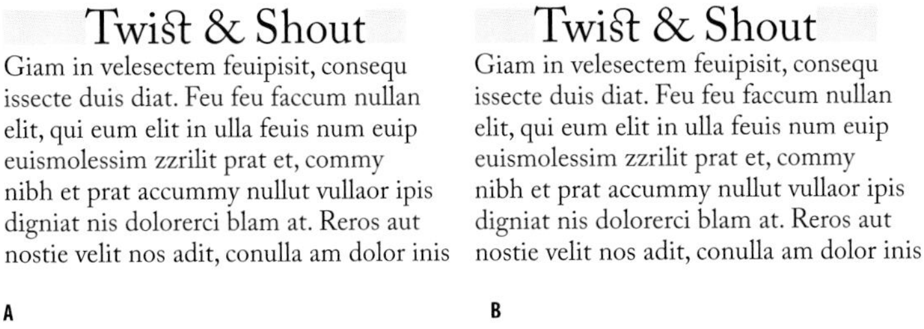

Twist & Shout

Giam in velesectem feuipisit, consequ issecte duis diat. Feu feu faccum nullan elit, qui eum elit in ulla feuis num euip euismolessim zzrilit prat et, commy nibh et prat accummy nullut vullaor ipis digniat nis dolorerci blam at. Reros aut nostie velit nos adit, conulla am dolor inis

A

Twist & Shout

Giam in velesectem feuipisit, consequ issecte duis diat. Feu feu faccum nullan elit, qui eum elit in ulla feuis num euip euismolessim zzrilit prat et, commy nibh et prat accummy nullut vullaor ipis digniat nis dolorerci blam at. Reros aut nostie velit nos adit, conulla am dolor inis

B

FIGURE 8.6 Optically centering a headline. In example **A**, the headline is mathematically centered. In example **B**, the headline has been optically centered—by adding a small amount of right indent—over the first line of type.

- Avoid using an italic headline over roman type because the slant of the italic can make the headline appear off-center.
- Centered lines that begin or end with punctuation may look off-center and require optical centering.
- Avoid centering paragraphs with too many lines, especially on a wide measure, because it is harder to find the beginning of the next line.
- Break lines into phrases that make sense.

Clean Shaven or Rugged: Justified vs. Ragged Type

Because centered alignment and right alignment have limited applications when it comes to continuous text, we are essentially concerned with the pros and cons of using Left or Left Justified type, and the main difference between them—what happens to the leftover space. On every line of type there will be leftover space—unless, like Jack Nicholson in *The Shining,* you're just typing the same line over and over. With Justified type the extra space is distributed between the words and varied to give you lines that are exactly the same width. With left-aligned type, the extra space is added at the end of the line, giving you lines of varying width.

Left-aligned type has the following characteristics:

- Consistent word spacing.
- Asymmetry. The ragged margin adds shape and interest—as well as white space—to what would otherwise by a rectangular block.
- Informal. The differing line lengths can give a casual feel.

Justified type has the following characteristics:

- Economical. You get more words on your page when you justify your text. The difference may be insignificant with a short document, but in a magazine or book your document may be several pages shorter.
- Symmetrical. Columns with smooth edges can make your document seem balanced.
- Formal. The uniformity of the smooth right-hand margin can cause your text to be perceived as more formal, which, depending on the text, may be a good or a bad thing.

How InDesign Justifies Type

Justification is achieved by varying the size of the word spaces on the line—or in the entire paragraph—in an attempt to get even word and letter spacing, or at least word and letter spacing that looks even. If justification can't be achieved by adjusting the Word Spacing alone, then InDesign will adjust the Letter Spacing according to your minimum, desired, and maximum settings. After that, it moves on to your Glyph Scaling settings. Too much variation in word or letter spacing will cause the tight lines to look darker than the rest of your text and disturb the paragraph's rhythm. At the other extreme, if the word spacing is too big, you will get unsightly "rivers" of white running through your lines. This is particularly problematic when the columns are narrow and/or when the word spacing exceeds the leading, because the eye is tempted to read down through the gaps rather than from left to right.

Good type color is essential regardless of what alignment you are using, but it's harder to achieve in justified text, because the space left over at the end of the line has to be redistributed across the line to give you a smooth right margin. The more words you have in a line the easier it will be to get even word spacing. You get more words either by making your type smaller or your column wider. It's a balancing act because if you make your column too wide relative to your type size, you'll be swapping one evil for another (see Chapter 15: "Set Up").

TIP: To check for rivers, turn your page upside down—without the distraction of actually reading the words, any problems should shout themselves out.

InDesign's Justification options can seem intimidating, but ultimately they are extremely logical. Using them well will make a dramatic difference in the appearance of your type.

Four score and seven years ago our fathers brought forth on this continent, a new nation, conceived in liberty, and dedicatedtotheproposition that allmen arecreatedequal.

Now we are engaged in a great civil war, testing whether that nation or any nation so conceived and so dedicated, canlongendure.

We are met on a great battlefield of thatwar.Wehavecometodedicateaportionofthatfield,asafinalrestingplacefor

A

Four score and seven years ago our fathers brought forth on this continent, a new nation, conceived in liberty, and dedicated to the proposition that all men are created equal.

Now we are engaged in a great civil war, testing whether that nation or any nation so conceived and so dedicated, can long endure.

B

FIGURE 8.7 Many rivers to cross. Word Spacing and Letter Spacing too tight (example **A**) and too loose (example **B**).

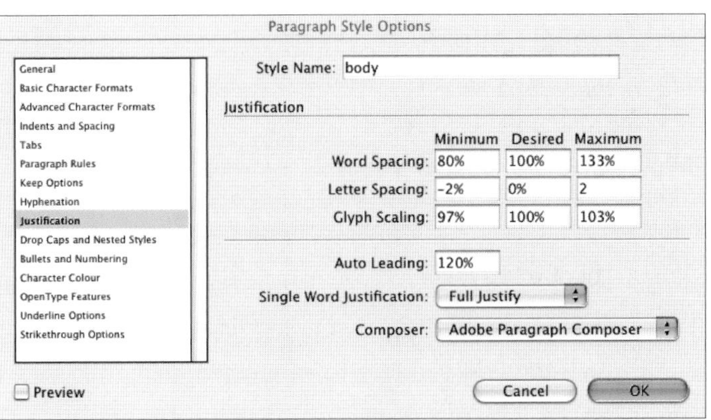

FIGURE 8.8 The Justification options specified as part of a style sheet definition.

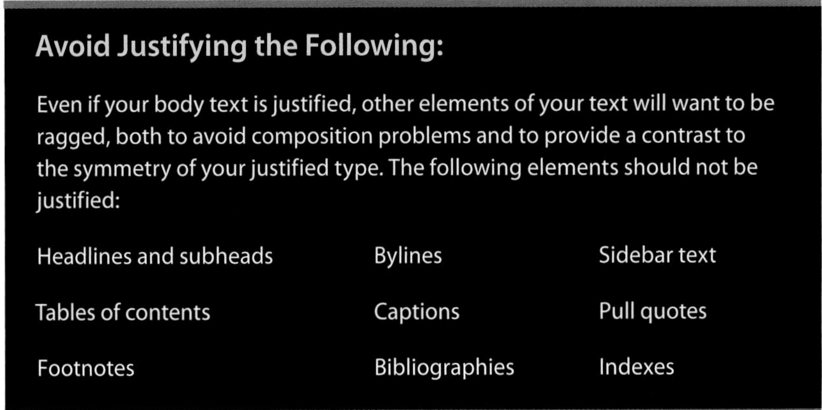

Avoid Justifying the Following:

Even if your body text is justified, other elements of your text will want to be ragged, both to avoid composition problems and to provide a contrast to the symmetry of your justified type. The following elements should not be justified:

Headlines and subheads	Bylines	Sidebar text
Tables of contents	Captions	Pull quotes
Footnotes	Bibliographies	Indexes

Word Spacing

No prizes for guessing that this refers to the space between words, i.e., the width of space you get when you press the spacebar.

If you make your word spacing too tight, words will blend together making it hard for the eye to distinguish one from the next. At the other extreme, word spacing that's too loose creates unsightly blocks of white space between words, which makes reading groups of words more difficult.

Determining word spacing is more of an aesthetic consideration than an exact science. A good starting point is 100 percent—the width of the *spaceband* designed by the font designer. However, you may want to reduce this from 60 to 80 percent in the following circumstances:

- If you're working with condensed type.
- If the weight of your typeface is relatively light.
- If your typeface is tightly fit, i.e., if you are using tight letter spacing, you will want your word spacing to be correspondingly tight.
- If you're working with larger point sizes.

Four score and seven years ago our fathers brought forth on this continent, a new nation, conceived in liberty, and dedicated to the proposition that all men are created equal.

Now we are engaged in a great civil war, testing whether that nation or any nation so conceived and so dedicated, can long endure.

We are met on a great battlefield of that war. We have come to dedicate a portion of that field, as a final resting place for those who here gave their lives that that nation might live. It is altogether fitting and proper that we should do this.

A

	Minimum	Desired	Maximum
Word Spacing:	50%	60%	90%
Letter Spacing:	0%	0%	0%
Glyph Scaling:	100%	100%	100%

Four score and seven years ago our fathers brought forth on this continent, a new nation, conceived in liberty, and dedicated to the proposition that all men are created equal.

Now we are engaged in a great civil war, testing whether that nation or any nation so conceived and so dedicated, can long endure.

We are met on a great battlefield of that war. We have come to dedicate a portion of that field, as a final resting place for those who here gave their lives that that nation might live. It is altogether fitting and proper that we should do this.

B

	Minimum	Desired	Maximum
Word Spacing:	80%	100%	133%
Letter Spacing:	0%	0%	0%
Glyph Scaling:	100%	100%	100%

FIGURE 8.9 Tight word spacing (example **A**) and using the default values (example **B**). (ITC Garamond Book Condensed).

Letter Spacing

This is the distance between letters and includes any kerning or tracking values you may have applied. A character's width is determined not just by the character itself, but also by the space that the font designer adds around the character—known as the *side bearing*.

A purist will tell you that come hell or high water all three values should be set to 0. That is, under no circumstances is any variation in letter spacing permissible. However, if you are working with a narrow measure you'll need to be more liberal with these settings. Depending on the font, you might try reducing the Desired Letter Spacing to –3, and set the minimum and maximum can be set to –5 and 0, respectively.

FIGURE 8.10 Letter Spacing: A slight adjustment to the Letter Spacing (example **A**) significantly improves the type color over example **B**, where InDesign has to rely solely upon the Word Spacing values to justify the type.

We need to stop the World Bank and International Monetary Fund (IMF) forcing poor countries to open their markets to trade with rich countries, which has proved so disastrous over the past 20 years; the EU must drop its demand that former European colonies open their markets and give more rights to big companies; we need to regulate companies — making them accountable for their social and environmental impact both here and abroad; and we must ensure that countries are able to regulate foreign investment in a way that best suits their own needs.

We need to stop the World Bank and International Monetary Fund (IMF) forcing poor countries to open their markets to trade with rich countries, which has proved so disastrous over the past 20 years; the EU must drop its demand that former European colonies open their markets and give more rights to big companies; we need to regulate companies — making them accountable for their social and environmental impact both here and abroad; and we must ensure that countries are able to regulate foreign investment in a way that best suits their own needs.

A

	Minimum	Desired	Maximum
Word Spacing:	80%	100%	133%
Letter Spacing:	-2%	0%	2%
Glyph Scaling:	100%	100%	100%

B

	Minimum	Desired	Maximum
Word Spacing:	80%	100%	133%
Letter Spacing:	0%	0%	0%
Glyph Scaling:	100%	100%	100%

With both Word and Letter Spacing you need to find a balance between being strict and being reasonable. There's no point in specifying restrictive settings if your text-to-column width ratio makes it impossible for InDesign to honor these settings.

Glyph Scaling

Glyph Scaling is the process of adjusting the width of characters in order to achieve even justification—and a little glyph scaling goes a long way. Entering a value other than 100 percent for your Desired Glyph Scaling when working with ragged text is the same as entering a value for Horizontal Scaling. In other words, it's a bad idea. Glyph scaling might sound like the kind of crime that the Type Police will bust you for in an instant. But in reality, moderate amounts of glyph scaling can—combined with your other justification settings—improve type color significantly. Moderation is the key: Keep your glyph scaling to 97, 100, 103 for Minimum, Desired, and Maximum, respectively. No one will ever know that you varied the horizontal scale of your type. They will, however, appreciate the splendidly even word spacing. Mum's the word.

We need to stop the World Bank and International Monetary Fund (IMF) forcing poor countries to open their markets to trade with rich countries, which has proved so disastrous over the past 20 years; the EU must drop its demand that former European colonies open their markets and give more rights to big companies; we need to regulate companies — making them accountable for their social and environmental impact both here and abroad; and we must ensure that countries are able to regulate foreign investment in a way that best suits their own needs.

A

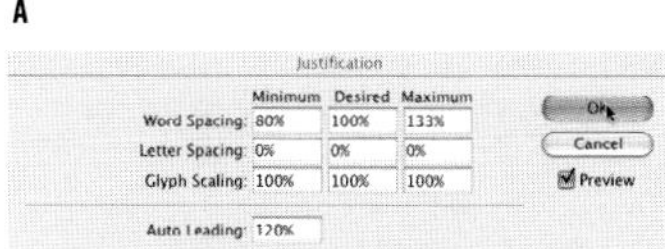

We need to stop the World Bank and International Monetary Fund (IMF) forcing poor countries to open their markets to trade with rich countries, which has proved so disastrous over the past 20 years; the EU must drop its demand that former European colonies open their markets and give more rights to big companies; we need to regulate companies — making them accountable for their social and environmental impact both here and abroad; and we must ensure that countries are able to regulate foreign investment in a way that best suits their own needs.

B

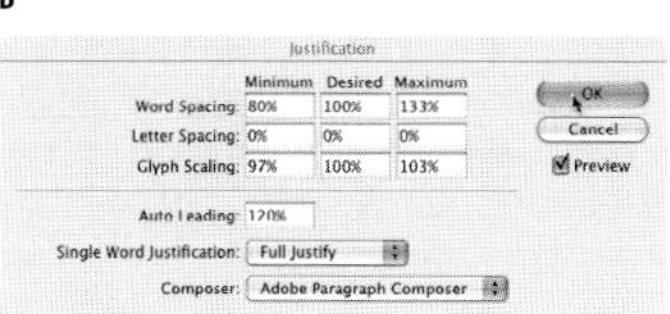

FIGURE 8.11 Glyph Scaling: Allowing glyphs to scale to a small degree (example **B**) allows for more even justification.

We need to stop the World Bank and International Monetary Fund (IMF) forcing poor countries to open their markets to trade with rich countries, which has proved so disastrous over the past 20 years; the EU must drop its demand that former European colonies open their markets and give more rights to big companies; we need to regulate companies — making them accountable for their social and environmental impact both here and abroad; and we must ensure that countries are able to regulate foreign investment in a way that best suits their own needs.

A

We need to stop the World Bank and International Monetary Fund (IMF) forcing poor countries to open their markets to trade with rich countries, which has proved so disastrous over the past 20 years; the EU must drop its demand that former European colonies open their markets and give more rights to big companies; we need to regulate companies — making them accountable for their social and environmental impact both here and abroad; and we must ensure that countries are able to regulate foreign investment in a way that best suits their own needs.

B

FIGURE 8.12 In example **B**, Letter Spacing and Glyph Scaling are combined with Word Spacing to produce an even type color.

The Adobe Paragraph Composer

The Adobe Paragraph Composer is the jewel in the crown of InDesign's typographic features. Before InDesign came along, page layout programs would compose paragraphs line by line. Because there was only a limited number of word spaces across which the extra space at the end of the line could be distributed, this often caused bad type color. Using the Adobe Paragraph Composer (it is the default choice of Composer), InDesign analyzes the word spaces across a whole paragraph, considering the possible line breaks, and optimizing earlier lines in the paragraph to prevent bad breaks later on. Not only does this mean fewer hyphens and better breaks where hyphens do occur, it also means better spacing. Because InDesign looks in the whole paragraph, there are more places where it can add or subtract an imperceptible amount of space. The default values of 80, 100, 133 for the Minimum, Desired, and Maximum word space allow the program enough latitude to distribute the space over a range of lines.

The Adobe Paragraph Composer works for both ragged and justified type, but it's with the latter that you really see its benefits.

FIGURE 8.13 Adobe Paragraph Composer

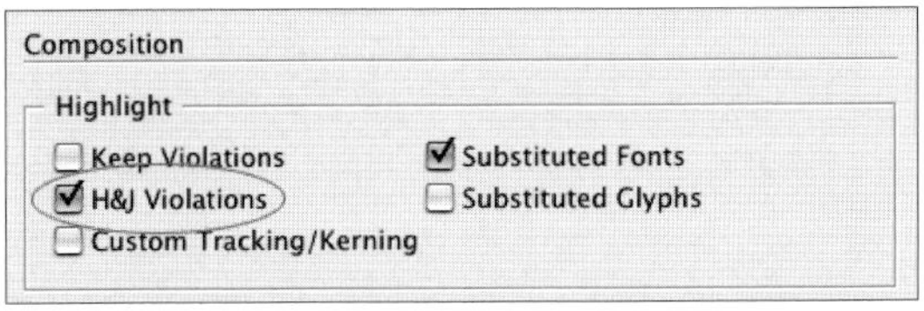

FIGURE 8.14 Show H&J Violations.

Show H&J Violations

As absolutely fabulous as the Adobe Paragraph Composer is, you shouldn't expect miracles. Good type color doesn't come easy, and you'll still have to fix some composition problems manually. This is where the Preference Show H&J Violations comes in handy. This composition preference allows you to easily identify the problems so that you can fix them—by any means necessary. As a final reality check, it's important to keep in mind that even with the most carefully considered column widths, the most scientifically proven justification options, and the most judicious use of InDesign's Composition preferences, spacing problems will still occur from time to time. So don't fire the proofreader.

Paragraph Composer Weirdness

In InDesign CS, there were some problems with the Adobe Paragraph Composer refusing to let short words be pulled back to the previous line, even when there was room enough to accommodate them. This issue has been resolved in InDesign CS2. However, you will still find that when editing text that is composed using the Adobe Paragraph Composer, the type before *and* after the cursor will move. This is because, while you are editing the text, the paragraph is in progress—InDesign is still figuring out how it can compose the spacing within the paragraph and adjusting spacing and line break on the fly. If it bothers you, you can always edit the type in the Story Editor—choose Edit > Story Editor, Cmd+Y (Ctrl+Y).

NOTE: It's important to bear in mind that InDesign's Justification and Hyphenation features work in conjunction with each other. Good word spacing will not be achieved by the Adobe Paragraph Composer alone, but rather by combining it with the other justification features in InDesign's toolkit.

Adobe Single-Line Composer

If you're going for that retro look of bad word spacing circa 1994, then this is the option to choose. Otherwise it's second best to the Adobe Paragraph Composer.

Balancing Ragged Lines

It is often necessary to break display type: either at logical places for meaning and/or to achieve a visual balance. InDesign's Balance Ragged Lines feature goes some way towards achieving the latter and is useful to include as part of the style definition of headings, pull-quotes, and centered paragraphs. Using Balance Ragged Lines will reduce the amount of manual intervention (in the form of forced line breaks, or nonbreaking spaces), but you're still going to need to check your display type carefully for meaning.

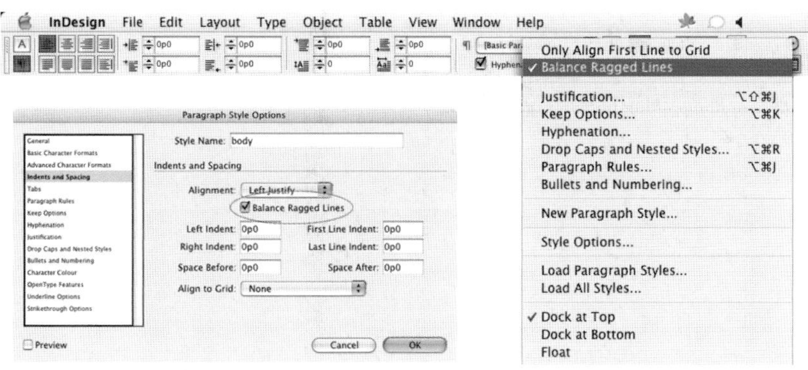

FIGURES 8.15 Balance Ragged Lines applied locally from the Control palette and incorporated into a Paragraph Style definition.

FIGURE 8.16 Unbalanced (example **A**); balanced (example **B**).

A **Everybody's Got Something to Hide Except for Me and My Monkey**

B **Everybody's Got Something to Hide Except for Me and My Monkey**

Balance Ragged Lines can also be used to adjust the line endings in left-aligned body text to produce a more even rag—what you're aiming for is a gentle ripple down the edge of your page. Note that Hyphenation settings also play an important role in determining the way a paragraph rags (see Chapter 11: "Don't Fear the Hyphen") as does your chosen method of composition: Adobe Paragraph Composer or Adobe Single-line Composer. Balance Ragged Lines has no effect in justified text.

The line lengths in ragged type should be clearly irregular, i.e., they shouldn't look like carelessly set justified type. On the other hand, they shouldn't be so irregular that they create distracting shapes that impede fast reading.

FIGURE 8.17 Balance Ragged Lines in body text. Both paragraphs are composed using the Adobe Paragraph Composer, and both permit hyphenation. Example **A** is without Balance Ragged Lines; example **B** has Balance Ragged Lines applied. Using Balance Ragged Lines for body text can yield unpredictable results—it is best applied locally, or, if incorporated into a Paragraph Style definition, to paragraphs that typically run only a few lines.

Scrooge was better than his word. He did it all, and infinitely more; and to Tiny Tim, who did *not* die, he was a second father. He became as good a friend, as good a master, and as good a man, as the good old city knew, or any other good old city, town, or borough, in the good old world. Some people laughed to see the alteration in him, but he let them laugh, and little heeded them; for he was wise enough to know that nothing ever happened on this globe, for good, at which some people did not have their fill of laughter in the outset; and knowing that such as these would be blind anyway, he thought it quite as well that they should wrinkle up their eyes in grins, as have the malady in less attractive forms. His own heart laughed: and that was quite enough for him.

A —Charles Dickens, *A Christmas Carol*

Scrooge was better than his word. He did it all, and infinitely more; and to Tiny Tim, who did *not* die, he was a second father. He became as good a friend, as good a master, and as good a man, as the good old city knew, or any other good old city, town, or borough, in the good old world. Some people laughed to see the alteration in him, but he let them laugh, and little heeded them; for he was wise enough to know that nothing ever happened on this globe, for good, at which some people did not have their fill of laughter in the outset; and knowing that such as these would be blind anyway, he thought it quite as well that they should wrinkle up their eyes in grins, as have the malady in less attractive forms. His own heart laughed: and that was quite enough for him.

B —Charles Dickens, *A Christmas Carol*

Right-Aligned Type

Right-aligned or flush-right type can be effective for short bursts of text like captions, pull quotes, or sometimes headlines. Because we read from the left, right-aligned type is hard going for anything more than a few lines. The unevenness of the rag becomes distracting and finding the beginning of lines is difficult.

Photo
Gallery
Right aligned
text can be
suitable for
short picture
captions..

FIGURE 8.18 Right-aligned type used for captions. The type is also set to align to the bottom of the text frame, making it easy to align the baselines of the type with the bottom of the picture frame. See below for vertical alignment.

Optical Margin Alignment

Ever notice how opening quotation marks and letters such as "W" or a "T" can make the left or right edges of a column appear misaligned? The problem—like all typographic problems more noticeable at large type sizes—exists because InDesign aligns characters mechanically, that is, by the edge of the character plus its side bearing (the built-in space that surrounds each letter). Also, when the line begins with punctuation, like an opening quotation mark, you can get a visual hole or indentation at the beginning of the line relative to the characters below.

Until recently these shortcomings were regarded as part of the price of progress. After all, we could all do so much more with our page layout programs, at the end of the day did it really matter that we had to forgo a few niceties? Along came InDesign to the rescue.

Optical Margin Alignment allows the edges of letters to hang outside the text margin so that the column edge actually looks straighter. And not only that: Optical Margin Alignment will hang punctuation marks such as periods, commas, quotation marks, hyphens, and dashes outside the right-hand text margin.

It looks at the shapes and alignment of all the characters on the left and right margins and adjusts the spacing optically according to their letter shapes. Fan-frickin-tastic! Surprisingly, some people don't like this look, preferring everything contained within the text block. But then some people have become so accustomed to the taste of instant coffee that they no longer like the real thing.

FIGURE 8.19 Without Optical Margin Alignment (example **A**); Optical Margin Alignment applied (example **B**).

"Farewell! I leave you, and in you the last of human kind whom these eyes will ever behold. Farewell, Frankenstein! If thou wert yet alive, and yet cherished a desire of revenge against me, it would be better satiated in my life than in my destruction. But it was not so; thou didst seek my extinction that I might not cause greater wretchedness; and if yet, in some mode unknown to me, thou hast not ceased to think and feel, thou wouldst not desire against me a vengeance greater than that which I feel. Blasted as thou wert, my agony was still superior to thine; for the bitter sting of remorse will not cease to rankle in my wounds until death shall close them for ever.

—Mary Shelly, *Frankenstein*

A

"Farewell! I leave you, and in you the last of human kind whom these eyes will ever behold. Farewell, Frankenstein! If thou wert yet alive, and yet cherished a desire of revenge against me, it would be better satiated in my life than in my destruction. But it was not so; thou didst seek my extinction that I might not cause greater wretchedness; and if yet, in some mode unknown to me, thou hast not ceased to think and feel, thou wouldst not desire against me a vengeance greater than that which I feel. Blasted as thou wert, my agony was still superior to thine; for the bitter sting of remorse will not cease to rankle in my wounds until death shall close them for ever.

—Mary Shelly, *Frankenstein*

B

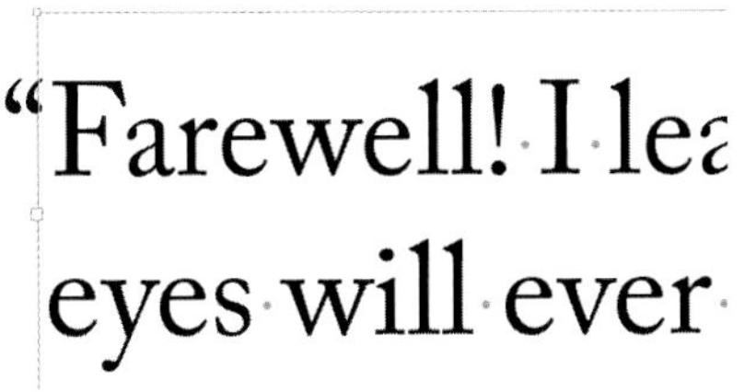

"Farewell! I lea
eyes will ever

FIGURE 8.21 The opening quotation mark "hangs" to the left of the column edge.

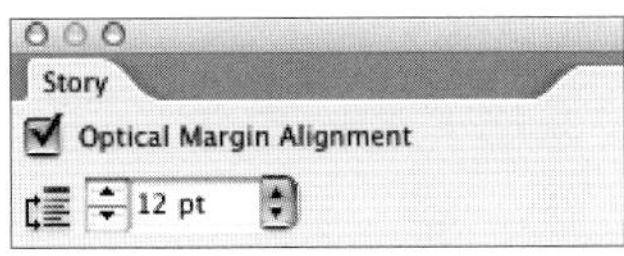

FIGURE 8.20 To optically align your type check Optical Margin Alignment.

To apply Optical Margin Alignment to a story, select a text frame, then choose Type > Story and check Optical Margin Alignment. The font size setting determines the amount of overhang. Usually this should be the same size as the text, but you'll want to eyeball it.

Indent to Here

To create hanging punctuation, for example on a pull quote, use the Indent to Here character—Cmd+\ (Ctrl+\). This special character indents all subsequent lines in the paragraph to the point where you added the character.

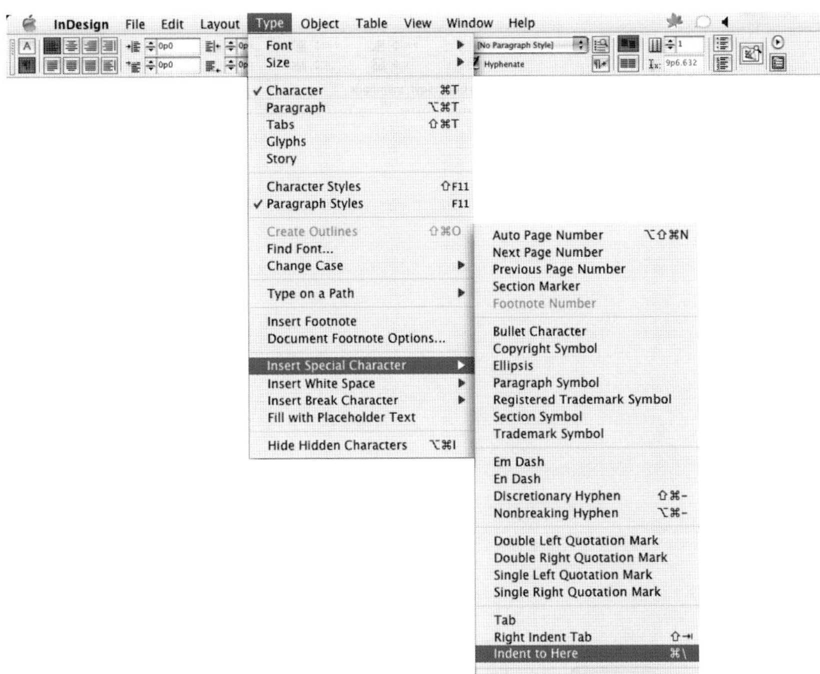

FIGURE 8.22 Indent to Here.

FIGURE 8.23 In example **A**, without the Indent to Here character the opening quote mark bites into the text block. Adding an Indent to Here character after the opening quotation (example **B**) allows the quote mark to "hang" in the left margin.

A

"Life is what happens while
you are making other plans."
—John Lennon

B

"Life is what happens while
you are making other plans."
—John Lennon

Vertical Alignment

NOTE: Vertical justification doesn't work in nonrectangular text frames.

When we talk of type alignment, for the most part we mean the horizontal alignment of the text. InDesign also gives you options for the vertical alignment of your type within a text frame. The default is for type to begin at the top of the frame, and this is appropriate in most instances, but there are times when Center or Bottom alignment of type within a text frame will be necessary. With a text frame selected or your pointer inserted into the text, choose Object > Text Frame Options—Cmd+B (Ctrl+B).

A fourth vertical alignment option—Justified—can be used on text frames with multiple columns to make text "bottom out" by adding extra space above paragraphs and potentially to the leading of your type.

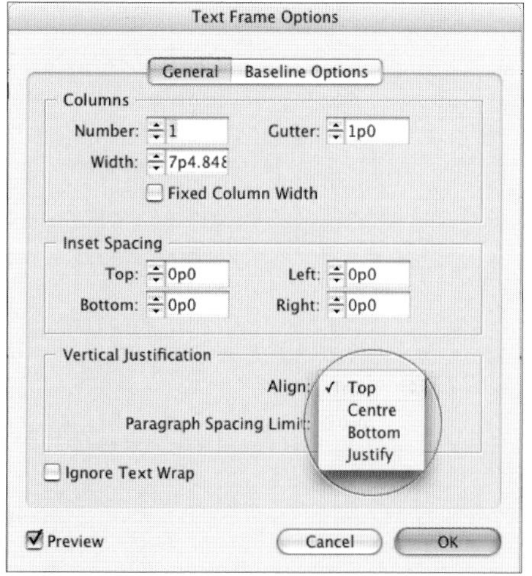

FIGURE 8.24 Text Frame Options. Vertical Justification.

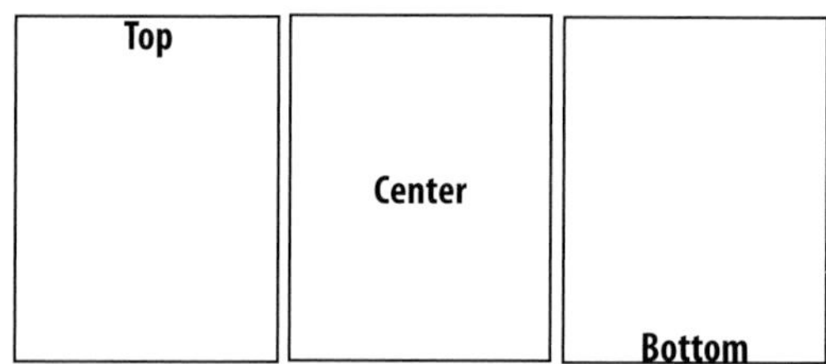

FIGURE 8.25 Vertical Justification applied to text frames.

This is a super-convenient feature and one that I confess to using when I think no one will notice and/or when time is tight. However, vertical justification is a something of a Faustian bargain—yes, it makes your columns end on the same baseline, but it does so at a price. Vertical justification overrides your leading, knocking your type off the baseline grid if you are using one, and potentially makes your type color uneven. That said, you do not surrender all control: Paragraph Spacing Limit lets you specify the maximum amount of space permissible between paragraphs. Once the Paragraph Spacing Limit has been reached, there's nowhere to go but to increase the leading. You can prevent this by setting a massive amount in this field (up to a maximum 8640 points). That way spacing will only be added between paragraphs (the lesser of the two evils) and your leading will remain unaffected.

How effective this is will depend on how many paragraphs you have in the column. If you have text with subheads and body text, for example, the extra space can usually be added unobtrusively above the subheads. If your column is a single paragraph, however, this approach isn't going to work.

FIGURE 8.26 Vertical Justification of this text frame causes the leading in the third column to open up in an unsightly way.

Rivera received an ultimatum: "As much as I dislike to do so," wrote John D., Jr.'s son, Nelson, "I am afraid we must ask you to substitute the face of some unknown man where Lenin's now appears." The mural became a cause for pickets and newspaper assaults both for and against; when Rivera refused to remove the offending Lenin, Rockefeller paid him the agreed fee of $21,000 and ordered work on the unfinished mural terminated. In the wake of the controversy Rivera found his other contracts in the U.S. cancelled. Despite assurances to the contrary, two months later the Rockefeller Center mural was blasted from the wall, later to be replaced by an inoffensive composition by Jose Sert.

Man At The Crossroads was recreated by Rivera in Mexico City using photographs of the destroyed New York mural. There are just a few changes. Second time around, besides Lenin, Rivera threw in Marx, Engels and Trotsky for good measure and, in the night club scene there is a depiction of a tall, slim, bespectacled figure holding a cocktail glass. Above the figure are a strain of syphilis germs. This was Diego's revenge: the figure is that of John D. Rockefeller, Jr. ■

Up Next

Moving along the Control Palette, we'll look next at the indents and spacing options, closely related to the type's alignment, and which further clarify the hierarchy and purpose of the type and enhance its readability.

CHAPTER 9

Paragraph Indents and Spacing

TYPOGRAPHY, LIKE ALL COMMUNICATIONS MEDIA, relies on established conventions that are understood, often unconsciously, by its audience. One such convention is the use of indents or spacing to distinguish one paragraph from another. Paragraphs represent units of thought, and a new paragraph signals the reader that a new idea is coming. While there are several ways to indicate a new paragraph, two methods are most prevalent: indenting the first line and adding spacing before the paragraph.

FIGURE 9.1 Two ways of differentiating paragraphs: First-line indents set to 1 pica for continuous reading text (example **A**) and Paragraph Spacing (example **B**) with a 6-point space above for more technical material.

Four score and seven years ago our fathers brought forth on this continent, a new nation, conceived in liberty, and dedicated to the proposition that all men are created equal.

Now we are engaged in a great civil war, testing whether that nation or any nation so conceived and so dedicated, can long endure.

We are met on a great battlefield of that war. We have come to dedicate a portion of that field, as a final resting place for those who here gave their lives that that nation might live. It is altogether fitting and proper that we should do this.

But, in a larger sense, we can not dedicate—we can not consecrate—we can not hallow this ground. The brave men living and dead, who struggled here, have consecrated it, far above our poor power to add or detract. The world will little note, nor long remember what we say here, but it can never forget what they did here. It is for us the living, rather, to be dedicated here to the unfinished work which they who fought here have thus far

A

To colour correct using an eyedropper tool:

1. (Optional) Place a colour sampler on a pixel in an area of the image that should be neutral gray. Choose a pixel in the shadows, midtone, or highlight, depending on the eyedropper tool that you plan to use. Use the Info palette to help you locate an appropriate pixel.
2. Choose Layer > New Adjustment Layer > Levels
3. Double-click the Set Black Point, the Set Gray Point, or the Set White Point Eyedropper tool. Use the Adobe Colour Picker to specify a neutral target colour.

If you're working in RGB, enter the same values for R, G, and B to specify a neutral colour. The neutral colour should be close as possible to the values of the colour sampler.

If you want to preserve specific details in the shadow or highlight, be sure to specify a values for the Set Black Point

B

First-Line Indents

The humble first-line indent plays a crucial role in the readability of documents, notifying the reader that one paragraph has ended and a new one is about to begin.

You wouldn't think there would be too much to say about first-line indents. They're indents on the first line of a paragraph. 'Nuff said. Not if you're Jan Tschichold. The famous typographer wrote several articles about first-line indents and was unequivocal on the subject: "The beginnings of paragraphs must be indented. Paragraphs without indent...are a bad habit and should be eliminated." And more: "Typesetting without indentation makes it difficult for the reader to comprehend what has been printed. And that is its most important disadvantage. While blunt beginnings seem to create a uniform and consistent impression when compared to normal typesetting, this impression is paid for with a serious loss of comprehension."

How Big Should They Be?

There is no hard and fast rule, but 1 em is a good starting point. If you're using 10-point type, a 10-point first-line indent is suitable. Anything less and the indent may be missed. Alternatively you can use your leading increment so that if your text is 10/12, then a 12-point first line indent is suitable. Some people prefer a slightly larger indent, especially if they're working with wide columns. Just make sure your first-line indent is not bigger than the exit lines of your paragraphs, as this will create ugly areas of trapped space between paragraphs.

How (and How Not) to Add First-Line Indents

First-line indents can be applied through the Control palette, or better yet, incorporated into a style sheet definition. Don't create your first-line indents with tabs, or worse, by pressing the spacebar multiple times.

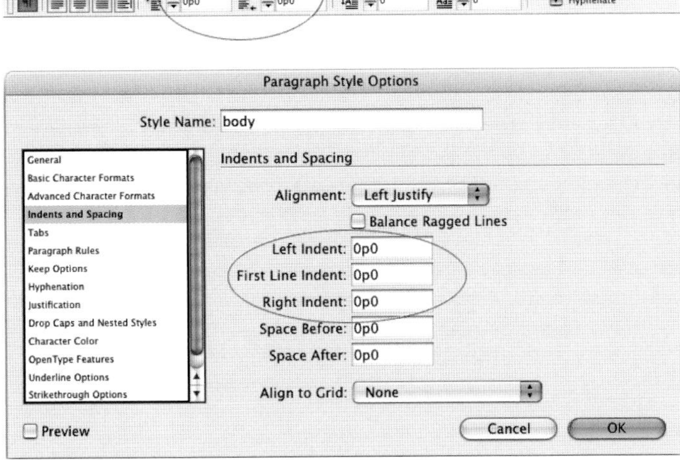

FIGURE 9.2 Control palette. Paragraph Style Options.

While first-line indents are generally more suited to reading matter, be it magazine or newspaper articles or literature, paragraph spacing may be more appropriate for reference material. To some degree it's a matter of preference, but here are some things to consider:

- Don't use first-line indents *and* paragraph spacing. It's an either/or proposition.
- Don't use first line-indents on centered or right-aligned type.

- Any paragraph spacing values will be overridden by the baseline grid if you align all the lines of your paragraph to the grid. Unless that is you ensure that your total paragraph spacing is a multiple of your baseline grid. (See Chapter 16: Everything in it Right Place: Using Grids.)
- If a paragraph follows a heading or subhead, the first-line indent is unnecessary to differentiate that paragraph and should be dropped.
- Dropping the first-line indent and adding a line of paragraph spacing before is a simple way to indicate a separation without implying a hierarchical difference between two paragraphs of type.

Alternatives to the First-Line Indent

Not everyone loves a first-line indent. In Germany, as well as in some newspapers where space is especially tight, it's popular to have the paragraphs flush left, without any indentation. This can be problematic if the last lines of the paragraphs run the full column measure, making it difficult for the reader to discern one paragraph from another.

Instead of indents, try separating paragraphs with an em or en space, or with a decorative paragraph mark. This can be effective for short passages of text where you want to maintain a flush look, but don't want to compromise the meaning of the text.

FIGURE 9.3 Flush paragraphs. Without first-line indents it is difficult to find the beginning of the line, especially when the last line of the previous paragraph is long (line 10).

Poverty will not be eradicated without an immediate and major increase in international aid. Rich countries have promised to provide the extra money needed to meet internationally agreed poverty reduction targets. This amounts to at least $50 billion per year, according to official estimates, and must be delivered now.

Rich countries have also promised to provide 0.7% of their national income in aid and they must now make good on their commitment by setting a binding timetable to reach this target.

However, without far-reaching changes in how aid is delivered, it won't achieve maximum benefits. Two key areas of reform are needed.

First, aid needs to focus better on poor people's needs. This means more aid being spent on areas such as basic healthcare and education. Aid should no longer be tied to goods and services from the donor, so ensuring that more money is spent in the poorest countries. And the World Bank and the IMF must become fully democratic in order for poor people's concerns to be heard.

One morning, when Gregor Samsa woke from troubled dreams, he found himself transformed in his bed into a horrible vermin. He lay on his armour-like back, and if he lifted his head a little he could see his brown belly, slightly domed and divided by arches into stiff sections. The bedding was hardly able to cover it and seemed ready to slide off any moment. His many legs, pitifully thin compared with the size of the rest of him, waved about helplessly as he looked. ¶ "What's happened to me?" he thought. It wasn't a dream. His room, a proper human room although a little too small, lay peacefully between its four familiar walls. A collection of textile samples lay spread out on the table—Samsa was a travelling salesman—and above it there hung a picture that he had recently cut out of an illustrated magazine and housed in a nice, gilded frame. It showed a lady fitted out with a fur hat and fur boa who sat upright, raising a heavy fur muff that covered the whole of her lower arm towards the viewer. ¶ Gregor then turned to look out the window at the dull weather. Drops of rain could be heard hitting the pane, which made him feel quite sad. "How about if I sleep a little bit longer and forget all this nonsense", he thought, but that was something he was unable to do because he was used to sleeping on his right, and in his present state couldn't get into that position. However hard he threw himself onto his right, he always rolled back to where he was. He must have tried it a hundred times, shut his eyes so that he wouldn't have to look at the floundering legs, and only stopped when he began to feel a mild, dull pain there that he had never felt before. ¶ "Oh, God", he thought, "what a strenuous career it is that I've chosen! Travelling day

FIGURE 9.4 Paragraph ornaments are one way of maintaining a flush look to the paragraph without sacrificing comprehension of the text.

Hanging Indents

Hanging indents (also known as *outdents*), are where all the lines of the paragraph are indented except for the first line, which sticks out beyond the left margin edge. Hanging indents are achieved by applying a left indent, then applying a first-line indent of a negative value, typically the same amount as you entered for the left indent. For example, if you specify a left indent of 1 pica, your first-line left indent will be –1 pica.

Poverty will not be eradicated without an immediate and major increase in international aid. Rich countries have promised to provide the extra money needed to meet internationally agreed poverty reduction targets. This amounts to at least $50 billion per year, according to official estimates, and must be delivered now.

Rich countries have also promised to provide 0.7% of their national income in aid and they must now make good on their commitment by setting a binding timetable to reach this target.

However, without far-reaching changes in how aid is delivered, it won't achieve maximum benefits. Two key areas of reform are needed.

First, aid needs to focus better on poor people's needs. This means more aid being spent on areas such as basic healthcare and education. Aid should no longer be tied to goods and services from the donor, so ensuring that more money is spent in the poorest countries. And the World Bank and the IMF must become fully democratic in order for poor people's concerns to be heard.

FIGURE 9.5 When used sparingly, hanging indents or *outdents* can be an effective way of emphasizing the beginning of a paragraph.

To create a hanging indent, use the Control palette or the Paragraph palette. You can also use the Tabs palette: Specify a left-indent value greater than zero and drag the top marker to the left.

The most common example of a negative first-line indent is a bulleted or numbered list, where the second and subsequent lines of the paragraph align under the first character rather than under the bullet point or number. Bullets are great for lists that don't require a sequence or hierarchy. In days of yore, you made bulleted lists by indenting the text, making the first-line indent the same as the left indent, but negative, then inserting a tab before the first character (after the bullet) to move it over to the left indent value. These days, a single-click using the Control palette or the PageMaker Toolbar will not only set the hanging indent but also add the bullet character.

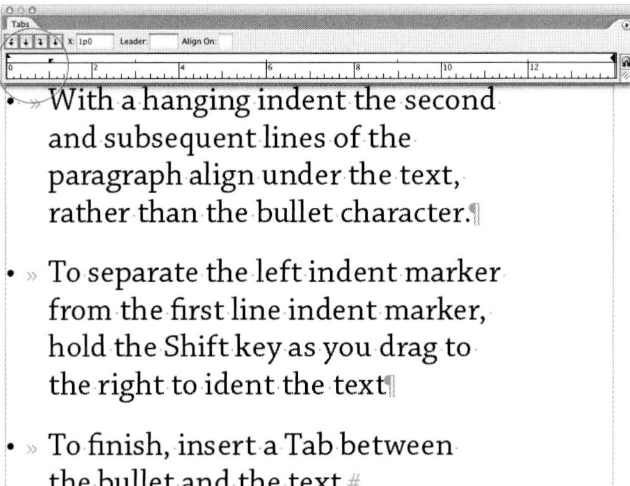

FIGURE 9.6 Using the Tabs palette to create a hanging indent.

FIGURE 9.7 The PageMaker Toolbar.

TIP: To remove bullets from a bulleted list created with the Bulleted List button in the PageMaker Toolbar, either click the Bulleted List icon again or apply a paragraph style that does not incorporate bullets.

Here's a bulleted list of things to consider when making a bulleted list:

- Sometimes, especially if your bullet character is a different font from the body text, the bullet may not vertically align perfectly. If necessary, adjust the vertical spacing of the bullet with Baseline Shift.
- If your items begin with a cap, center the bullet on the cap height.

- If your items begin with lowercase characters, center the bullets on the x-height.
- Don't indent the text too far from the bullet—an em space is usually sufficient.
- You are not limited to the standard bullet character. There are many picture or dingbat fonts available. Common picture fonts include Carta, Zapf Dingbats, Symbol, Wingdings, and Davy's Dingbats, to name just a few.
- New in CS2: Bullets (and Numbering) formatting can now be incorporated into the Paragraph Style definition. You can specify a specific font, size, and color for your bullet, and then apply this with a single click to multiple paragraphs. This is especially useful when you have specific paragraphs that always begin with a certain bullet. Defining a paragraph style with Bullets and Numbering saves you having to key in the bullet character every time. See Chapter 13: "Stylin' with Style Sheets" for more on Paragraph Styles.

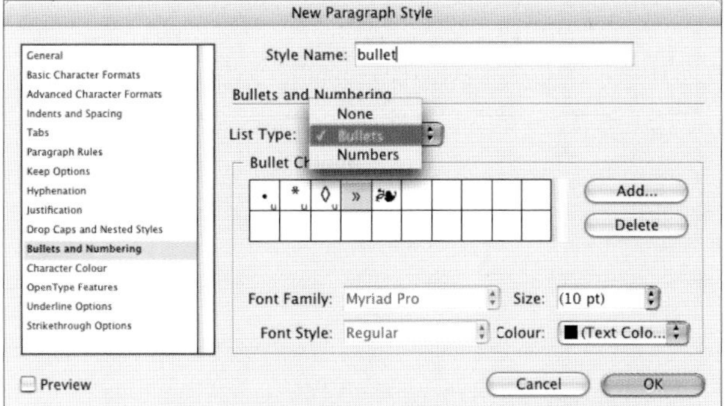

FIGURES 9.8A AND 9.8B Bullets and Numbering options can be incorporated into a Paragraph Style definition. You can also add bullets from multiple fonts to the available bullet list by clicking the Add button in the Bullets and Numbering section of the Paragraph Style Options dialog.

- An attribute that cannot, as yet, be incorporated into the Bullets and Numbering formats of a Paragraph Style is baseline shift. This means that if your bullet character requires vertical adjustment to make it align, as mentioned above, with either the cap height or x-height of the type, your best option is the old-school method of defining your bullet as a Character Style. Once a Character Style is set up, you can easily apply the same formats to the subsequent bullets in the document, saving time and making sure that their formatting is consistent. You can go a step further and make a Nested Style, where the Character Style is incorporated into the Paragraph Style definition, and both are applied with a single mouse click. See Chapter 13: "Stylin' with Style Sheets" for more on Character Styles and Chapter 14: "More Styles" for information on how to create Nested Styles.

Hanging indents are also used for dictionaries and other reference sources, and sometimes on résumés.

FIGURE 9.9 A Dictionary entry.

Politics, n. A strife of interests masquerading as a contest of principles. The conduct of public affairs for private advantage.

Politician, n. An eel in the fundamental mud upon which the superstructure of organized society is reared. When we wriggles he mistakes the agitation of his tail for the trembling of the edifice. As compared with the statesman, he suffers the disadvantage of being alive.

Polygamy, n. A house of atonement, or expiatory chapel, fitted with several stools of repentance, as distinguished from monogamy, which has but one.

—Ambrose Bierce, *The Devil's Dictionary*

Space Before and Space After

Time for another sweeping pronouncement: Never, ever, under any circumstances should you have more than one consecutive carriage return in your document. Or to put it another way, Never create line spaces by pressing Return (Enter). No exceptions—at least none that I can think of. If text that you import into InDesign has extra carriage returns (very likely), then zap 'em with Find/Change.

Now, you might be thinking, what's the big deal? Why not type a harmless extra carriage return between paragraphs—no one gets hurt. And it's true; the sun will still rise if you insist on this bad habit. But there are good reasons why not:

- Using carriage returns for paragraph spacing allows no flexibility in the size of the space between paragraphs. Every time you create a new paragraph by pressing Return, the new (blank line) paragraph has the same formats (including the leading) as the paragraph before it.
- If your text flows into multiple columns and/or pages, a carriage return at the top of the column or page creates an unwanted space.

Instead of pressing Return (Enter) twice, or—heaven forbid—more than twice, use Space Before or Space After. I say *or* because using both, while occasionally necessary, is apt to get confusing. Most of the time, I use Space Before; only when working with a baseline grid do I use both. As well as giving you complete flexibility in the size of the space between paragraphs, paragraph spacing is smart enough to disappear when not needed, i.e., at the top or bottom of a column or page.

Today, the gap between the world's rich and poor is wider than ever. Global injustices such as poverty, AIDS, malnutrition, conflict and illiteracy remain rife.¶
¶
Despite the promises of world leaders, at our present sluggish rate of progress the world will fail dismally to reach internationally agreed targets to halve global poverty by 2015.¶
¶
World poverty is sustained not by chance or nature, but by a combination of factors: injustice in global trade; the huge burden of debt; insufficient and ineffective aid. Each of these is exacerbated by inappropriate economic policies imposed by rich countries.¶
¶
But it doesn't have to be this way. These factors are determined by human decisions.¶
¶
2005 offers an exceptional series of opportunities for the UK to take a lead internationally, to start turning things around. Next year, as the UK hosts the annual G8 gathering of powerful world leaders and heads up the European Union (EU), the UK Government will be a particularly influential player on the world stage.¶
¶
A sea change is needed. By mobilising popular support across a unique string of events and actions, we will press our own government to compel rich countries to fulfil their obligations

FIGURE 9.10 Don't use extra carriage returns. The spacing between the paragraphs is too big, and you can get blank lines at the tops of columns.

Proximity

Make sure any paragraph spacing accentuates rather than detracts from the connection between different pieces of text. Simply put, things that belong together get placed together. Organizing your type into clusters of information—subhead and paragraph, for example—will help establish the rhythm of your type. The reader will interpret the spaces between such clusters as representing a pause, the next cluster as being a new idea. To reinforce the relationship your subhead should always be closer to the text that follows it than to the text that precedes it. An obvious point, but this rule is frequently broken.

And to ensure that this relationship is never broken—by a column or page break, for example—set your Keep Options for the style definition of your subheads to Keep With Next 2 lines. (See Chapter 13: "Styling with Style Sheets.")

remains of the Blackfriars Rail Bridge, which once ran parallel, are the red columns in the river and the brightly colored cast-iron insignia of the company: London, Chatham and Dover Railway.

9 Tate Modern

Giles Gilbert Scott, 1947-63

Jacques Herzog and Pierre de Meuron, 1995-2000

The Tate Modern is now one of the most successful and popular art galleries in the world and London's most popular free tourist attraction. The building was

A

remains of the Blackfriars Rail Bridge, which once ran parallel, are the red columns in the river and the brightly colored cast-iron insignia of the company: London, Chatham and Dover Railway.

9 Tate Modern

Giles Gilbert Scott, 1947-63

Jacques Herzog and Pierre de Meuron, 1995-2000

The Tate Modern is now one of the most successful and popular art galleries in the world and London's most popular free tourist attraction. The building was

B

FIGURE 9.11 Creating a visual relationship. In example **A**, the subhead floats ambiguously between the text before and after it. In example **B**, the subhead is closer to the text that follows, establishing a visual connection between the two paragraphs..

10 Shakespeare's Globe
Jon Greenfield, 1997
This is a working reconstruction of the original playhouse used by Shakespeare four centuries ago and where, in the summer, you can see world class, open-air Shakespeare for as little as £5. The original Tudor playhouse was built in 1598, financed by a consortium that included William Shakespeare and was the venue of many of his theatrical works. The globe burnt down in 1613, and after its replacement was demolished by the Puritans in 1642 the site remained empty for the next three centuries. American director Sam Wanamaker began the project to re-create an accurate, functioning reconstruction of the Globe. The new Globe was built using contemporary craftsmen's techniques and features the first thatched roof London has seen since the Great Fire of 1666.

11 Millennium Bridge

A

Foster And Partners, Anthony Caro, Arup, 2000-01
The first completely new pedestrian bridge to be built over the Thames for a hundred years, the Millennium Bridge is a combination of art, design and technology. The three main contributors: engineer, architect and sculptor, designed the bridge to be streamlined, using an innovative and complex structure to achieve a simple form: a shallow suspension bridge that spans the river as an 'elegant blade.' The bridge was opened on June 10, 2000 (2 months late) and became the butt of many a joke when it closed two days later due to unexpected lateral vibrations. The movements were produced by the sheer numbers of pedestrians (90,000 users in the first day, with up to 2,000 on the bridge at any one time). The initial small vibrations encouraged the users to walk in synchronisation with the sway, increasing the effect. This swaying motion earned it the nickname the Wobbly Bridge. After the installation of a 'passive dampening solution' and a period of testing the bridge was successfully re-opened

---

10 Shakespeare's Globe
Jon Greenfield, 1997
This is a working reconstruction of the original playhouse used by Shakespeare four centuries ago and where, in the summer, you can see world class, open-air Shakespeare for as little as £5. The original Tudor playhouse was built in 1598, financed by a consortium that included William Shakespeare and was the venue of many of his theatrical works. The globe burnt down in 1613, and after its replacement was demolished by the Puritans in 1642 the site remained empty for the next three centuries. American director Sam Wanamaker began the project to re-create an accurate, functioning reconstruction of the Globe. The new Globe was built using contemporary craftsmen's techniques and features the first thatched roof London has seen since the Great Fire of 1666.

11 Millennium Bridge
Foster And Partners, Anthony Caro, Arup, 2000-01
The first completely new pedestrian bridge to be built over the Thames for a hundred years, the Millennium Bridge is a combination of art, design and technology. The three main contributors: engineer, architect and sculptor, designed the bridge to be streamlined, using an innovative and complex structure to achieve a simple form: a shallow suspension bridge that spans the river as an 'elegant blade.' The bridge was opened on June 10, 2000 (2 months late) and became the butt of many a joke when it closed two days later due to unexpected lateral vibrations. The movements were produced by the sheer numbers of pedestrians (90,000 users in the first day, with up to 2,000 on the bridge at any one time). The initial small vibrations encouraged the users to walk in synchronisation with the sway, increasing the effect. This swaying motion earned it the nickname the Wobbly Bridge. After the installation of a 'passive dampening solution'

B

FIGURE 9.12 Using Keep Options. In example **A**, no Keeps are specified and the subhead is stranded at the bottom of the first column. In example **B**, the Subhead is set to Keep With Next 2 lines.

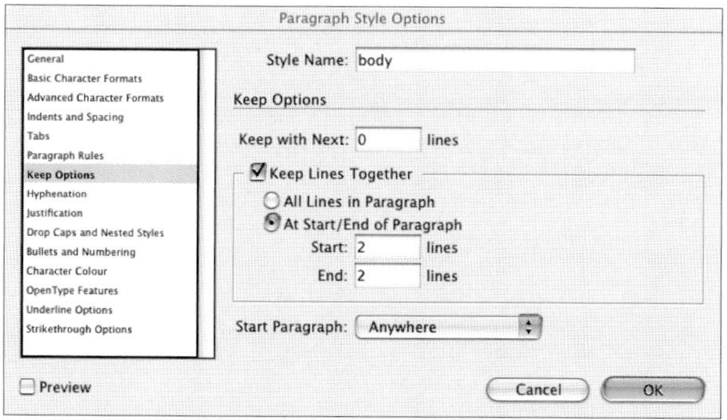

FIGURE 9.13 The Keep Options section of the Paragraph Style Options dialog.

Paragraph Indents

Indenting your text on the left and/or right is appropriate in the following situations:

- To indicate a quoted passage of text or extract. Typically the type will be 1 point smaller than the body text with an even amount of paragraph space—usually a half-line space—added before and after.
- To indicate hierarchy. Especially in tables of contents or technical documents, indenting signifies a lower level of the hierarchy.
- Bibliography entries should be set with a hanging indent of 1 em space.

FIGURE 9.14 A table of contents using indents.

Table of Contents

Introduction

What is typography?
Type anatomy diagram
Why InDesign?
Who should read this book?
Conventions used in this book
An InDesign Type map: Where to find stuff on the menus

PART 1: CHARACTER FORMATS

Getting Started

A map of InDesign's type menus and palettes
Getting text on your page
Choosing and sizing type
Case
Underline and Strikethrough
Baseline Shift
Sidebar: No more faux styles
Viewing your page
Zooming in and out
Visual aids
Tip: Shortcuts for sizing type
Tip: Trim your text frame
Wish List: Initial Caps style
Text selection techniques

Placing and flowing text

Manual
Auto
Semi
Tip: Save yourself the trouble: don't draw a Text Frame
Tip: Unloading your cursor
Tip: Checking over matter with the Info palette
Threading Text Frames
Threading empty Text Frames

Text Insets

Text insets are an inner margin on your text frame. They give you the same result as applying left and/or right indents, but might be more convenient if you are working with type in a framed or colored rectangle.

TIP: If you use a rounded rectangle or any kind of custom text frame shape you will only be able to specify a single dimension for the text inset.

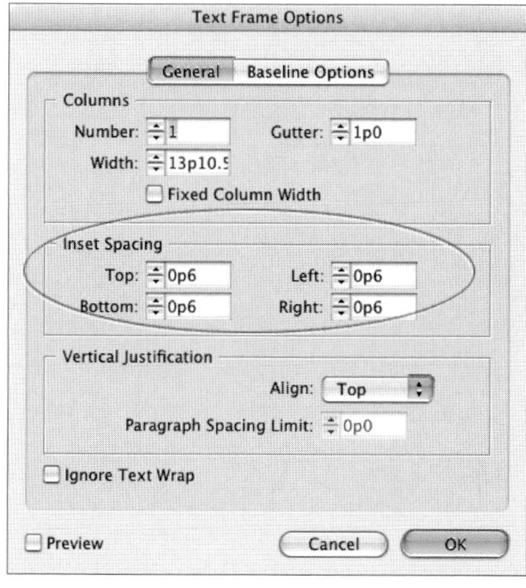

FIGURE 9.15 Text Frame Options.

FIGURE 9.16 A sidebar text frame using Inset Spacing.

Up Next

We take a look at how to make a splash with opening paragraphs: their function and the things to consider when creating them.

CHAPTER 10

First Impressions:

Creating Great Opening Paragraphs

THE APPEARANCE OF AN OPENING PARAGRAPH is almost as important as its content for hooking the reader, or, if you are marking a section break, for providing visual relief from a continuous body of text. This chapter looks at initial capitals, specifically drop caps—those created manually and those created automatically using InDesign's Drop Caps feature.

Drop caps are part of a long tradition of decorative first letters stretching back to before the invention of the printing press. Before printing, books were dictated to, and subsequently copied by, scribes and each book was regarded as a unique treasure. The scribes incorporated individual flourishes to distinguish their work from others. In medieval times the ornamentation of manuscripts was a monastic discipline; each major section of a book usually began with an illuminated letter made with metallic, mineral, or vegetable pigments, which were bound by glue or gum to the paper or parchment.

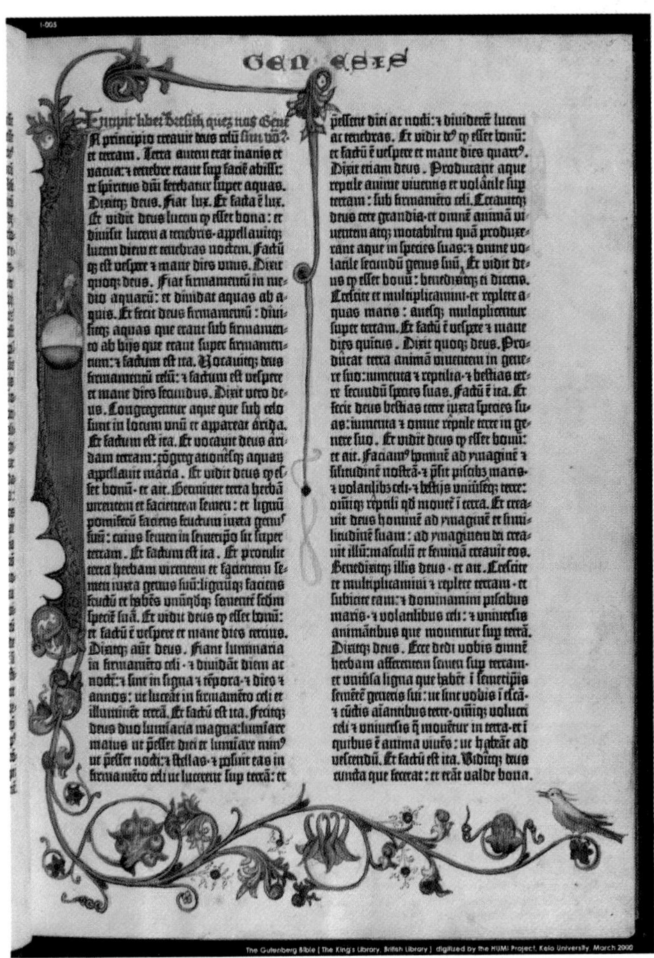
The Gutenberg Bible (The King's Library, British Library) digitized by the HUMI Project, Keio University March 2000

FIGURES 10.1A AND 10.1B
Two pages from the Gutenberg Bible (1455), the first (this page) showing an illuminated first character painted by a scribe, the second (page 135) showing smaller initial characters in red to indicate new sections.

By the fourteenth century, initial letters or *versals* had evolved from enlarged heavy letters into elaborate illustrated works of art, most often used to decorate religious texts. An illuminated *versal* might flow down the whole side of a page, or extend up and around the top of the page. Sometimes they included illustrations and took over the entire page. In 1455, when Gutenberg printed his 42-line-per-page Bible—the first book to be printed in the western world with moveable type—he acknowledged the importance of this tradition by leaving space in the printed text for the scribe to add a decorative first letter.

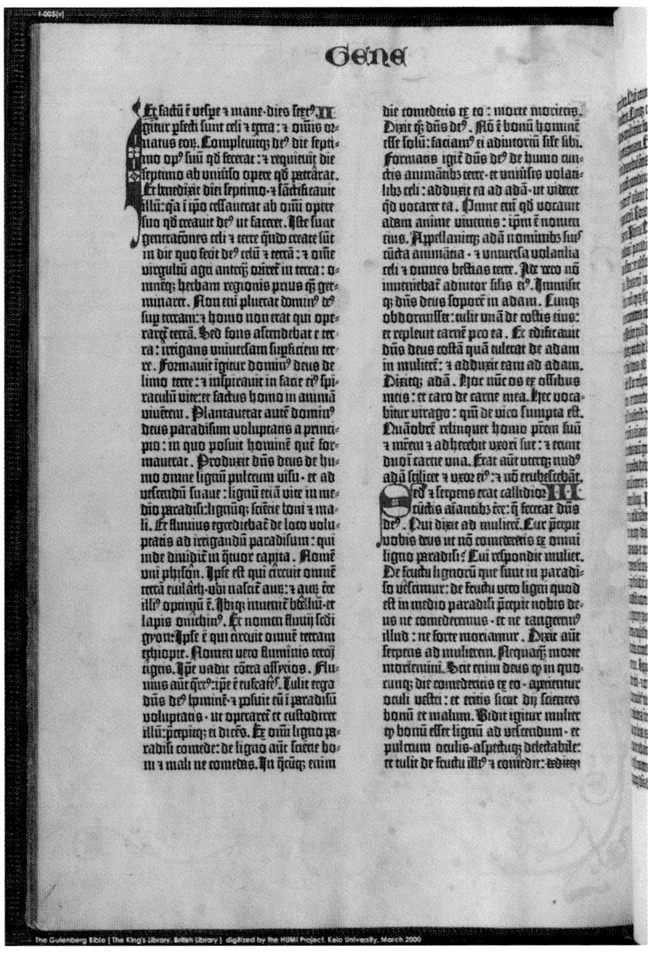
Gene
The Gutenberg Bible | The King's Library, British Library | digitized by the HUMI Project, Keio University, March 2000

Creating a Simple Drop Cap

Contemporary magazine and book publishing continues this centuries-old tradition with the convention of beginning chapters and articles with large initial letters. Creating a simple drop cap is a breeze in InDesign and can be applied locally or incorporated into a style sheet definition.

You create drop caps locally using the Control palette or the Paragraph palette. I prefer the Control palette—that way I don't need my Paragraph palette open, cluttering up my workspace.

If you plan to apply the same formatting to more than one paragraph in your document, it saves time (and ensures consistency) to incorporate the drop cap attributes into a paragraph or style definition. The drop cap style is commonly based on your body text style with any first-line indent removed and with some space added before the paragraph.

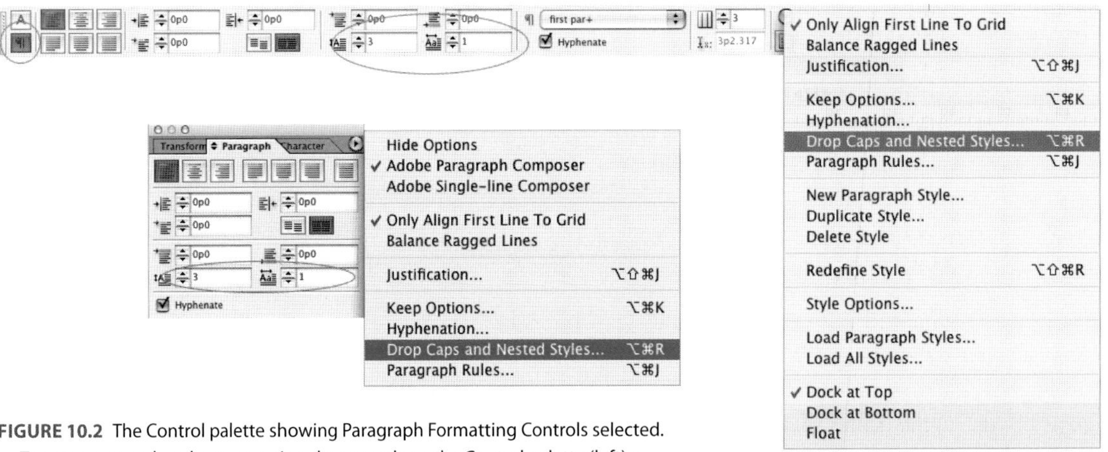

FIGURE 10.2 The Control palette showing Paragraph Formatting Controls selected.

Two ways to apply a drop cap: using the controls on the Control palette (left) or using the palette fly-out menu (right). Type a number for Drop Cap Number of Lines, then specify the number of drop cap characters you want—usually one, but as we'll see this isn't always the case.

The Paragraph palette found under the Type menu (Cmd+Option+T/Ctrl+Alt+T), showing the drop cap fields (Drop Cap Number of Lines, Drop Cap One or More Characters), as well as the Drop Caps and Nested Styles palette menu option.

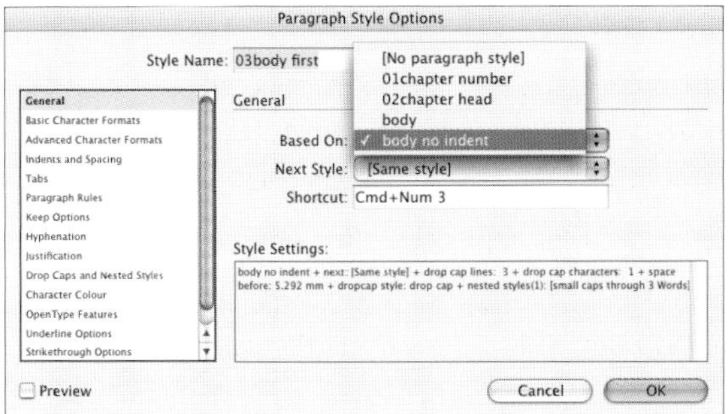

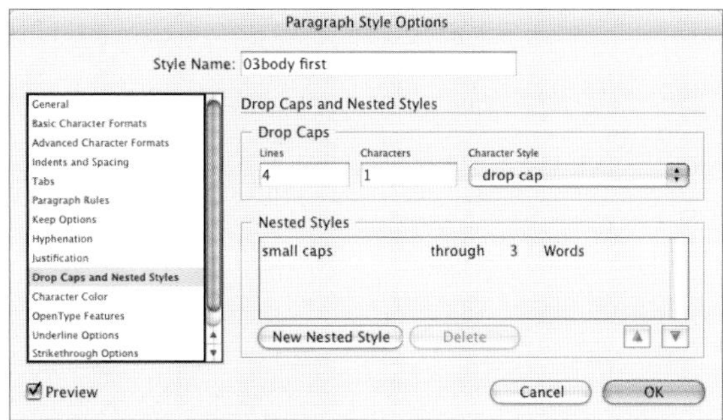

FIGURES 10.3A AND 10.3B Applying a drop cap as part of a style sheet definition:

Choose New Paragraph Style from the Paragraph Styles palette. To edit an existing style, Ctrl-click (right mouse click) on the style and choose Edit.

Name the style—"first par," "body first" are common naming conventions. If you have your body text style, you may want to base your "body first" on this. Choose body from the Based On: pull down menu—in the example shown I am basing the drop cap on the no indent version of the body text style, which itself is based on "body."

Choose Drop Caps and Nested Styles from the list in the left column. Specify the number of lines, i.e., how many lines to sink the first character, and the number of characters—how many characters you want to make big.

If you have a character style defined you can apply that here, too, using the Character Style pull-down menu—see below. In InDesign terminology, this is "nesting" the character style inside the paragraph style. (See Chapter 14: Mo' Style)

Drop Cap Aesthetics

There are no hard and fast rules concerning how big a drop cap should be, but common sense should prevail. Size matters, although in this context bigger isn't always better. The purpose of the drop cap is to signal to the reader where to begin. To do so, the drop cap doesn't need to scream at the reader and shouldn't overwhelm any headline that precedes it. The drop cap comes below the headline in terms of page hierarchy; usually, though not always, it will be smaller than the headline. Also, don't repeat the letter you use as the drop cap at the beginning of the body text.

Too Much of a Good Thing?

In addition to the initial drop cap for the first paragraph of a chapter or article, designers often use smaller drop caps as section markers—set up as a style sheet based on the parent drop cap style. This is visually effective, necessary even, if the text doesn't have illustrations, subheads, or other graphic elements to break up the monotony of columns of type. That said, if you sprinkle your drop caps too

Different Types of Initial Caps

A drop cap is just one type of initial letter. Here are some variations on a theme:

1. Raised Drop Cap Hybrid
In this case the drop cap has been scaled (Cmd+Shift+>/Ctrl+Shift+>) and the text kerned under the shade of the T's horizontal bar.

2. Raised Cap
A raised cap or stick-up letter sits on the same baseline as the first line of text. When using this technique avoid using auto-leading. Although the initial is usually set to align flush left, you can also indent the first line.

3. Hung Initials
Here the initial character is in a separate text frame, which is positioned in the left margin.

THERE WAS NO POSSIBILITY of taking a walk that day. We had been wandering, indeed, in the leafless shrubbery an hour in the morning; but since dinner (Mrs. Reed, when there was no company, dined early) the cold winter wind had brought with it clouds so sombre, and a rain so penetrating, that further out-door exercise was now out of the question.

THERE WAS NO POSSIBILITY of taking a walk that day. We had been wandering, indeed, in the leafless shrubbery an hour in the morning; but since dinner (Mrs. Reed, when there was no company, dined early) the cold winter wind had brought with it clouds so sombre, and a rain so penetrating, that further out-door exercise was now out of the question.

THERE WAS NO POSSIBILITY of taking a walk that day. We had been wandering, indeed, in the leafless shrubbery an hour in the morning; but since dinner (Mrs. Reed, when there was no company, dined early) the cold winter wind had brought with it clouds so sombre, and a rain so penetrating, that further out-door exercise was now out of the question.

THERE WAS NO POSSIBILITY of taking a walk that day. We had been wandering, indeed, in the leafless shrubbery an hour in the morning; but since dinner (Mrs. Reed, when there was no company, dined early) the cold winter wind had brought with it clouds so sombre, and a rain so penetrating, that further out-door exercise was now out of the question.

THERE WAS NO POSSIBILITY of taking a walk that day. We had been wandering, indeed, in the leafless shrubbery an hour in the morning; but since dinner (Mrs. Reed, when there was no company, dined early) the cold winter wind had brought with it clouds so sombre, and a rain so penetrating, that further out-door exercise was now out of the question.

FIGURE 10.4 Some different approaches to a drop cap.

liberally throughout your document, they cease to be an elegant and functional graphic device and start to become a repetitive annoyance. One drop cap per length of copy or long section is enough.

Kerning Drop Caps

A common problem with automatically generated drop caps is that the big first character may collide with the body text that follows. Where necessary, you'll need to kern to avoid such problems. Note that when you kern between the drop cap and the first character of the text, kerning is applied to all the lines adjacent to the drop cap.

A

WHETHER I shall turn out to be the hero of my own life, or whether that station will be held by anybody else, these pages must show. To begin my life with the beginning of my life, I record that I was born (as I have been informed and believe) on a

B

WHETHER I shall turn out to be the hero of my own life, or whether that station will be held by anybody else, these pages must show. To begin my life with the beginning of my life, I record that I was born (as I have been informed and believe) on a

FIGURE 10.5 Kerning a drop cap. Example **A** shows the result of applying a 4-line drop cap in Adobe Caslon Pro. Note, the serif of the W collides with the "h." Insert your type cursor between the two letters and press Option+Right Arrow/Alt+Right Arrow to kern the letters, inserting space between the W and the "h" (example **B**).

Using Optical Margin Alignment

Certain letters will not look optically aligned because the left sidebearing (space to the left of the character shape that is incorporated into the letter's design) can cause the letter to appear slightly indented. There are two potential solutions:

1. InDesign's Optical Margin Alignment is a quiet and unassuming feature, but one of those typographic refinements that raises the bar for digital typesetting and sets InDesign apart from its competitors. We saw in Chapter 8: Aligning your Type how optical margin alignment can be used to create hanging punctuation and to allow your hyphens to extend beyond the right edge of your text frame. For now, we're concerned with how optical margin alignment can improve the appearance of a drop cap. Just how beneficial it is depends on the shape of your drop cap letter. With something like a W, which would otherwise have an unsightly island of trapped white space on its left side, Optical Margin Alignment is indispensable, allowing the letter to "hang" outside the margin, thus giving a more even appearance to the edges of the text block.

2. Sometimes, Optical Margin Alignment may not be enough and, in addition, you'll want to kern the drop cap to the left margin. To do this you'll first need to add a space before the drop cap. Note that adding a space will mean you have to drop two characters instead of one—if you see yourself likely to do this more than once, make an alternate paragraph style with this specification. You can then insert your cursor between the space and the drop cap and kern [Option-Left Arrow/Alt-Left Arrow] until the character is optically aligned with the left margin edge. Instead of adding a regular space, you can add a thin space (Cmd-Shift-Option-M [Ctrl-Shift-Alt-M]) that way, you won't have to kern as much.

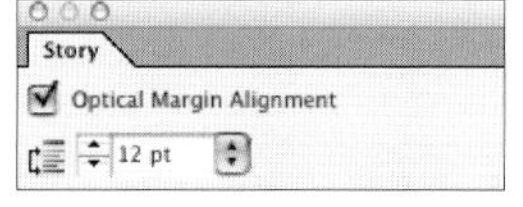

FIGURES 10.6A AND 10.6B Optical Margin Alignment. Turned off (example **A**). Turned on and set to 12 point (example **B**).

THE NELLIE, A cruising yawl, swung to her anchor without a flutter of the sails, and was at rest. The flood had made, the wind was nearly calm, and being bound down the river, the only thing for it was to come to and wait for the turn of the tide.

A

THE NELLIE, A cruising yawl, swung to her anchor without a flutter of the sails, and was at rest. The flood had made, the wind was nearly calm, and being bound down the river, the only thing for it was to come to and wait for the turn of the tide.

B

FIGURE 10.7 Before kerning the space in front of the drop cap (example **A**) and after (example **B**) to optically align the first letter.

IT WAS THE best of times, it was the worst of times, it was the age of wisdom, it was the age of foolishness, it was the epoch of belief, it was the epoch of incredulity, it was the season of Light, it was the season of Darkness, it was the spring of hope, it was the winter of despair, we had everything before us, we had nothing before us, we were all going direct to Heaven, we were all going direct the other way—in short, the period was so far like the present period, that some of its noisiest authorities insisted on its being received, for good or for evil, in the superlative degree of comparison only.

A

IT WAS THE best of times, it was the worst of times, it was the age of wisdom, it was the age of foolishness, it was the epoch of belief, it was the epoch of incredulity, it was the season of Light, it was the season of Darkness, it was the spring of hope, it was the winter of despair, we had everything before us, we had nothing before us, we were all going direct to Heaven, we were all going direct the other way—in short, the period was so far like the present period, that some of its noisiest authorities insisted on its being received, for good or for evil, in the superlative degree of comparison only.

B

Creating a Contoured Drop Cap

Putting your drop cap character in its own text frame gives you the option of contouring the text to the shape of the drop cap. Apply a text wrap to the drop cap text frame, then use the Direct Selection tool to sculpt the text wrap outline to conform to the diagonal of the W. Make sure that the space around the drop cap is optically the same on the side as it is on the bottom. Note that using this technique will change the location of the start of successive lines of text, which can impede readability.

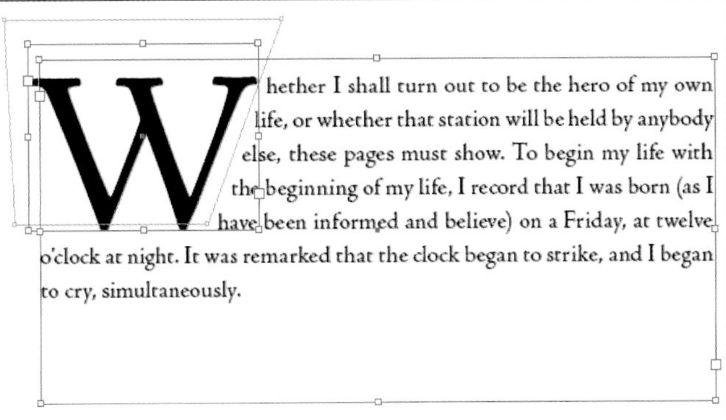

FIGURES 10.8 Contoured drop cap. The W is in its own text frame. A text wrap is applied and then adjusted to correspond to the letter shape.

If you are working with a document that contains several custom drop caps you can take things a step further by turning the drop cap into an anchored object. That way, if your text reflows, the drop cap moves with it—no wasting time chasing after missing text blocks. Here's how:

1. Prepare your custom drop cap in its own text frame and apply a text wrap to the frame. Choose the third text wrap option Wrap Around Object Shape.
2. Cut the text frame Cmd/Ctrl+X.
3. Insert your cursor at the beginning of the main text block and paste Cmd/Ctrl+V the text frame. The text frame is now a generic inline graphic appearing at the beginning of the line of text.
4. To adjust it's horizontal position use the Direct Selection tool to shape the text wrap border. For example, to make the letter shape hang in the left margin, reduce the text wrap offset on the left.
5. To adjust the vertical position of the drop cap choose Object>Anchored Object>Options. For position, choose Inline or Above Line. To sink the drop cap into the paragraph make the Y offset a negative value.

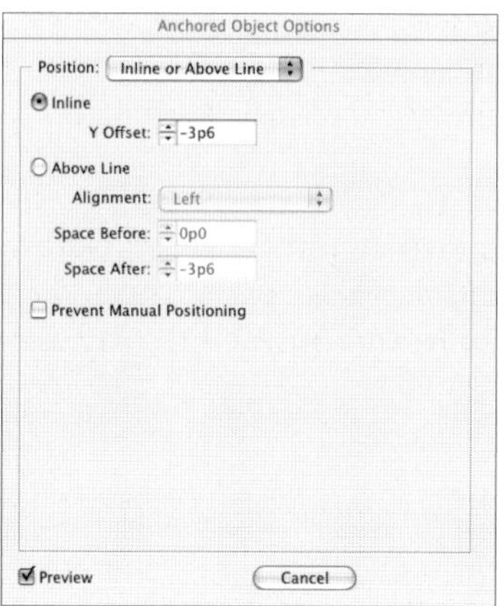

FIGURE 10.9 Anchored Object Options. Defining the custom drop cap as an anchored object ensure that it will move as part of the text flow. For more on anchored objects see Chapter 16: Text Wraps: The Good, the Bad, and the Ugly.

Adding Small Caps

An often-used device to create a visual bridge between the drop cap and the text is to put the words following the drop cap in small caps. This creates a transition from the large decorative character into the upper- and lowercase of the body text without which the drop cap may look like an isolated graphic. Just how many characters are put into small caps is a matter for discretion—it may be just the first word, the first phrase, a specified number of words, or the first line. Whatever you choose, make sure you are consistent throughout your publication.

Back in the old days—pre-2003—adding small caps after a drop cap was fiddly and time consuming, especially when working on long documents with many chapter or article heads. You would find yourself applying character styles locally all the while thinking that there had to a better way. And now there is: As I've already mentioned, if you want a drop cap character to have a different color and/or font than the rest of the paragraph, you can define a character style with these attributes then *nest* the character style in a paragraph style. You can also use Nested Styles to automatically apply a character style to a specified number of words after the drop cap. InDesign lets you incorporate a character style inside a paragraph style. This way, your small caps character style is added to your first paragraph style definition and applied with a single mouse click.

The possibilities here are mind-boggling—enough to distract a type and automation geek for the better part of a Friday night—and we'll look at nested styles in more detail in Chapter 14: Mo' Style.

A Four score and seven years ago our fathers brought forth on this continent, a new nation, conceived in liberty, and dedicated to the proposition that all men are created equal.

B FOUR SCORE AND SEVEN years ago our fathers brought forth on this continent, a new nation, conceived in liberty, and dedicated to the proposition that all men are created equal.

FIGURE 10.10 Adding Small Caps: No small caps (example **A**); small caps applied through four words (example **B**) to ease the transition from big first character to the upper- and lowercase text. (The drop cap is also changed to an italic swash and the kerning between drop cap and text adjusted.)

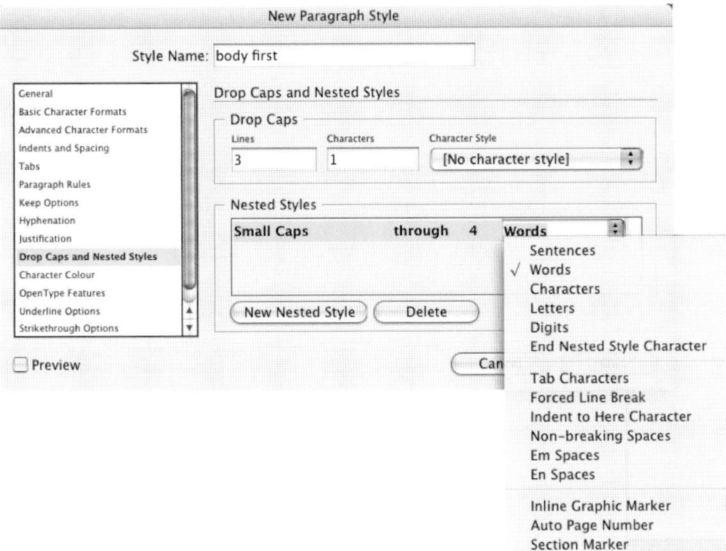

FIGURE 10.11 Nested Styles: Choose a character style to apply to a specified number of words.

Nesting Small Caps

1. Create a small caps character style. If you are using an OpenType font, choose OpenType All Small Caps from the Case pull-down menu to keep the case of your small cap range consistent without having to re-key any initial caps as lowercase letters.

2. To "nest" your small caps character style in your "body first" paragraph style, right click (ctrl+click) the paragraph style in the Paragraph Styles palette to edit the style, then choose Drop Caps and Nested Styles.

3. Click New Nested Style and specify the number of words you want the nested style applied to.

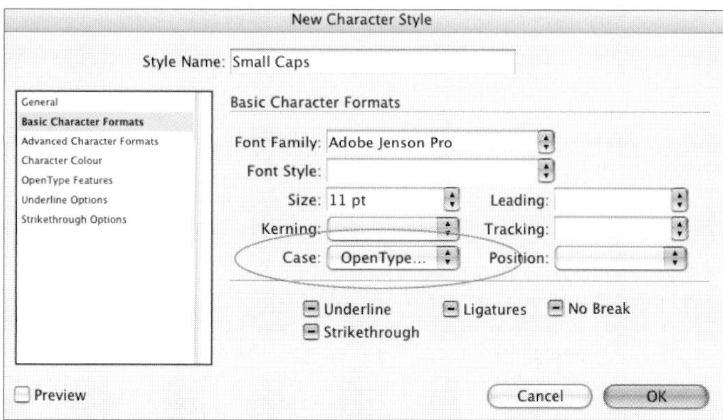

FIGURE 10.12 Using OpenType Small Caps.

Currently there is no way of automating the application of small caps to a single line. You can insert an End Nested Styles character (Type > Insert Special Character) at any point in the text so that the character style is applied up to that point, but this requires the discretion of manual input on a case-by-case basis.

Tricks with Drop Caps

InDesign's drop cap feature can be used for more than just drop caps at the beginning of articles or sections. Here are a few ideas for other uses that can be great time savers when included as part of a paragraph style definition.

FIGURE 10.13 Drop caps used for question and answer section. In this example a tab stop has been set to push the question text away from the Q, the baseline of the Q has been raised by 1 point.

Q **What's the difference between Optical and Metrics kerning?**

Metrics kerning uses a font's built-in kerning information. For this reason it's effectiveness depends upon how much kerning information the font contains (how many kerning pairs). Optical kerning, on the other hand, ignores the built-in kerning information and adjusts the space between the characters based upon the character shapes.

Q **How do I prevent certain text frames from being effected by a text wrap?**

Select the text frame then Choose Object>Text Frame Options (-B), then check Ignore Text Wrap.

Q **What is the floppy disk icon in Paragraph and Character Styles palette?**

This is the symbol that appears when you bring in text from a Microsoft Word document. To remove them simply edit the style.

Sorry!

We're sorry you are stuck in your car in a traffic jam. Gridlock is more and more common these days...it'll probably go on getting worse, unless we do something.

We're sorry if we've contributed to your delay, but please recognize that we bicyclists are ignored, obstructed and physically threatened ALL THE TIME, EVERY DAY. This "Critical Mass" ride home is an organized coincidence that happens once a month, giving bicyclists of all persuasions the chance to see that we are not alone, and that we, too, have a right to the road.

We're sorry that absurd and mean-spirited decisions about how we live are made behind the closed doors of the corporate and government elite, leading to a suicidal dependence on the automobile and the oil industry, a cancer epidemic and general ecological catastrophe. We know there are better alternatives, and our monthly ride demonstrates one of them.

We're sorry that we all go on reproducing this silly and self-degrading way of life, instead of throwing it over and making a life worth living. Why should we do jobs which make our lives worse due to toxic waste or pollution? Why are our best intentions always corrupted by the need to "make a living"? These questions have complex and difficult answers, answers worth looking into. But for now...

We're sorry you're not already out here on your bicycle riding with us! But we heartily invite you to join us next time.

Remember, every day is a good bicycling day! Meet at the foot of Market Street on the last working Friday of the each month at 5:30 p.m.

FIGURE 10.14 Words used as drop caps. Because of the repetition in this example, it's possible to make a paragraph style with the drop cap character count set to 11. The drop cap character style that is nested in the paragraph style includes a small amount of baseline shift as well as changing the Character Color to a 50 percent tint. For the last paragraph, the drop cap is modified locally.

DESTINATIONS

27 The look Hilary, Cate and friends dazzle at the Oscars and BAFTAs

37 COVER STORY Style file: The right stripes Get in line for the designer's pattern of choice

45 COVER STORY High street must-haves We've shopped around to find you all the biggest trends

60 Summer style strategy Actress Sarah Parish shows you how to outshine everyone in the season's best occasionwear

FIGURE 10.15 Drop caps used for numbers in a contents page.

Coming Unstuck with Drop Caps

Drop caps are just one way of kicking off a paragraph and not always the best solution. There are times when drop caps don't work well:

- When the opening paragraphs of your chapters or articles begin with quotations or dialog or numbers. If you have the occasional opening paragraph that begins with a quotation mark, making it an exception is no big deal—so long as it is an exception. If you find yourself having to fuss over every chapter or article opening, then use another type of opening device.
- When opening paragraphs begin with punctuation, you will need to drop two characters. The opening quotation mark will probably look disproportionately large and you'll want to reduce its size and adjust its baseline using Baseline Shift. Exact amounts will vary according to the nature of the font, so there's some (time-consuming) subjectivity involved here. You should also hang the punctuation. Alternatively, another solution is to drop the opening punctuation altogether.
- When opening paragraphs are short-one or two lines. Trying to sink a drop cap three lines into a one-line paragraph can be tricky and create some visual confusion, although InDesign does an excellent job of coping. If you find you are repeatedly using a three-line drop cap on paragraphs that are only two lines deep, then you need another solution.
- When your articles or chapters begin with poetry, song lyrics, or other quoted material. You can still use the drop cap, but it is no longer signaling the beginning of the chapter, article, or section, and can tend to look fussy as a result.

‘Curiouser and curiouser!’ cried Alice (she was so much surprised,
that for the moment she quite forgot how to speak good English);
‘now I’m opening out like the largest telescope that ever was! Good-
bye, feet!’ (for when she looked down at her feet, they seemed to be
almost out of sight, they were getting so far off). ‘Oh, my poor little feet,
1 I wonder who will put on your

‘Curiouser and curiouser!’ cried Alice (she was so much
surprised, that for the moment she quite forgot how to
speak good English); ‘now I’m opening out like the largest telescope that ever was! Good-bye, feet!’ (for when
she looked down at her feet, they seemed to be almost out of sight, they
2 were getting so far off). ‘Oh, my poor little feet, I wonder who will put

‘Curiouser and curiouser!’ cried Alice (she was so much
surprised, that for the moment she quite forgot how to speak
good English); ‘now I’m opening out like the largest telescope that ever was! Good-bye, feet!’ (for when she looked
down at her feet, they seemed to be almost out of sight, they were getting
3 so far off). ‘Oh, my poor little feet, I wonder who will put on your

‘Curiouser and curiouser!’ cried Alice (she was so much
surprised, that for the moment she quite forgot how to speak
good English); ‘now I’m opening out like the largest telescope that ever was! Good-bye, feet!’ (for when she looked
down at her feet, they seemed to be almost out of sight, they were getting
4 so far off). ‘Oh, my poor little feet, I wonder who will put on your

‘Curiouser and curiouser!’ cried Alice (she was so much
surprised, that for the moment she quite forgot how to speak
good English); ‘now I’m opening out like the largest telescope
that ever was! Good-bye, feet!’ (for when she looked down at
her feet, they seemed to be almost out of sight, they were getting so far
5 off). ‘Oh, my poor little feet, I wonder who will put on your

FIGURE 10.16 Dealing with quotation marks. **1.** Because this paragraph begins with a quotation, it is the quote mark that is "dropped." **2.** This is fixed by changing the number of dropped characters to two, but there's an unsightly amount of space to the left of the C and the punctuation is too big. **3.** The optical alignment of the C is partially fixed by applying Optical Margin Alignment to the story. **4.** The punctuation is reduced in size and its baseline adjusted using Baseline Shift. **5.** The space between the punctuation and the C is kerned.

CHAPTER III

"He is well, quite well!" Zossimov cried cheerfully as they entered. He had come in ten minutes earlier and was sitting in the same place as before, on the sofa. Raskolnikov was sitting in the opposite corner, fully dressed and carefully washed and combed, as he had not been for some time past. The room was immediately crowded, yet Nastasya managed to follow the visitors in and stayed to listen.

FIGURE 10.17 Dealing with short opening paragraphs. InDesign copes elegantly, bringing the second paragraph up next to the drop cap and maintaining its first line indent. If you find yourself making many such "exceptions," you probably need a different device.

Up Next

More fiddly stuff: we turn our attention to hyphens, those small and underappreciated servants of readability.

CHAPTER 11

Don't Fear the Hyphen

THERE'S A LOT OF PREJUDICE against the poor hyphen. Some designers feel that hyphens are ugly and to be avoided at all costs, as if a broken word is somehow inferior to a word with no hyphens. I believe the humble hyphen is our friend. We live in a world of compromises and—as long as the hyphenation breaks make sense—hyphens are preferable to the evils of bad word spacing in justified type, or uneven rags in ragged type. Besides, we're used to reading hyphenated text. We do it without thinking, rarely if ever pausing to consider the hyphen's service to the cause of readability. Hyphenation also allows more words to fit on a line, which saves space. That said, a hyphen is only as good as its settings, so it's important to be familiar with InDesign's hyphenation options.

Hyphenation rules vary from one style manual to another and from one language to another—the English UK dictionary will hyphenate differently than the English USA dictionary. So make sure you're familiar with your house style and that you have the correct dictionary applied to your type.

Good hyphenation can be labor-intensive. Manually adjusting hyphenation should be one of the fine-tuning stages of your publication. Because text invariably gets edited throughout the production process, line endings will change. There's no point investing time in getting the hyphenation right until you know exactly what you're up against. Try to get your client to sign off on the text content before you start manually tweaking the hyphenation. And—an obvious point—always start at the beginning of the story and work forward.

Hyphenation Options

Words with at Least _ Letters

This refers to the minimum number of characters for hyphenated words. Changing this number from 5 to 6 will result in less hyphenation.

After First and Before Last

These rather confusingly named options refer, respectively, to the minimum number of characters at the beginning of a word and the minimum number of characters at the end of a word that can be broken by a hyphen. The golden rule is to leave at least two characters behind and take at least three forward.

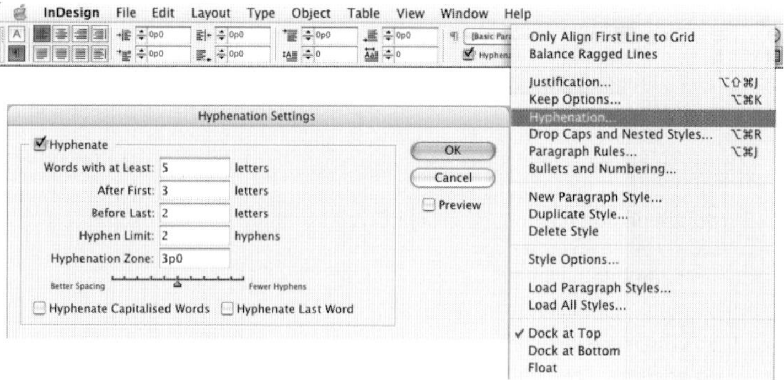

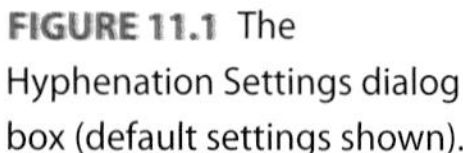
FIGURE 11.1 The Hyphenation Settings dialog box (default settings shown).

Hyphen Limit

This determines the maximum number of hyphens that can appear on consecutive lines so that you can avoid a stepped effect (ladders) on your column edge. While you'd never want more than two consecutive hyphens, it's debatable whether this option is the best method of preventing consecutive hyphens. You might want to set this option to 0, allowing unlimited consecutive hyphens, then manually fix any problems through a combination of tracking and/or rewriting and/or discretionary hyphens.

TIP: Applying No Break to a word that you don't want to hyphenate is preferable to using line breaks, which can later come back to bite you if the text is edited , causing the line break to occur in the middle of a line rather than at the end. Because No Break is buried away on the Control palette menu you'll save a lot of time by assigning it a keyboard shortcut.

Here are some options for fixing ladders:

- Find a better break a few lines above and insert a discretionary hyphen.
- Find a line(s) where you can tighten the letter spacing with manual tracking.
- Take the tightest hyphenated line and set the last word to No Break. This will turn the word over to the next line. You can do the same thing with line breaks (Shift+Return/Enter), but these can cause problems if the text is later edited, with line breaks showing up in the middle of a line.
- Rewrite, if you have the authority and it's appropriate.

A But the Web wasn't the only place in which customers were gravitating toward Acrobat and PDF. Print
publishers, too, started using the format as a convenient means of distributing complex pages via email or
on CD-ROM. A growing number of businesses recognized that they could send advertisements to publishing enterprises in a single PDF file with images, logos,
and pricing information intact. PDF was an economi-

B But the Web wasn't the only place in which customers
were gravitating toward Acrobat and PDF. Print publishers, too, started using the format as a convenient
means of distributing complex pages via email or on
CD-ROM. A growing number of businesses recognized
that they could send advertisements to publishing
enterprises in a single PDF file with images, logos, and
pricing information intact. PDF was an economical

FIGURE 11.2 Add Discretionary Hyphens. In example **A**, lines 4 and 5 have consecutive hyphens. In example **B**, inserting a discretionary hyphen before "recognized" (line 5) turns that word over to the next line, fixing the problem and—because the Adobe Paragraph Composer is applied—recomposing the preceding lines.

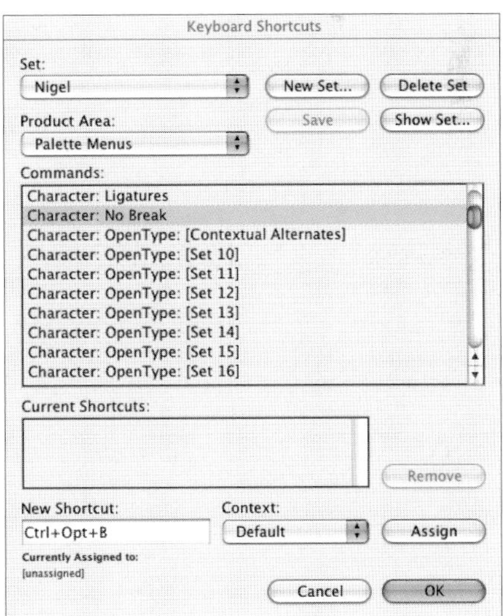

FIGURE 11.3 Assigning a shortcut to No Break.

Hyphenation Zone

Despite the alluring name, this is nothing more than an invisible boundary set from the right margin. A larger Hyphenation Zone creates a hard rag, allowing more words to be pulled down to the next line, thus requiring fewer words to be hyphenated. A smaller Hyphenation Zone will create a softer rag, with more hyphenated words. Note: The Hyphenation Zone is relevant only if you're using ragged text.

FIGURE 11.4 Hyphenation Zone.

This then is what the ANC is fighting. Their struggle is a truly national
one. It is a struggle of the African people, inspired by their own suffering
and their own experience. It is a struggle for the right to live.
During my lifetime I have dedicated myself to this struggle of the
African people. I have fought against
white domination, and I have fought
against black domination. I have cherished the ideal of a democratic and
free society in which all persons live
together in harmony and with equal
opportunities. It is an ideal which I
hope to live for and to achieve. But if
needs be, it is an ideal for which I am
prepared to die.
–Nelson Mandela, April 20, 1964

Hyphenation Zone set to 0. Single Line Composer.

This then is what the ANC is
fighting. Their struggle is a truly
national one. It is a struggle of the
African people, inspired by their own
suffering and their own experience. It
is a struggle for the right to live.
During my lifetime I have
dedicated myself to this struggle of
the African people. I have fought
against white domination, and I have
fought against black domination. I
have cherished the ideal of a democratic and free society in which all persons live together in harmony and
with equal opportunities. It is an ideal
which I hope to live for and to
achieve. But if needs be, it is an ideal
for which I am prepared to die.
–Nelson Mandela, April 20, 1964

Hyphenation Zone set to 3 picas. Single Line Composer.

The Hyphenation Slider

This enables you to alter the balance between better spacing and fewer hyphens. With justified text the spacing is adjusted between the words. With left-aligned text the rag (the right edge of the text) is adjusted. When working with left-aligned text avoid any gaping holes, long sloping edges, or words that stick out unattractively. Aim for a gentle wave that makes slight in-and-out adjustments as the eye travels down the column.

FIGURE 11.5 The Hyphenation Slider.

This then is what the ANC is fighting. Their struggle is a truly national
one. It is a struggle of the African people, inspired by their own suffering
and their own experience. It is a struggle for the right to live.
During my lifetime I have dedicated myself to this struggle of the
African people. I have fought against
white domination, and I have fought
against black domination. I have cherished the ideal of a democratic and
free society in which all persons live
together in harmony and with equal
opportunities. It is an ideal which I
hope to live for and to achieve. But if
needs be, it is an ideal for which I am
prepared to die.
–Nelson Mandela, April 20, 1964

Better Spacing

This then is what the ANC is
fighting. Their struggle is a truly
national one. It is a struggle of the
African people, inspired by their own
suffering and their own experience. It
is a struggle for the right to live.
During my lifetime I have dedicated myself to this struggle of the
African people. I have fought against
white domination, and I have fought
against black domination. I have cherished the ideal of a democratic and
free society in which all persons live
together in harmony and with equal
opportunities. It is an ideal which I
hope to live for and to achieve. But if
needs be, it is an ideal for which I am
prepared to die.
–Nelson Mandela, April 20, 1964

Fewer Hyphens

Hyphenate Capitalized Words

This does exactly what it says. Generally you want to avoid breaking proper nouns, but if they occur frequently and/or if there are a lot of them, checking this option yields better word spacing.

Hyphenate Last Word

Just what the doctor ordered when it comes to preventing word breaks at the end of a paragraph. Uncheck this to prevent the last word of a paragraph being hyphenated.

> **Not all Hyphens are Born Equal**
>
> The hyphen character in most fonts is nasty, brutish, and short, and could easily be swapped with the hyphen from another font without anyone even noticing. Certain fonts, however, have very distinctive—and beautiful—hyphens.

FIGURE 11.6 Hyphen examples.

Discretionary Hyphens and Nonbreaking Hyphens

Discretionary hyphens are useful when a word at the end of a line is not in your hyphenation dictionary, or when you want to break the word at a place different than that chosen by InDesign. Discretionary hyphens have the good manners to disappear when not needed. If the text is edited so that the word is no longer at the end of the line, the discretionary hyphen disappears.

A discretionary hyphen also serves another purpose: You can prevent a word from breaking by placing a discretionary hyphen in front of its first letter—Cmd+Shift+Hyphen (Ctrl+Shift+Hyphen). You can also prevent an individual word, or a string of words, from breaking by selecting it and then choosing No Break from the Character palette fly-out menu.

Multilingual Documents

InDesign CS2 comes with 35 dictionaries representing 28 languages (there are several flavors of English—legal, medical, British, Canadian) and the one you have applied to your type will determine how that type is hyphenated and spellchecked. If you are working on a multilingual document, as is common in countries like Canada or Switzerland, make sure you apply the appropriate language dictionary to the appropriate passages of text. But even if you have only an excerpt, a single

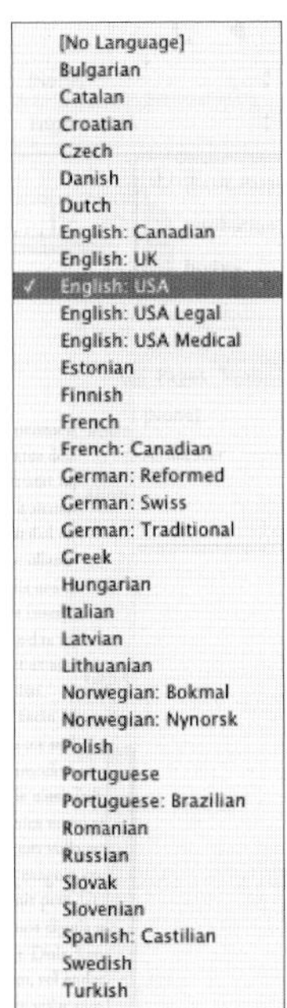

FIGURE 11.7 InDesign's Language Dictionaries.

paragraph in a second language for example, you can specify the appropriate language dictionary for that range of text so that the text hyphenates with the right syllable breaks and so that it is spell-checked in the right language.

Hyphenation and User Dictionaries

Hyphenation and spelling are controlled by the language dictionary associated with your text. When a word—usually a technical term, proper noun, or expletive—is not found in your language dictionary, you may wish to add it to your User Dictionary. Click Add and the word is added to the chosen language's user dictionary.

If you wish to add and word *and* specify its hyphenation breaks. Click Dictionary and then click Hyphenate to view the word's suggested hyphenation points. You can add your own hyphenation points by inserting tildes and ranking them: One tilde indicates the best break, two tildes the second best, and so on. If you don't want the word to be hyphenated, add a tilde before its first character.

You can also customize the hyphenation of words already in the language dictionary by typing (or pasting) the word into the Word field and clicking Hyphenate. If appropriate, insert tildes as above to customize the hyphenation. You can also import a word list (saved as a text file) by clicking Import, then quickly add these words to you user dictionary.

FIGURE 11.8 Adding a Word.

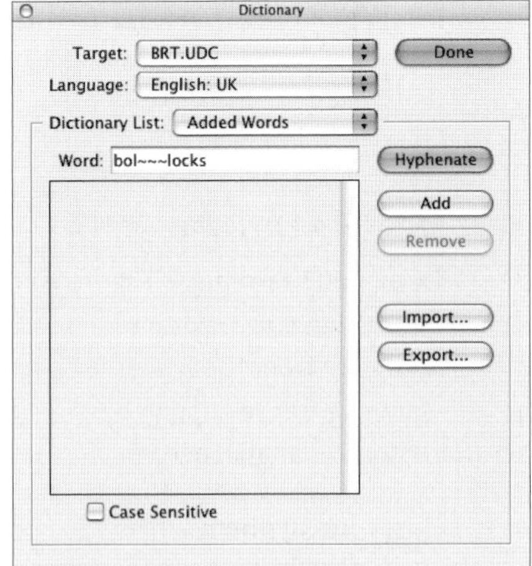

FIGURE 11.9 Adding a Word and choosing its hyphenation breaks.

Sharing User Dictionaries

If you are part of a workgroup, make sure that each user has the same customized user dictionary installed so that the same spelling and hyphenation rules are applied to a particular document regardless of who is working on it. Dictionary file names end with the extensions UDC and are stored in the InDesign Preferences folder.

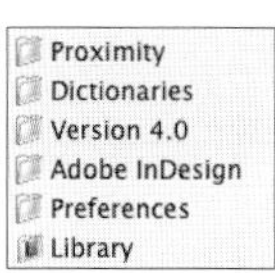

FIGURE 11.10 The path to the user dictionary (Mac).

Alternatively, you can merge the user dictionary into the InDesign document. Choose InDesign > Preferences > Dictionary and check Merge User Dictionary into Document. The advantage of this approach is that you don't have to worry about sharing user dictionaries.

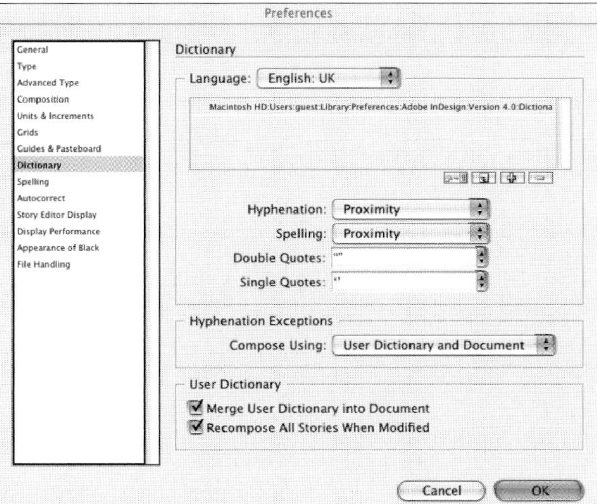

FIGURE 11.11 Dictionary Preferences.

Hyphenation Dos and Don'ts

Do: Check your language dictionary. Hyphenation (and spelling) rules are based on the language dictionary specified for the text. You can choose which language to use from the Language menu on the Control palette or in the Character palette. Better yet, apply this as part of a Paragraph Style definition. You can specify a default language in your Preferences.

Do: Hang your hyphens. When hyphenating, don't forget about Optical Margin Alignment to hang the hyphens (and other punctuation) in the right margin. Choose Type > Story and check Optical Margin Alignment.

TIP: Check Spelling and Ligatures: InDesign is smart enough to recognize ligatures in your text and won't flag words containing ligatures as being misspelled.

In Spelling Preferences (InDesign > Preferences > Spelling) you can specify the kind of problems you want InDesign to look for. You can also turn on Dynamic Spelling, which will underline potential spelling errors in your text. This is a feature that has been available in word processing applications for some time, but is of limited utility in a page layout application. Likewise the Autocorrect feature, which you can turn on in Preferences, second-guesses you on any unorthodox spellings—often with comical results.

Spell Checking

It's always a good idea to run a spell check before going to print, even if you haven't edited the text content, since it's easy for errors to creep into a layout during design and production. There's not a whole lot to say about InDesign's Check Spelling, except that it does what you'd expect a spell checker to do. You can specify whether you want to spell check one word or from where you place the pointer to the end of the story. You can also check a story, the entire document, or all open documents. When InDesign flags words not in its assigned language dictionary, you can ignore just one instance, ignore all instances, accept its suggestion, or type in your own substitution. If it's a word you'll be using frequently, you can add it to your User Dictionary. If you are adding a proper noun you can check Case Sensitive, so that the word will still be flagged if it is spelled in lowercase or with extra caps.

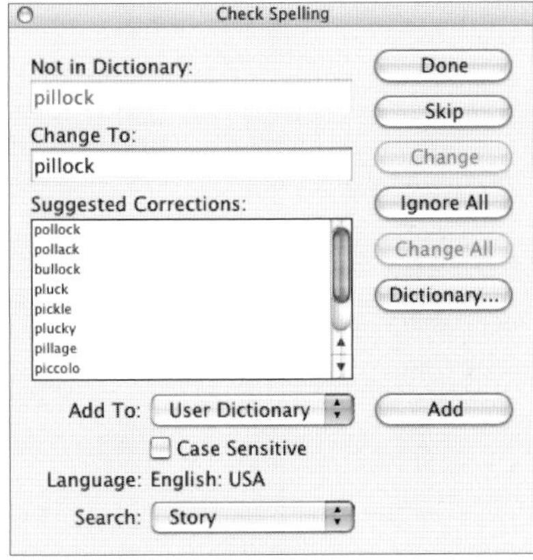

FIGURE 11.12 Check Spelling.

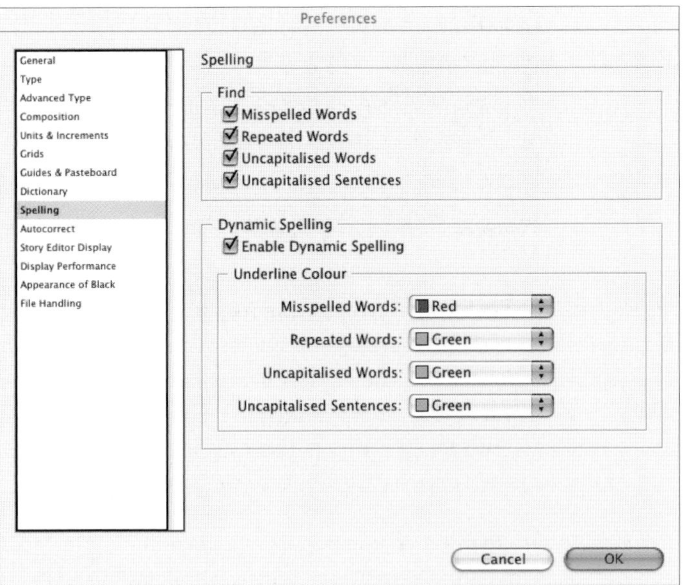

FIGURE 11.13 Spelling Preferences. Dynamic Spelling—godsend or minor irritation? You decide.

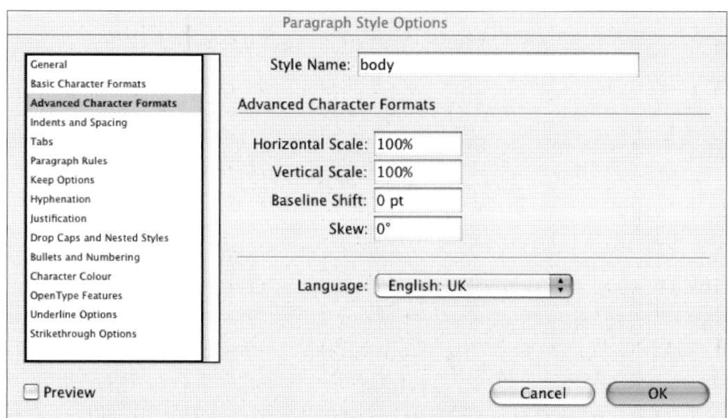

FIGURE 11.14 Advanced Character Formats.

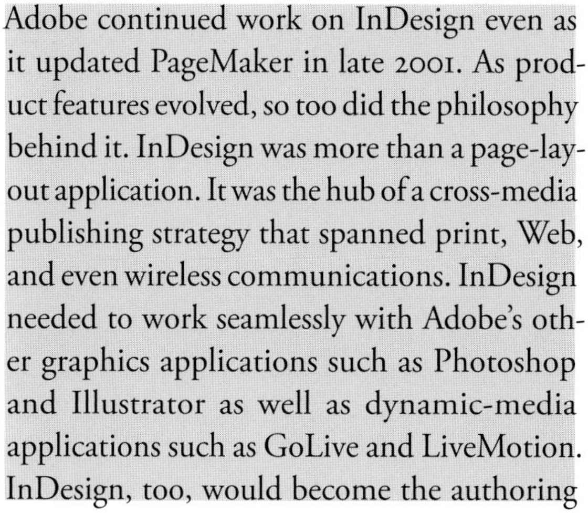

Adobe continued work on InDesign even as it updated PageMaker in late 2001. As product features evolved, so too did the philosophy behind it. InDesign was more than a page-layout application. It was the hub of a cross-media publishing strategy that spanned print, Web, and even wireless communications. InDesign needed to work seamlessly with Adobe's other graphics applications such as Photoshop and Illustrator as well as dynamic-media applications such as GoLive and LiveMotion. InDesign, too, would become the authoring

FIGURE 11.15 Hanging punctuation.

Do: Consult a dictionary for hyphenation breaks. When inserting discretionary hyphens divide the word after a vowel, turning over the consonant to the next line. In present participles, turn over -ing, as in walk-ing, driv-ing, design-ing. When two consonants come together, put the hyphen between them. Try to divide the word so that the first part of the division suggests what is following: conserva-tion not con-servation, re-appear not reap-pear, cam-ellia not camel-lia.

Do: Use Nonbreaking Hyphens (Cmd+Option— [Ctrl+Alt—--]) in phone numbers and Web addresses to prevent them breaking over a line.

Don't: Use stupid hyphenations like crap-ulous or the-rapist

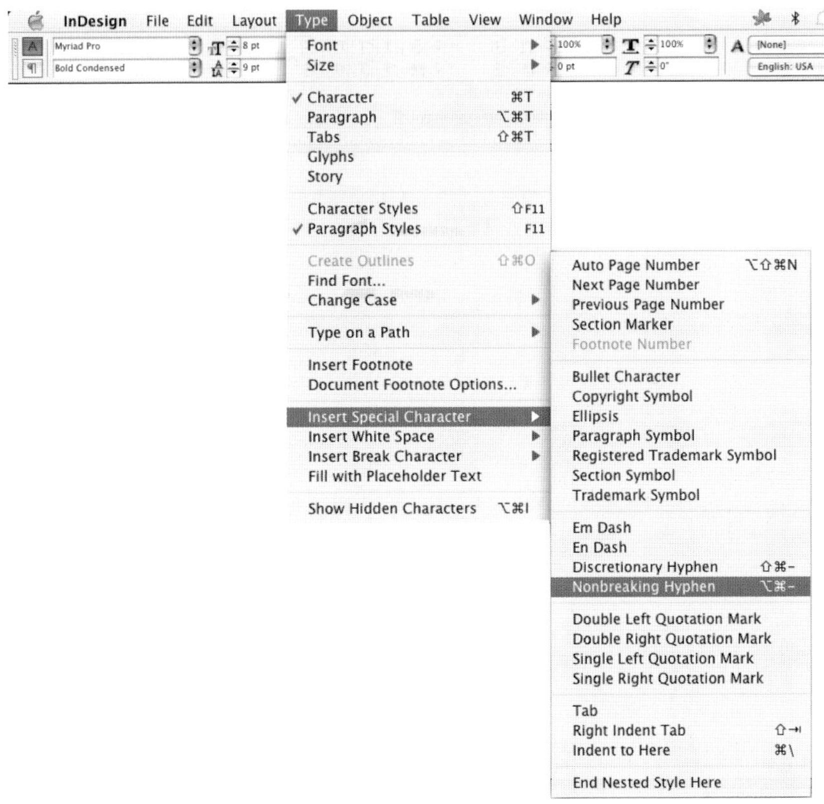

FIGURE 11.16 Insert Nonbreaking Hyphen.

Don't: Hyphenate headlines or subheads. Be sure to uncheck Hyphenation in the relevant Style Sheet definitions.

Don't: Hyphenate a word at the end of a paragraph. Uncheck the Hyphenate Last Word option in the Hyphenation dialog box to prevent this.

Don't: Hyphenate a word at the bottom of a column or page break.

Don't: Double-hyphenate a word. This can happen if you have a long compound word that contains a hard hyphen occurring at the end of the line and requiring a second hyphen. Select the type on either side of the hyphen and choose No Break to prevent this.

Don't: Use more than two consecutive hyphens. Hyphens set in a row cause an ugly stepped effect down your right margin. Turn over one of the words by selecting it and choosing No Break, or by inserting a discretionary hyphen at the beginning of the word.

Using the Story Editor

The Story Editor, a word processor within InDesign, is a feature borrowed from PageMaker (may it rest in peace) and a useful, no nonsense tool. To view text in the Story Editor, select a text frame with your Type pointer or Selection tool and choose Edit > Edit in Story Editor —Cmd+Y (Ctrl+Y). In the Story Editor window there's only one view size, and all the text is in the same font and size.

It may not be pretty but when all you want to do is edit text, it can be lot quicker to do so without the visual distraction of graphics, column breaks, and text formatting. You don't have to worry about zooming in and out, navigating from page to page, or redrawing screens. It's pure content. Any changes made in the Story Editor window are automatically reflected in the layout and visa versa.

The Story Editor is also useful when you want to quickly apply paragraph and/or character styles to a long document or when troubleshooting text composition problems, like mysterious line breaks or spacing gaps.

TIP: When switching back and forth between the Story Editor and the layout use the keyboard shortcut Cmd/Ctrl+Y rather than closing the Story Editor window. This way InDesign will automatically scroll to your Type cursor position, rather than leaving you to find your place in the text you were just editing.

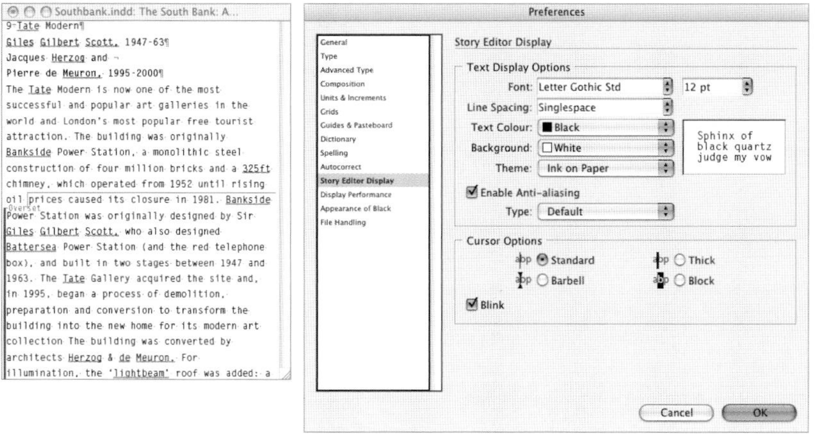

FIGURE 11.17 Part of a story viewed in the Story Editor and the associated Story Editor preferences. The Story Editor is a good place to check your spelling as well as view overset text (redlined) and quickly apply Paragraph and Character Styles. When you have Spelling preferences set up to Enable Dynamic Spelling, words not found in InDesign's dictionary are underlined in red.

Up Next

We visit InDesign's often overlooked table formatting functions, starting with the progenitor of all these tabular, the tab ruler.

CHAPTER 12

Mastering Tabs and Tables

WE LIVE IN A WORLD OF LISTS: the Top Ten this, the 100 greatest that, 12-step programs, 50 ways to leave your lover, etc. Tabs and tables are invaluable tools when it comes to working with anything list-like—from a simple bullet list to a complex financial table. In this chapter we'll look first at tabs and some of their common uses, and then take a look at InDesign's robust and versatile table formatting features.

Tabs are for positioning a piece of text in a specified place on the line. They are used to create bullet or numbered lists, reply forms, or for aligning numbers on a decimal point. Tabs can also be used to separate columns of information into a table-like layout. However, these days it's usually easier to use an InDesign table to do this.

Tabs come in several flavors: left, center, right, and decimal or special-character tabs.

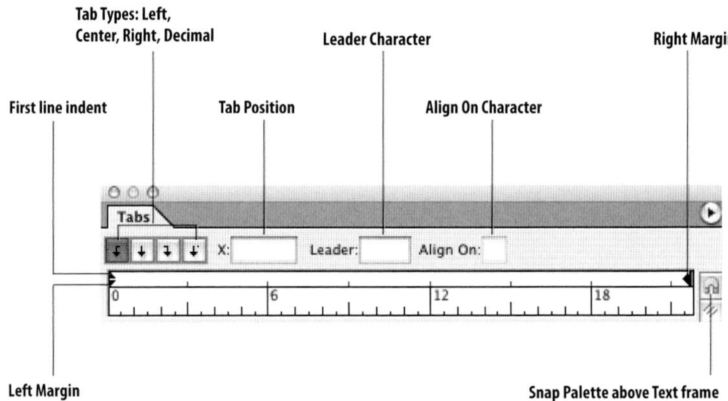

FIGURE 12.1 The Tabs Palette Cmd+Shift+T (Ctrl+Shift+T)

Setting Tabs

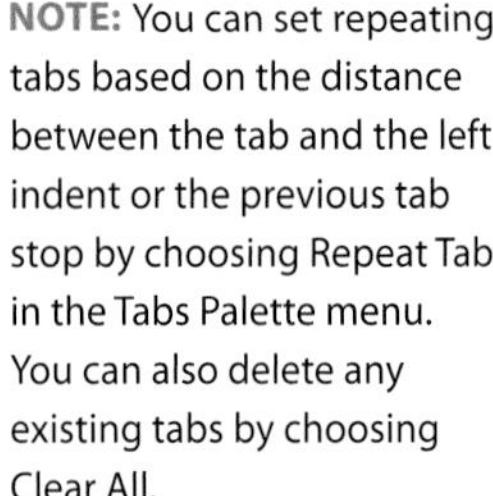

NOTE: You can set repeating tabs based on the distance between the tab and the left indent or the previous tab stop by choosing Repeat Tab in the Tabs Palette menu. You can also delete any existing tabs by choosing Clear All.

1. Place your pointer where you want to add horizontal space and press the Tab key.
2. Choose Type > Tabs. With your Type cursor in the text frame, click the magnet symbol at the bottom right of the Tab Ruler to snap the Tab Ruler above the text frame.
3. On the Tab Ruler, choose the type of tab you want and click a location on the ruler to position the tab.

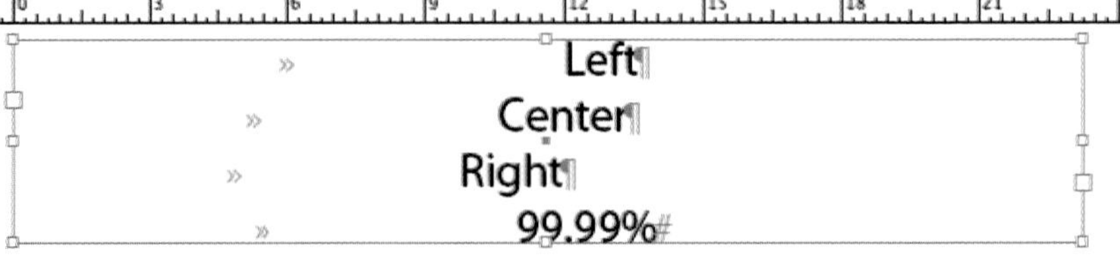

FIGURE 12.2 Types of Tabs. In each case the tab stop is set at 12 picas.

Creating Decimal Tabs

A decimal tab aligns characters on a decimal or another character you specify: Select a decimal tab on the Tab ruler, then, in the Align On box, type the character you want to align on—typically a decimal point, but you can use anything.

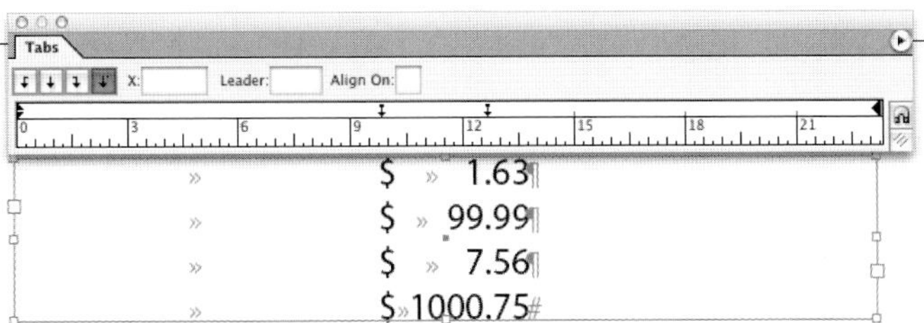

FIGURE 12.3 Align On. This example uses two decimal tabs, the first set to align on the $ symbol.

Using Tab Leaders

Tab leaders are used on menus, price lists, and contents pages. Their purpose is to guide the eye from one piece of text to the next. There are other solutions, arguably preferable, that don't introduce gaping holes between the item and its page number or price, but so long as the distance between the text and the number isn't too wide, this can be a good solution.

Caribbean Pumpkin Curry Served over a quinoa corn cake with a red Calypso bean, smoked pepper sofrito, a spicy mango-coconut mojo, and crispy plantain slices $15.25

Wild Mushroom Roulade Marinated seitan, wild mushroom ragout, truffled mashed potatoes and celery root wrapped in yuba and baked in a crisp phyllo dough. Served with grilled pears and a porter porcini mushroom sauce. $16.50

Portobello Potato Salad Breaded portobello mushrooms, pan sautèed and served over a warm gold and purple potato salad with cucumbers, tomatoes, Mandarin oranges, French lentils, mint, and winter greens. $13.95

North African Tempeh Berbere crusted tempeh, pan-seared and served with a saffron millet pilaf over ginger pomegranate sauce with preserved lemon pear chutney, peanuts, and seasonal vegetables $14.95

FIGURE 12.4 This menu uses a right tab with leader characters (a period followed by a space) to separate the menu item and its price.

Reply Forms

If you've ever tried to create a form with the underscore character, you've doubtless found it's impossible to have the lines perfectly aligned at the right column edge, giving you an ugly, stepped effect. This is because, unlike with typewriters, proportional-spaced fonts are not of a fixed width. With different characters on each line, the likelihood of your underscores ending at the same position is remote. The solution, or one of them, is to use a right tab with an underscore as the leader character.

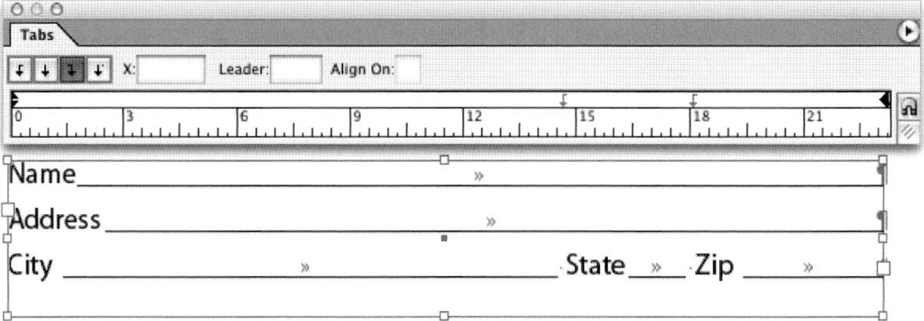

FIGURE 12.5 Reply Form. The first two lines have a right tab set at the right margin with an underscore as the leader character. Line 3 (selected) has three tabs, each with an underscore as the leader character.

Numbered Lists

When you have numbered lists that mix one-, two-, and possibly three-digit numbers you'll need two tabs, combining the right alignment of the numbers and the left alignment of the text.

A	B
1. Airbag	1 Airbag
2. Paranoid Android	2 Paranoid Android
3. Subterranean Homesick Alien	3 Subterranean Homesick Alien
4. Exit Music (For A Film)	4 Exit Music (For A Film)
5. Let Down	5 Let Down
6. Karma Police	6 Karma Police
7. Fitter Happier	7 Fitter Happier
8. Electioneering	8 Electioneering
9. Climbing Up The Walls	9 Climbing Up The Walls
10. No Surprises	10 No Surprises
11. Lucky	11 Lucky
12. Tourist, The	12 Tourist, The

FIGURE 12.6 A numbered list before formatting (example **A**) and the same text using a right and a left tab (example **B**). Note that the periods after the numbers are redundant and have been removed. Using the Control palette or the PageMaker Toolbar to convert the text to a numbered list adds numbers before each paragraph, but does not add tabs or formatting. The numbers are static—that is, they do not update should you change the order of the text.

Right Indent Tab

A right-aligned tab allows you to align all subsequent text to the right edge of the text frame. You won't find it in the Tabs palette, but under the Insert Special Character menu. Alternatively you can press Shift-Tab in the text. To use a Right Indent Tab with a tab leader (CS2 only), set a tab stop anywhere in the paragraph and apply a leader character to it. When you press Shift-Tab the leader character will appear.

> Part of the reason for the ugliness of adults, in a child's eyes, is that the child is usually looking upwards, and few faces are at their best when seen from below. — George Orwell

FIGURE 12.7 A Right Indent Tab (Shift-Tab) is inserted before the attribution to align the author's name to the right column edge.

Working with Tables

Working with tables in InDesign is so much more than just making financial spreadsheets readable, although if that's what you need to accomplish InDesign is more than up to the task. Tables can be used in all sorts of creative ways beyond the obvious: crossword puzzles, reply coupons, television listings, calendars, and forms of all kinds. Just because you use a table to design all or part of your document doesn't mean that document has to *look like* a table. In fact, tables are useful when you have content that needs to be updated yet remain in the same location on the page. The rows, columns, and cells that make up the structure of your table can be visible as such, or they can merely serve as an underlying grid to your design. Tables used to be a thorn in the side of the graphic designer, but InDesign offers such powerful and intuitive table formatting features that this is no longer the case.

Tables are always contained in a text frame and move with the flow of the text. To align the table within the text frame, insert the Type tool to the right or left of the table and click the appropriate alignment option on the Paragraph formats section of the Control Palette.

A table is edited with the Type tool. Formatting text within a table is the same as formatting text in a text frame. Paragraph and Character Styles, as well as local formatting, can be applied to the text.

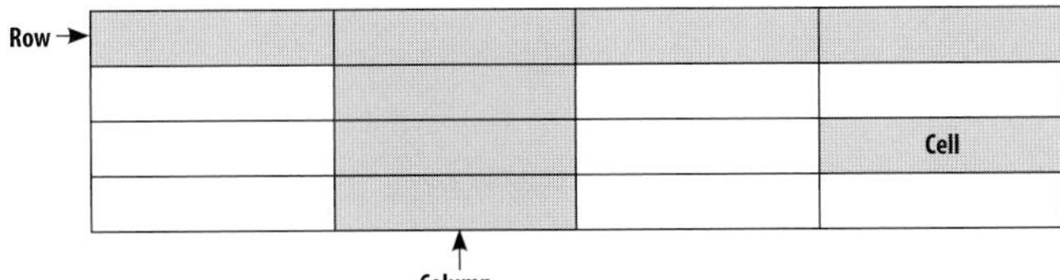

FIGURE 12.8 Anatomy of a Table.

Working with tables, you can add or delete rows and columns, cut or copy and paste selected cells, change the column and row height, split or merge cells, add header and footer rows, and much more.

When you create a table, it fills the width of your column. The default height of a row is determined by the leading of your text at the insertion point, but this can be easily changed.

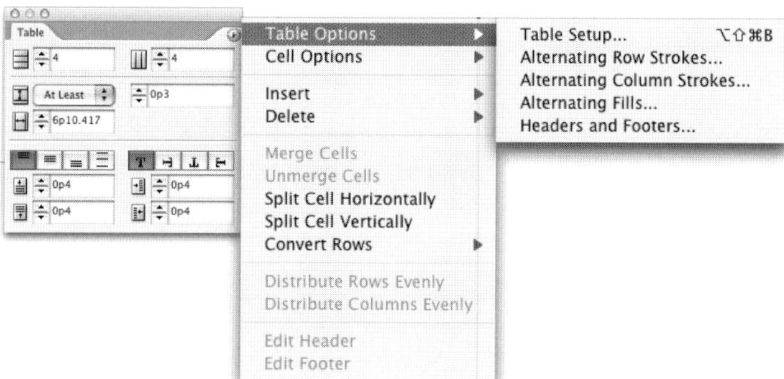

FIGURE 12.9 The Table palette (Window > Type & Tables > Table).

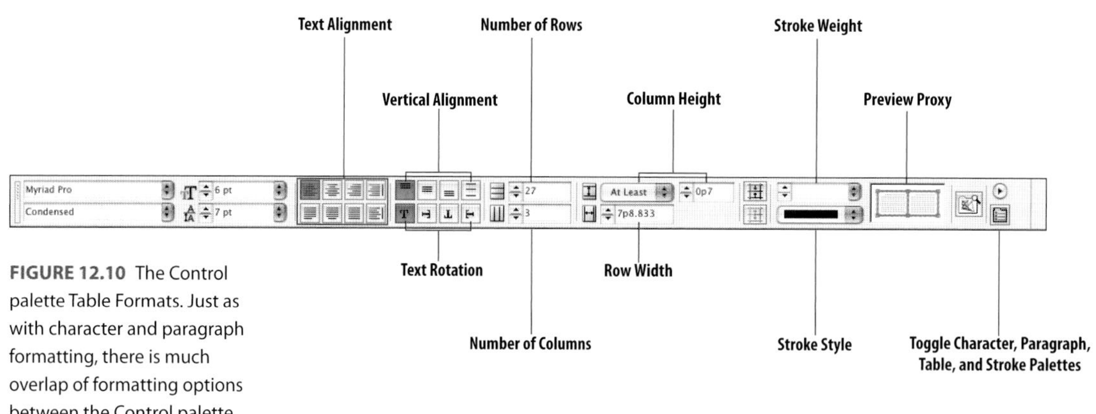

FIGURE 12.10 The Control palette Table Formats. Just as with character and paragraph formatting, there is much overlap of formatting options between the Control palette and the Table palette.

Creating a Table

There are three approaches to creating a table: from scratch, converting existing text to a table, or importing a table from Microsoft Word or Excel.

From Scratch

1. Draw a text frame with the Type Tool, or insert your type pointer into an existing text frame.

2. Choose Table > Insert Table.
3. Specify the numbers of rows and columns and click OK. Optionally, if the table will span more than one column or frame, specify the number of (repeating) header or footer rows.

Each table cell is like a text frame. You type or paste text, or place text into a table cell just as you would do with a text frame. You can also paste or place (File > Place) graphics into table cells.

NOTE: If you add a graphic that is larger than the cell, the cell height expands to accommodate the graphic, but the cell width remains fixed, causing the graphic to extend beyond the right side of the cell. If the row is set to a fixed height, a graphic that is taller than the row height causes the cell to be *overset*.

Converting Text to a Table

If you are going to convert text to a table, it pays to set up the text properly with tabs separating the columns and paragraph returns separating the rows. Once your tabs and carriage returns are in the right place, select your text and choose Table > Convert Text to Table.

It's rare that you'd want to, but you can also make this conversion in reverse by inserting your Type Tool in a table and choosing Table > Convert Table to Text.

Premier League 2004–2005

			Home					Away						
	Team	P	W	D	L	F	A	W	D	L	F	A	GD	PTS
1	Chelsea	38	14	5	0	35	6	15	3	1	37	9	57	95
2	Arsenal	38	13	5	1	54	19	12	3	4	33	17	51	83
3	Man Utd	38	12	6	1	31	12	10	5	4	27	14	32	77
4	Everton	38	12	2	5	24	15	6	5	8	21	31	-1	61
5	Liverpool	38	12	4	3	31	15	5	3	11	21	26	11	58
6	Bolton	38	9	5	5	25	18	7	5	7	24	26	5	58
7	Middlesbrough	38	9	6	4	29	19	5	7	7	24	27	7	55
8	Man City	38	8	6	5	24	14	5	7	7	23	25	8	52
9	Tottenham	38	9	5	5	36	22	5	5	9	11	19	6	52
10	Aston Villa	38	8	6	5	26	17	4	5	10	19	35	-7	47
11	Charlton	38	8	4	7	29	29	4	6	9	13	29	-16	46
12	Birmingham	38	8	6	5	24	15	3	6	10	16	31	-6	45
13	Fulham	38	8	4	7	29	26	4	4	11	23	34	-8	44
14	Newcastle	38	7	7	5	25	25	3	7	9	22	32	-10	44
15	Blackburn	38	5	8	6	21	22	4	7	8	11	21	-11	42
16	Portsmouth	38	8	4	7	30	26	2	5	12	13	33	-16	39
17	West Brom	38	5	8	6	17	24	1	8	10	19	37	-25	34
18	Crystal Palace	38	6	5	8	21	19	1	7	11	20	43	-21	33
19	Norwich	38	7	5	7	29	32	0	7	12	13	45	-35	33
20	Southampton	38	5	9	5	30	30	1	5	13	15	36	-21	32

FIGURE 12.11 Tab Delimited Text.

FIGURE 12.12 The same text converted to a Table (it looks worse than it is).

Pre-mier														
		P	W	D	L	F	A	W	D	L	F	A	GD	PTS
1	Chel-sea	38	14	5	0	35	6	15	3	1	37	9	57	95
2	Arse-nal	38	13	5	1	54	19	12	3	4	33	17	51	83
3	Man Utd	38	12	6	1	31	12	10	5	4	27	14	32	77
4	Ever-ton	38	12	2	5	24	15	6	5	8	21	31	-1	61
5	Liv-er-pool	38	12	4	3	31	15	5	3	11	21	26	11	58
6		38	9	5	5	25	18	7	5	7	24	26	5	58

FIGURE 12.13 The cleaned-up table: Column Widths and Row Heights adjusted. Cell Inset Spacing reduced. Paragraph Styles Applied. Table Border, Row, and Column Strokes removed. Alternating Fills of 20 percent cyan applied.

Premier League 2004–2005

		Home						Away						
	TEAM	P	W	D	L	F	A	W	D	L	F	A	GD	PTS
1	Chelsea	38	14	5	0	35	6	15	3	1	37	9	57	**95**
2	Arsenal	38	13	5	1	54	19	12	3	4	33	17	51	**83**
3	Man Utd	38	12	6	1	31	12	10	5	4	27	14	32	**77**
4	Everton	38	12	2	5	24	15	6	5	8	21	31	-1	**61**
5	Liverpool	38	12	4	3	31	15	5	3	11	21	26	11	**58**
6	Bolton	38	9	5	5	25	18	7	5	7	24	26	5	**58**
7	Middlesbrough	38	9	6	4	29	19	5	7	7	24	27	7	**55**
8	Man City	38	8	6	5	24	14	5	7	7	23	25	8	**52**
9	Tottenham	38	9	5	5	36	22	5	5	9	11	19	6	**52**
10	Aston Villa	38	8	6	5	26	17	4	5	10	19	35	-7	**47**
11	Charlton	38	8	4	7	29	29	4	6	9	13	29	-16	**46**
12	Birmingham	38	8	6	5	24	15	3	6	10	16	31	-6	**45**
13	Fulham	38	8	4	7	29	26	4	4	11	23	34	-8	**44**
14	Newcastle	38	7	7	5	25	25	3	7	9	22	32	-10	**44**
15	Blackburn	38	5	8	6	21	22	4	7	8	11	21	-11	**42**
16	Portsmouth	38	8	4	7	30	26	2	5	12	13	33	-16	**39**
17	West Brom	38	5	8	6	17	24	1	8	10	19	37	-25	**34**
18	Crystal Palace	38	6	5	8	21	19	1	7	11	20	43	-21	**33**
19	Norwich	38	7	5	7	29	32	0	7	12	13	45	-35	**33**
20	Southampton	38	5	9	5	30	30	1	5	13	15	36	-21	**32**

Importing a Table

There's no point in reinventing the wheel: If you already have a table in a Microsoft Excel spreadsheet or in Microsoft Word, choose File > Place to import it into InDesign, either retaining the formatting (probably not a good idea) or stripping out the formatting—the information will appear as tabbed text—and then using InDesign's Table tools to prettify it.

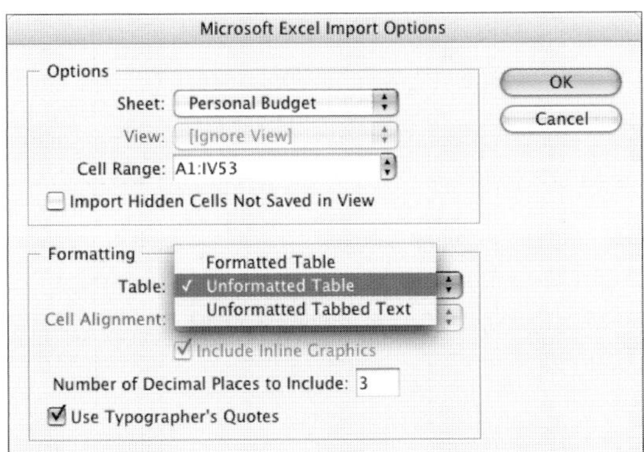

FIGURE 12.14 Table Import Options.

Selecting a Table

Selecting a whole table allows you to change the formatting of all the table's cells. To do so, move your pointer to the upper left corner of the table—it becomes a southeast pointing arrow—and click. Alternatively, with your pointer inside the table, choose Table > Select > Table (Cmd+Option+A/Ctrl+Alt+A).

Breaking Tables Across Frames

Large tables can be a pain, but, thankfully, if the table is taller than the text frame in which it resides, you can thread the frame with another frame—in the same way as you would thread a regular text frame—to continue the table.

TIP: Tabs in Tables When you're working in a table, pressing Tab moves your cursor to the next cell. If you want to insert a tab in a cell, choose Type > Insert Special Character > Tab.

Keep Options determines how many rows should remain together. You can also specify where a row breaks, such as at the top of a column or frame.

If you want a header or footer row to repeat information in the new frame, choose Table > Headers and Footers.

If you didn't set up a header or footer row first time around, you can easily convert an existing row to a header or footer row by choosing Table > Convert Rows > To Header or To Footer.

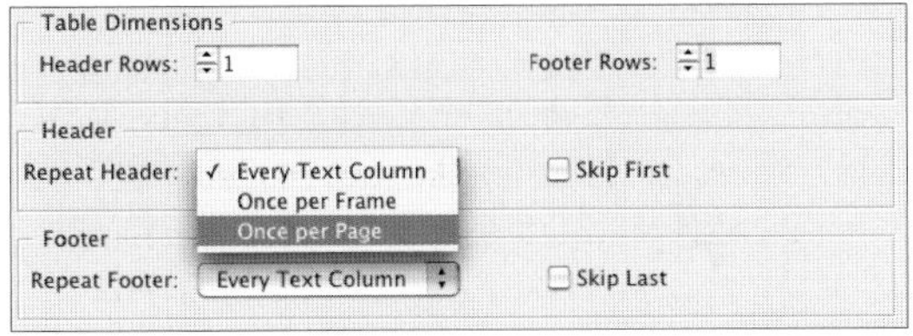

FIGURE 12.15 Header and Footer Options.

NOTE: Unless you choose Preserve Local Formatting, any formatting previously applied to individual table cells will be overridden by the row and column formatting.

Adding Borders, Strokes, and Fills to a Table

In the Table Options dialog box, you can change the stroke of the table border and add alternating strokes and fills to columns and rows.

To enhance the readability of a complicated table with a wide measure, use alternating strokes and/or fills to help the eye to track along the table rows. Depending on the nature of your data, you may want to experiment with Alternating Patterns. You can apply your fills or strokes to every other row, every second row, every third row, or, using the First and Next menus, come up with a Custom Row pattern. The same is true with columns.

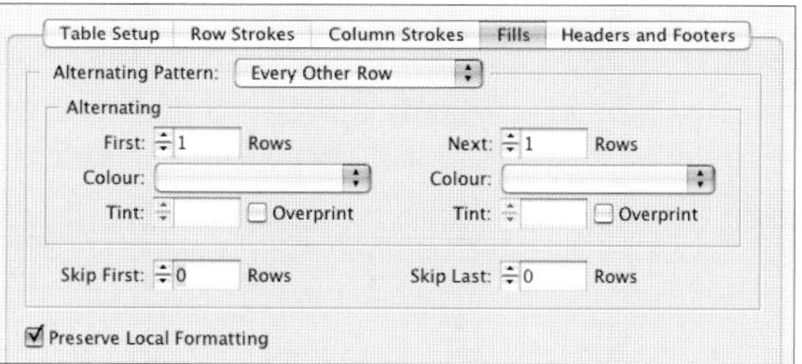

FIGURE 12.16 Preserve Local Formatting. Note that the Fill Color and Tint are shown as blank when this option is checked.

TIP: Tables and Text Wraps Text wraps do not work in tables without first jumping through a few hoops. Let's say you have a graphic and some text that you want to wrap around that graphic and you want to insert both items into a single table cell. Create your text frame and graphic outside the table, and then group them together (Cmd+G/Ctrl+G). Select the group, and copy and paste into the table cell—the relationship between the type and graphic is preserved.

Confusingly, row strokes are set on even when Alternating Pattern is set to None. To turn off row strokes, columns strokes, and the table border at the same time, select the whole table and then target the Stroke swatch on the Swatches palette or at the bottom of the Tool Palette, and then choose None.

To turn off just row strokes, choose Every Other Row as the Alternating Pattern, and then choose None as the color for the First and the Next row. If you want row strokes on, but want to change their weight and/or color, make sure you change both the First and the Next row. Likewise when working with column strokes: They are on even though Alternating Pattern is set to None. To change their stroke weight, choose a different alternating pattern and change the options for the First and the Next column stroke weights.

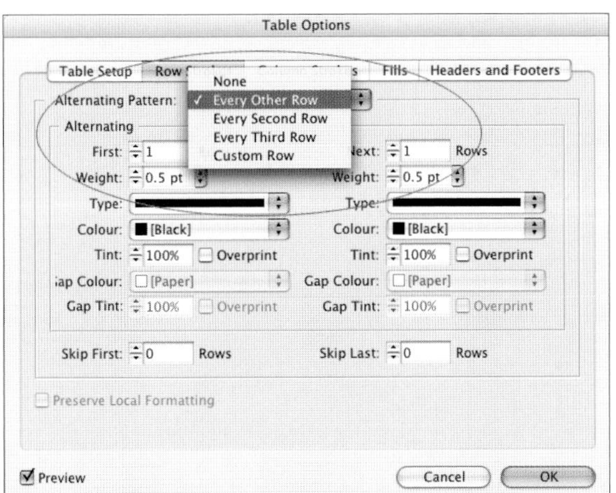

FIGURE 12.17 Changing the weight of row strokes.

Table Keyboard Shortcuts

Action	Mac	Windows
Insert Table	Cmd-Shift-Option-T	Ctrl-Shift-Alt-T
Table Setup	Cmd-Shift-Option-B	Ctrl-Shift-Alt-B
Cell Options Text...	Cmd-Option-B	Ctrl-Shift-Alt-B
Insert Row	Cmd-9	Ctrl-9
Insert Column	Cmd-Option-9	Ctrl-Alt-9
Delete Row	Cmd-Backspace	Ctrl-Backspace
Delete Column	Shift-Backspace	Shift-Backspace
Select Cell	Cmd-/	Ctrl-/
Select Row	Cmd-3	Ctrl-3
Select Column	Cmd-Option-3	Ctrl-Alt-3
Select Table	Cmd-Option-A	Ctrl-Alt-A
Insert or delete rows or columns while dragging	Begin dragging row or column border, and then hold down Option as you drag	Begin dragging row or column border, and then hold down Alt as you drag
Resize rows or columns without changing the size of the table	Shift-drag interior row or column border	Shift-drag interior row or column border
Resize rows or columns proportionally	Shift-drag right or bottom table border	Shift-drag right or bottom table border
Move to next/previous cell	Tab/Shift+Tab	Tab/Shift+Tab
Move to first/last cell in column	Option+Page Up/Page Down	Alt+Page Up/Page Down
Move to first/last cell in row	Option+Home/End key	Alt+Home/End key
Move to first/last row in frame	Page Up/Page Down key	Page Up/Page Down key
Move up/down one cell	Up Arrow/Down Arrow key	Up Arrow/Down Arrow key
Move left/right one cell	Left Arrow/Right Arrow key	Left Arrow/Right Arrow key
Select cell above/below the current cell	Shift+Up Arrow/Down Arrow key	Shift+Up Arrow/Down Arrow key
Select cell to the right/left of the current cell	Shift+Right Arrow/Left Arrow key	Shift+Right Arrow/Left Arrow key
Start row on next column	Enter (numeric keypad)	Enter (numeric keypad)
Start row on next frame	Shift+Enter (numeric keypad)	Shift+Enter (numeric keypad)
Toggle between text selection and cell selection	Esc	Esc

FIGURE 12.18 Table Formatting Shortcuts

FIGURE 12.19 Tables and Text Wraps. This section of a film calendar shows a grouped text frame and graphic with text wrap pasted into a single table cell.

CASTING BY A.N. OTHER SPECIAL VISUAL EFFECTS AND ANIMATION BY JOE BLOGGS

FIGURE 12.20 Using a table in a film poster is the best way to get a "double baseline" with the small credits. Without a table it would be necessary to position separate text frames next to the big credits, an approach that is cumbersome and difficult to edit.

CONTENTS

DESTINATIONS

27 Na facillan er sim quis eu feui euis am inim ad et praestis diatem adigna at.

37 COVER STORY Consectet, susto et alit praesent autpatis autet iriustrud tat.

40 Esequam nis at velis am quatummolor

45 COVER STORY Velenibh exeros num veraese quatuer sendrer aessit veriusci tinci ero dit aliquisit

60 Modionse dolessi. Ommod exerat. Ut vel e

MUSIC

62 Na facillan er sim quis eu feui euis am inim ad et praestis diatem adigna at.

65 Esequam nis at velis am quatummolor

70 COVER STORY Velenibh exeros num veraese quatuer sendrer aessit veriusci tinci ero dit aliquisit

"The quick brown fox jumps over the lazy dog."

FASHION

18 Na facillan er sim quis eu feui euis am inim ad et praestis diatem adigna at.

76 COVER STORY Consectet, susto et alit praesent autpatis autet iriustrud tat.

MOVIES

78 Na facillan er sim quis eu feui euis am inim ad et praestis diatem adigna at.

82 COVER STORY Consectet, susto et alit praesent autpatis autet iriustrud tat.

90 Esequam nis at velis am quatummolor

FIGURE 12.21 This table of contents page uses a clearly defined grid that is a good candidate for a table. Using a table in such a context can make it easier to edit the contents of individual cells in the publication's next issue.

Working with Rows and Columns

To select a column or columns, move the pointer to the top edge of the table, and your pointer becomes an arrow shape. Click to select the entire column. To select a row, move your pointer to the left edge of the table and click to select the row. Alternatively, you can click inside a table and choose Table > Select > Column or Row.

To specifically select Header, Body, or Footer rows, click inside the table and choose Table > Select > Header Rows, Body Rows, or Footer Rows.

Inserting and Deleting Rows and Columns

You can insert rows and columns using the menu options, or, if you want to be flash, on the fly by dragging while holding down Option (Alt) as you drag a row or column border. In addition, you can also create a new row by pressing Tab when the insertion point is in the last cell of the table.

NOTE: When adding columns, if you drag more than one and one-half times the width of the column being dragged, new columns with the same width as the original column are added.

To delete all or selected parts of your table, choose Table > Delete > Row, Column, or Table.

To delete cell contents without deleting cells, select the cells containing the text you want to delete and press Backspace or Delete.

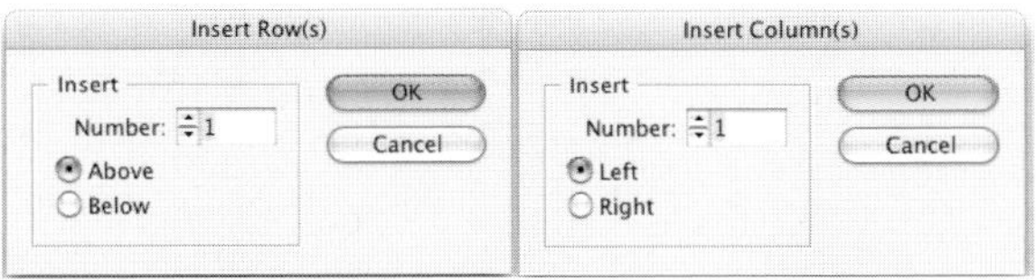

FIGURE 12.22 Inserting Rows and Columns

Resizing Rows and Columns

To resize rows and columns, drag the row or column border to change the row height or column width. To keep the table at the same size, hold Shift while you drag. This affects only two rows (or two columns) at once—one row or column gets bigger while the other gets smaller. To resize all the rows and columns proportionally, hold Shift while dragging the bottom table edge or the right table edge respectively.

To resize the whole table, position the pointer over the lower right corner of the table so that the pointer becomes an arrow, and then drag to increase or decrease the table size. To maintain the table's height and width proportions, hold Shift. Note, this doesn't work if your table spans more than one frame.

TIP: Choosing Exactly from the Control palette or Table palette sets a fixed row height. Fixed row heights don't grow when you add text, and a small red dot will appear in the lower right corner of the cell if it is overset. With an overset cell you have two options: Make the content smaller or the table cell bigger.

Changing Row Height

Choosing At Least specifies a minimum row height that will grow as you add text or increase the point size of the text you already have. If you copy or Place a graphic into the table cell, the row height will grow to accommodate the graphic. But the column width will not. With an overset graphic you can either choose to Clip Contents to Cell to crop the graphic to the table cell width or adjust the column width to fit the graphic.

Distributing Rows or Columns Evenly

If you want your selected rows or columns to have a uniform height or width, choose Table > Distribute Rows Evenly or Distribute Columns Evenly.

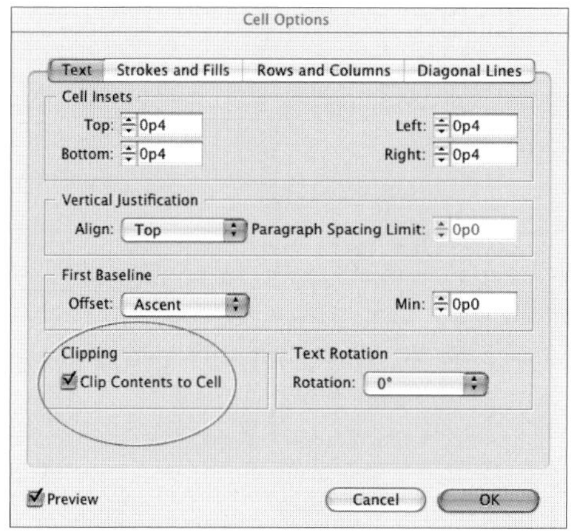

FIGURE 12.23 Clip Contents to Cell.

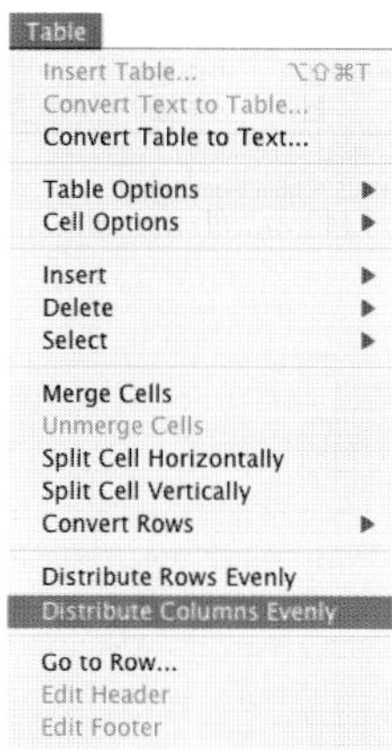

FIGURE 12.24 Distribute Columns Evenly.

NOTE: Selecting the Cell and the text within the cell are two distinct things. To select the cell, drag from the top left of the cell. Alternatively, because it's all too easy to inadvertently resize the rows and columns when trying to select individual table cells, especially if your table is complex, put your Type cursor in the cells and choose Table > Select > Cell (Cmd+/ [Ctrl+/]).

Working with Table Cells

The building blocks of a table are cells, and each cell in your table is like an individual text frame. Using Cell Options, you can determine the Cell Inset Spacing, the Vertical Alignment, Row Strokes, Column Strokes, the First Baseline Options, and Diagonal Lines. Table text can be formatted in exactly the same way as text in a text frame, and paragraph and character styles are equally beneficial—see Chapters 13 and 14. The only restriction on the formatting of tables is that text can be rotated only in increments of 90°, 180°, or 270°. (If you really must have text rotated at any other angle, format the text in its own frame, then cut and paste the text frame as an inline frame into a cell.)

Merging and Splitting Cells

You can merge two or more cells in the same row or column into a single cell. You can also split cells horizontally or vertically.

	7	8
Crime Thriller Discoveries! **Guilty As Hell** (82) "Hidden hands ended her life! Whose were they?" **(2:00), 5:15, 8:35** **Billion Dollar Scandal** (81) Paroled convict, employed as a financier's masseur, learns secrets of a giant oil stock scandal. **(3:40), 7:00** **Surprise Mystery Bonus feature 10:10**		**One Hour With You** (80) Lubitsch classic offers deliciously risque dialogue and songs by Maurice Chevalier and Jeanette MacDonald. **(2:10), 5:20, 8:35** **This Is The Night** (80) Cary Grant finds wife Thelma Todd with her lover in this rediscovered farce. **(3:45), 7:00**

14	15
Torch Singer (71) "Lips that had kissed more men than Claudette Colbert could remember, crooned lullabies no one could forget!" **(3:50), 7:00** **Kick In** (75) Clara Bow is terrific in this noirish lost film. **(2:20), 5:25, 8:35** **Betty Boop cartoon** (8) 	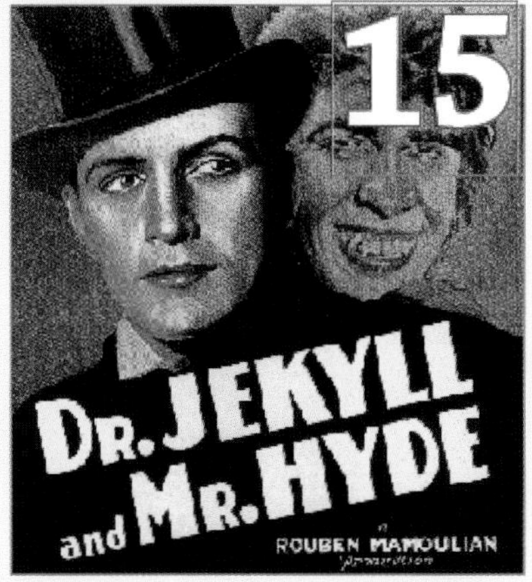 **Dr. Jekyll and Mr. Hyde** (97) Classic horror film with Frederic March and Miriam Hopkins. **(1:35), 5:00, 8:30** **Murder By The Clock** (76) Lost Atmospheric chiller. **(3:30), 7:00**

FIGURE 12.25 Tables Within Tables. This section of a film calendar shows a three-column single-row table that has been pasted into a merged cell above the two columns in the second row. A similar effect may have been possible by Splitting Cells vertically (not the same as Unmerging, which will restore the cells to their premerged state), but does not allow the same degree of independence when adjusting the column widths of the individual rows.

Adding Diagonal Lines to a Cell

Choose Table > Cell Options > Diagonal Lines. From the Draw menu, you can specify Diagonal in Front or Content in Front to position the diagonal line in front of or behind the cell contents.

For Line Stroke, specify desired weight, type, color, and gap settings; specify a Tint percentage and Overprint options, and then click OK.

FIGURE 12.26 Diagonal Lines.

SPECIAL OFFER PRICES!				
Postal Region	You Pay	Full 1 Year Price	You Save	You Pay
UK	57.65	£41.40	30%	£28.80
Rest of World	£139.02	£92.68	23%	£71.36

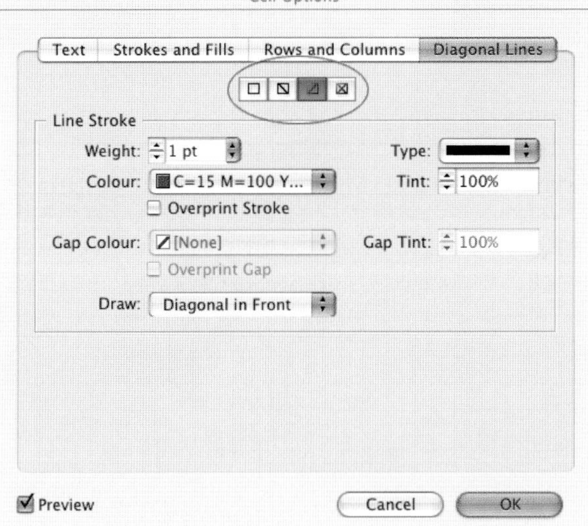

Working with Table Cells

Just like a regular text or picture frame, each table cell has fill and stroke properties. Choose the cell (Cmd+/[Ctrl+/]), or drag your pointer across a range of cells to select multiples, and use the Fill and Stroke boxes on the bottom of the Tool palette to change the properties of a cell. To modify specific sides of the cell border, determine which stroke line(s) you are affecting with the Preview Proxy at the bottom of the Stroke palette. Selected lines appear in blue; deselected lines in gray. To deselect all lines, triple click the Preview Proxy. Alternatively, you can use the Cell Options dialog box, which has all these options in one place.

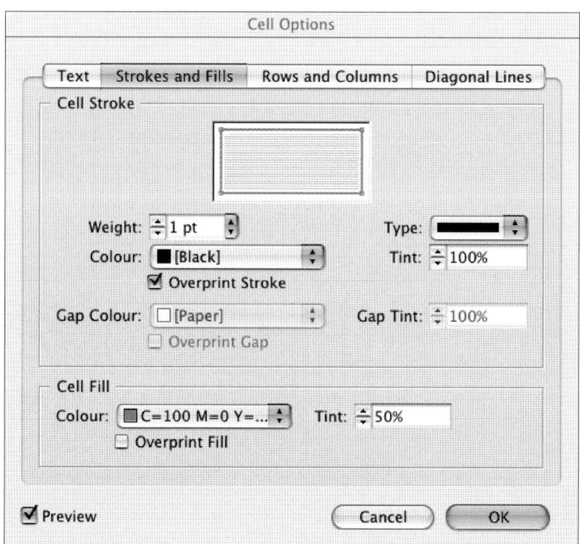

FIGURE 12.27 Cell Options: Your one-stop shop for table cell formatting.

Tables are extremely versatile and can be used for much more than just "tables." For example, putting a screen behind a single paragraph is a common request that is easy in Word, but has long proved problematic for the more heavyweight layout applications. Until now, that is. With InDesign the solution is simple.

> Make the paragraph into a single cell table using Convert Text to Table and then apply a fill color (and a stoke) to that cell. Using Cell Options you can control the inset spacing of the text.

FIGURE 12.28 A shaded paragraph.

Like all tables, the single cell table will move with the flow of text. What's more, the table cell—and it's shading—will expand and contract as necessary if you edit the paragraph.

TIP: Shading a Paragraph If you want to put a screened background behind a specific paragraph, a table is an elegant solution. Select the text in the paragraph—but not the final hidden carriage-return character—and choose Table > Convert Text To Table to make a one-cell table. You can then stroke and/or fill the table as you wish and—because it's a table—it will grow as you add type and move as part of the text flow. You control the paragraph spacing between the table and the paragraphs above and below using Table Options >Table Setup.

Table Aesthetics

Here are some rules of thumb that may be useful when working with tables that really look like tables.

- Table text is typically one or two points smaller than body text.
- Condensed sans serif faces work well.
- Use lining numbers, not proportional old style numbers.
- Keep it simple. Establish the hierarchy of information by the way the table is constructed, rather than changing fonts, weights, and point sizes.
- Use borders, column rules, row rules, and cell tinting sparingly.
- Don't try to cram too much into a finite amount of space. Just because it's a table doesn't mean it shouldn't be readable.
- Don't justify text—table cells are too narrow.
- Don't use first line indents. If table cell entries run to more than one paragraph, break them into separate cells.
- If a table runs across several pages, repeat the header row on each subsequent page on which the table appears.
- When tables run more than one page, a footer row is only necessary at the end of the complete table.

Up Next

See how you can let InDesign take the strain with its super array of Styles. Veterans of page layout programs will find paragraph and character styles as they would expect, but in addition, InDesign offers such delights as nested styles, sequential styles, and object styles—features that can make formatting even the longest, most complicated documents a joy.

PART III

Styles

CHAPTER 13

Stylin' with Paragraph and Character Styles

STYLES HAVE BEEN AROUND since the dawn of desktop publishing. Over the years they have evolved in their ease of use and range of capabilities. A bedrock feature of any page layout program, styles represent humankind's greatest advance in the field of digital page layout. Styles are to graphic designers what fire was to prehistoric people.

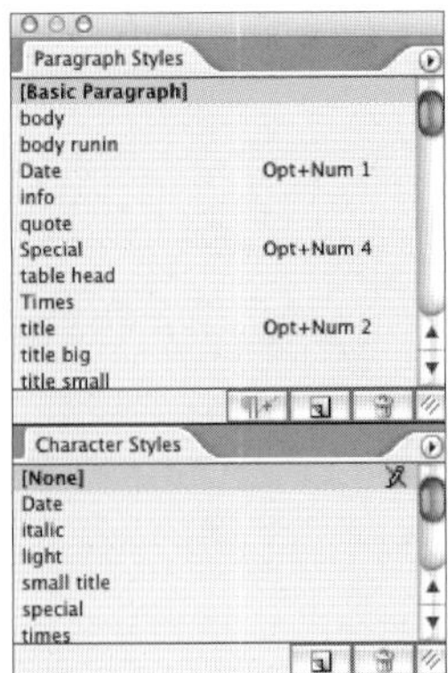

FIGURE 13.1 Paragraph and Character Styles Palettes (small palette rows chosen)

Defining Our Terms

Paragraph Styles and Character Styles are a collection of attributes that can be applied to text with a single click. Paragraph Styles, as their name suggests, are applied to the whole paragraph; Character Styles are applied to a *selected range of text* within a paragraph. Collectively I will refer to the Paragraph Styles, Character Styles, and Object Styles (see Chapter 14) in a document as a Style Sheet.

When you select text or click an insertion point, the style that has been applied to that text is highlighted in the Paragraph and/or Character Styles palette. If you select a range of text covering multiple styles, no style is highlighted.

By default the [Basic Paragraph] style is applied to text you type. You can't rename or delete this style, but you can edit it: Ctrl/Right Mouse+click on the style name to change its definition. You can also designate a different style to be the default style. To do so simply choose that style when you have no text or text frame selected.

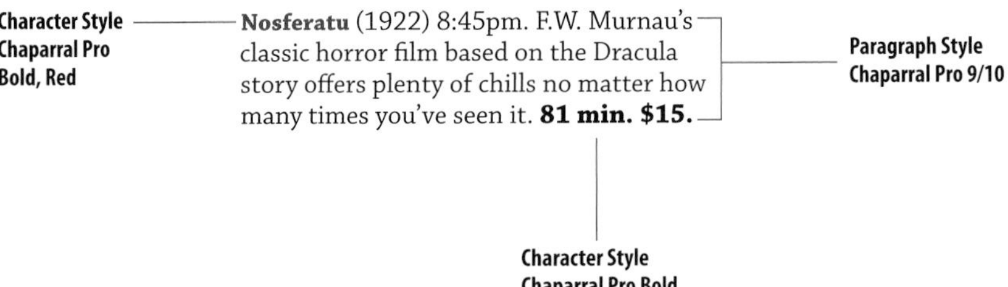

FIGURE 13.2 Paragraph Styles, Character Styles.

Using style sheets and not using styles sheets is the difference between you controlling InDesign and InDesign controlling you. Here are some reasons to use styles:

- Styles ensure consistency in formatting throughout your document, making for a better-designed piece.
- Styles enable you to change in seconds the entire formatting of your document, no matter how large, by changing your style definitions.
- And, as I mentioned before, the best reason of all: Styles save you hours and hours of drudgery.

Despite these irrefutable facts, many designers either underutilize or avoid styles altogether. I'm frequently amazed by the number of designers—many of whom should know better—who don't use styles, or who use them in a half-assed way. What's up with you people? You like the grind of unnecessary repetitive work?

I've had designers tell me: "I don't like to use styles, because I like to experiment with different designs," or "I don't want my pages to all look the same." These are exactly the reasons you *should* use styles. Far from stifling creativity, styles enhance it by making experimentation quick and easy. And just because your style names may be the same or similar from one document to the next doesn't mean the style definitions can't be completely different.

Creating Styles

Time spent creating style sheets is an investment that will repay you many times over throughout the lifespan of the publication. Though you should set up your Styles at the beginning of the design process, it is easy to add to your Style Sheet and edit your styles as your document evolves. There are several different approaches:

Creating a Style Based on Existing Text

1. Format the paragraph the way you want it to look.
2. Click the Create New Style icon at the bottom of the Paragraph Styles palette: "Paragraph Style 1" will appear in your Paragraph Styles palette.
3. Double click "Paragraph Style 1" to type a name for your Style and (optionally) specify a shortcut keystroke. If you want to add additional formatting, click the attributes list on the left and specify the options you want to add to your style. With Preview checked, you can see your formatting changes added to the paragraph.

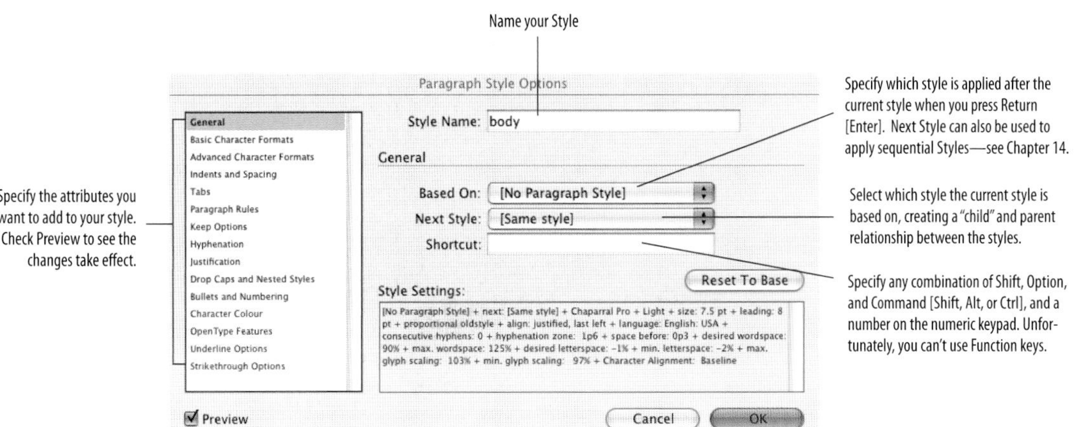

FIGURE 13.3 Paragraph Style Options.

TIP: Style Naming Conventions

- Name your styles in a logical way. Keep in mind that it's likely you'll need to come back to a document months or even years down the road, so you'll want a style-naming strategy that is transparent. Alternatively, you may need to hand over your InDesign document to someone else to finish. So that you don't spend a long time on the phone explaining why you named your styles after your favorite Radiohead songs, keep them simple.
- Because InDesign lists your styles in alphanumeric order, consider putting a two digit number in front of your most commonly used styles to force them to the top of the list in the Styles palette. Putting a unique two character identifier at the beginning of your style names also makes it easier to access those styles using Quick Apply by simply pressing Cmd-Return (Ctrl-Enter) then typing the first two characters to access the style.
- Styles are case-sensitive: Body Text and body text are recognized as two distinct styles, so be precise when naming your styles, or you may end up with two versions of the style and no idea which is the real one.

Choosing and Combining Typefaces

Setting up a Style Sheet for your document involves choosing what typeface—or combination of typefaces—to use. A well-constructed Style Sheet will make it easy to experiment with different font options. Here are some factors to consider when making your choices:

Versatility

The more complex the document, the more important the versatility of your typeface. Choosing a font is a bit like choosing a pair of shoes. If you are planning to go to the beach, then a pair of flip-flops may be all you need. But if you're going to the beach, then rock climbing, then out for a formal dinner, you'll need footwear that's more versatile—likewise with a typeface.

A versatile typeface will have a range of weights available: light, regular, semibold, bold, etc. You'll still be able to achieve the necessary contrast to indicate hierarchy of information. When The Guardian newspaper in London went through a major redesign in the fall of 2005, it switched to using a single font family—Guardian Egyptian—with 96 different weights and widths. Obviously, the demands of a daily newspaper and its associated supplements are more than is typical, but you get the idea.

Do the extras come as Standard?

A PostScript Type 1 font has a character set of only 256; an OpenType font has thousands—up to a maximum of 65,000. Those real small caps, old style numbers, and extra glyphs might really come in handy. Another huge advantage of OpenType fonts is that they are cross-platform.

Historical Connotations

Depending on the nature of your text, you might use history to inform your choice of font. For example, a book on modernist architecture could suggest Futura, while a book of 18th Century Italian poetry may be more appropriate in Bodoni.

Same Type Designer

In a similar vein, when looking for a complement to a given typeface, start by looking at other typefaces designed by the same type designer—the rationale being that the two faces will have a related sensibility. Some fonts are designed to be used together, their pairings suggested by their names: for example, Stone Serif and Stone Sans.

Contrast

Contrast is one of the most effective ways of establishing hierarchy. Choosing different fonts is just one way of adding contrast. Other parameters to mix and match are size, weight, structure, color, and form—for example, caps contrasted with lowercase, roman contrasted with italic. If you want contrast, then go for it. Don't use typefaces that are too similar—your readers won't pick up on the change, or the difference will be so subtle as to be disconcerting. Worse, it might look like you've chosen the "contrasting" font by mistake. Likewise, if you are mixing weights within the same font family, a black or heavy weight combined with a light weight will have far more impact than a bold mixed with a semibold.

Same X-Height

If you plan to use contrasting typefaces on the same line—for example, in a run-in head—make sure they have the same x-height, or adjust their relative sizes accordingly. Another example: with run-in heads, to ensure there are no jarring transitions from one font to the next.

A Tortured Tale: Em am eum quissendigna core er ing.

Out of Favor: Ut wis nullummy nim quisit wisl dolore te euguero do eugait ulputat.

Terror Strike: Lobor sed mincillum duismod ipissed tissi eugiamc onsenissi tincilis alit.

A

A Tortured Tale: Em am eum quissendigna core er ing.

Out of Favor: Ut wis nullummy nim quisit wisl dolore te euguero do eugait ulputat.

Terror Strike: Lobor sed mincillum duismod ipissed tissi eugiamc onsenissi tincilis ali.

B

FIGURE 13.4 Mixing x-heights. In example **A**, the run-in head (Helvetica Neue Black Condensed) is the same size (10 pt.) as the body text (Minion), creating a disparity in x-heights. In example **B**, the run-in head has been reduced by 1 point to equalize the x-heights of the two fonts.

Loading Styles from Another InDesign Document

If you have an InDesign file with a style sheet already created, there's no need to reinvent the wheel. You can load those styles from one document to another. You can even import styles from Microsoft Word and RTF documents. Choose Load All Styles (to bring in Paragraph, Character and Object styles from the source document), then navigate to it and click Open. Note, you will not be able to load styles from an InDesign CS2 document into a CS document; you can do it in the other direction.

With InDesign CS2 you can import specific styles and determine how to deal with any style name conflicts: Where the style name is the same in both documents, you can choose to use the Incoming Style Definition or to rename the incoming style, which will have "copy" appended to its style name. (You can rename the style later if you wish.)

Creating the Style "Blind"

Using the Paragraph Style Options dialog box, you can create as many styles as you need without having a single character on your page. With experience, you can visualize what a style will look like without needing to see it formatted on your page, which makes setting up a Style Sheet much faster.

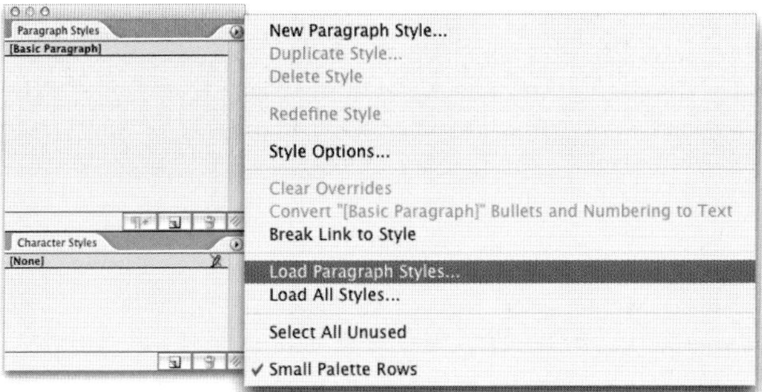

FIGURE 13.5 Load Styles.

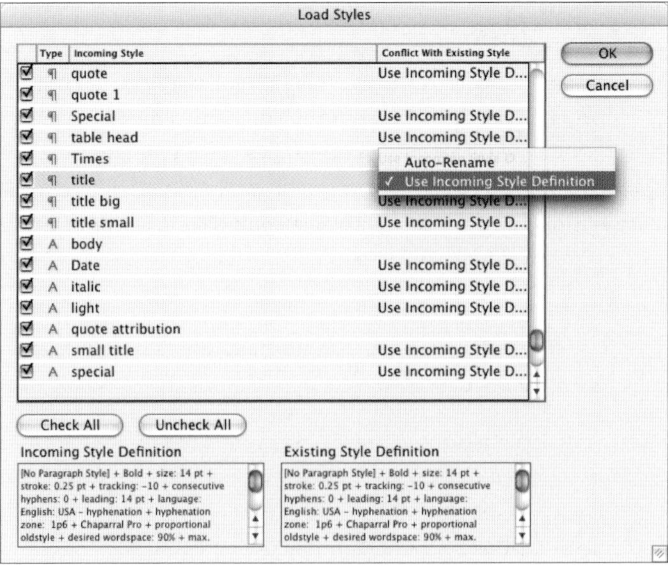

FIGURE 13.6 Mapping Styles.

Basing Styles on Other Styles

Hierarchy is a big concept in typography. Hierarchy gives your documents structure. Hierarchy is not about working for the Man—it's about effective communication. Take a simple example: Your headings and subheadings will probably use the same font. For this reason you need to consider carefully the relationship between them. By basing one style on another, you create more than just a visual link between the styles. When you edit the base or "parent" style, the attributes that it shares with its "offspring" styles will also change. To establish this relationship between styles, choose the parent style in the Based On menu. The new style becomes the "child" style.

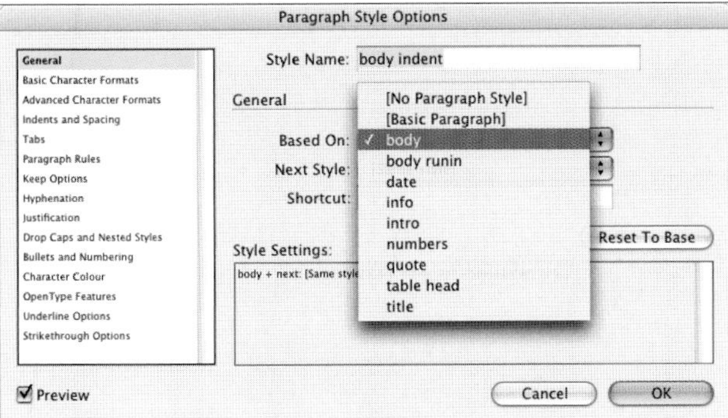

FIGURE 13.7 Basing one style upon another. The "child" inherits all the formatting of its "parent" style.

Applying Styles

To apply a paragraph style, place your Type Tool cursor anywhere inside the paragraph then click on the Style name in the Paragraph Styles palette. There is no need to select the whole paragraph—unless of course you like doing things the hard way. If you want to apply a paragraph style to more than one contiguous paragraph, drag your cursor through those paragraphs. Again, you don't need the whole paragraph selected; you just need to make contact with at least a part of each of the paragraphs.

To apply a character style, you need to first select the text. Character styles are applied to specific ranges of text, so no sloppiness allowed here.

Applying a paragraph style doesn't remove any existing character formatting or character styles applied to that paragraph—unless you clear overrides (see below). When you apply the style, if the text has additional formatting that is not part of the style definition, a plus sign (+) appears next to the current paragraph style in the Paragraph Styles palette.

Headlines

When chapter headings, headlines, and subheads are set in upper and lower-case, there are a couple of different case conventions:

Up Style: The most common approach, where every major word is capitalized.

Down Style: Also known as Sentence Style, where only the initial cap and proper nouns are capitalized. This style is gaining in popularity and has the obvious editorial appeal that no one has to agonize over whether a word is a "major" word and thus needs to be capitalized.

Unfortunately, InDesign doesn't allow you to specify the case of the type as part of a style definition. However, you can change the case of a selected range of text by choosing Type > Change Case.

FIGURE 13.8 Up Style (example **A**) vs. Down Style Heads (example **B**).

A **How the Brain Builds its Image of the Body**

B **How the brain builds its image of the body**

TIP: Assign a keyboard shortcut to your styles and you'll be able to apply them even faster. However, only keys on the numeric keypad (in combination with modifier keys) can be used for style shortcuts. To really speed things up, try applying your styles in the Story Editor. (I wonder why can't you assign F-keys as shortcuts for Style names. What's up with that?)

Character styles, on the other hand, replace any local formatting, and because you can't apply two Character Styles to the same text as soon as you apply a new Character Style, the old one is removed.

Clearing Overrides

When you add formatting to text that already has a paragraph or character style applied, you are overriding the style definition. To put it another way: You've defined a paragraph style, applied it to a piece of text, and then contradicted your style definition by adding additional formatting. You can tell which text has overrides applied because when selected a plus sign (+) appears next to its style name. Maybe this local formatting is what you want, maybe not. Maybe you've inherited the document from someone else—someone who hasn't used styles as effectively as you would have liked and you want to clear the overrides.

FIGURE 13.9 The Overrides Button.

There are several ways to approach this:

To clear all local formatting, but retain any Character Styles applied to the paragraph, Option/Alt+click the style name in the Paragraph Styles palette. Alternatively, click once on the Clear Overrides button in the Control palette.

To remove just the local character formatting (retaining any local paragraph formatting), Command/Ctrl+click the Overrides button.

To remove just the local paragraph formatting (retaining the character formatting), Command+Shift+click/Ctrl+Shift+click the Clear Overrides button.

This works the same way with Character Styles.

To clear all local formatting *and* Character Styles: Option+Shift (Alt-Shift) +click the style name in the Paragraph Styles palette.

TIP: The Plus Sign Curious about exactly what the + refers to? Hover the cursor over the style in the Paragraph Styles palette and a tool tip pops up with details of the local formatting.

FIGURE 13.10 Find/Change can be used to "map" local formatting (perhaps imported with a Word or RTF file) to paragraph styles.

TIP: Using Find/Change Find/Change is a great way to find all instances of a particular style and replace it with another. You can also use Find/Change to convert local formatting into styles. For example, if you inherit a document where the "subheads" have been locally styled in a particular font, you can look for that formatting and replace it with a specific style name.

Quick Apply

When you have a lot of styles—Paragraph, Character, and Object (see next chapter)—it can mean scrolling through long lists to get to the one you're after. To dramatically speed up your workflow use Quick Apply, a simple new feature in InDesign CS2 that allows you to find a style quickly by typing the first few characters of its name.

Select the text or frame to which you want to apply the style, choose Cmd+Return (Ctrl+Enter), start typing the name of the style, and you'll be taken to the closest match. You can use the Up and Down Arrow keys on the keyboard to move through the list. Simply press Return/Enter to apply the style.

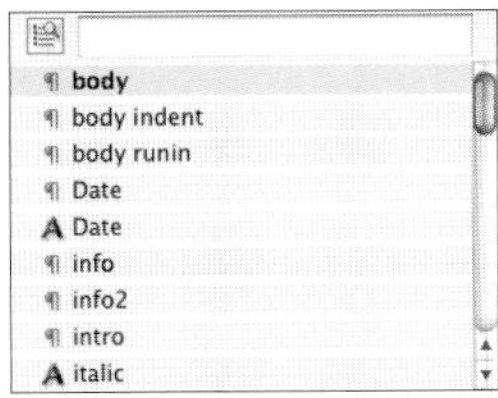

FIGURE 13.11 Quick Apply.

Editing Styles

The beauty of styles is that you can change their definition at any time. Changing a style definition means that all the text formatted with that style changes to match the new style definition. This has been a staple feature of all page layout programs since the Stone Age. Yet it still blows me away.

Styles allow you unprecedented flexibility in experimenting with the appearance of your document. A few simple clicks and you can totally transform the appearance of your pages. It's a beautiful thing.

There are several ways to edit a style, but to my mind the best (and safest) is to Control+Click (Right Mouse+Click) on the style name in the appropriate Styles palette. That way, there's no danger of inadvertently applying the style where you don't want it.

Once you're in the Styles Options box, make as many or as few changes as you want, click OK, and, as they say in cockney gangster movies, "Bob's your uncle."

Redefining Styles

Alternatively, and just to shake things up a bit, instead of editing the style, you can modify a paragraph with local overrides, decide that's how you'd like the style to look, then redefine the style based on the modified paragraph: With the paragraph selected choose Redefine Style from the fly-out menu of the Paragraph Styles palette.

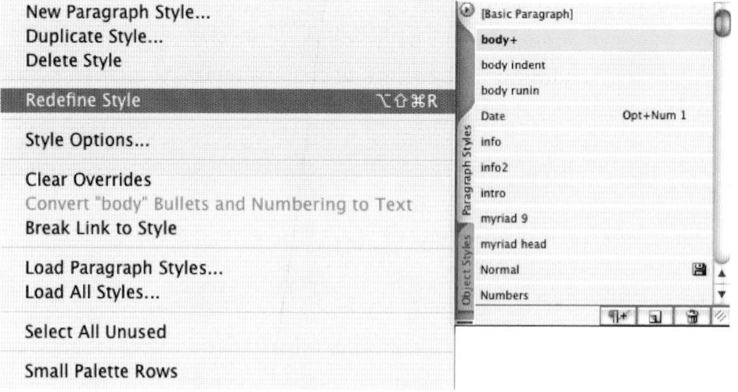

FIGURE 13.12 Redefine Style.

Creating Default Styles

If you create paragraph styles, character styles, or color swatches with no document open, the styles and swatches will be in every new document. Most documents have a similar structure: heads, subheads, body text, captions, sidebar text, etc. So it might be worth creating a default style sheet so you're ready to go every time you create a new document. Just because their styles names may be the same doesn't mean they have to look the same from one document to another. What's important is the hierarchy of the styles.

Make sure you have no InDesign document open when you create your styles or load them from an existing InDesign document. That way they will show up in every InDesign document you create thereafter. Of course this doesn't mean that all your documents will look the same. You have infinite choices for how you define your styles, but just about all documents will have such features as headlines, subheads, body text, captions, etc. What you make them look like is entirely up to you.

A Typical Style Sheet

This type of style sheet would be appropriate for a magazine or newspaper publication. These are just the basic styles; typically there would be styles defined for all standard type elements.

Head1

Heads will likely be in the bold or even black weight. Depending on the typeface, they may be negatively tracked and tightly leaded—contributing to a dark type color. The purpose of the Head1 headline is to make the reader want more. Typically such headlines do this by posing a question or telling part—the best part—of the story.

Head2

A secondary level head or subhead will be in the same typeface as the first-level head, its size reduced to indicate a lower level on the hierarchy and space added before (and possibly after) to separate it from the preceding text. The secondary level head will help the reader navigate the body text and break it up into chunks to provide visual relief.

Head3

A third level of heading could be a run-in head, one in which the heading is part of the same paragraph as the body text that follows. The run-in head would need to be a Character Style, which could be nested in the paragraph style definition.

Body

This will likely (though not necessarily) be a serif face in the regular or book weight at a size of 8 to 11 points. First line indents indicate the beginning of a new paragraph.

Body No Indent

Based on Body, with first line indent set to 0.

Body First

Based on Body, with no first line indent and with some kind of drop cap treatment.

Byline

The author's credit, typically based on body style, differentiated by bold weight and paragraph spacing above and/or below.

Caption

With so many competing demands on peoples' time, captions may be what people read first, so a caption should provide enough information for the browsing reader to decide whether to continue reading. More than just stating the obvious, a caption should clearly establish the relationship between the image and the text.

Intro

In magazines, to create an entry point for the reader the opening paragraph, or the first lines of the opening paragraph, are often set in larger type, possibly in bold type, possibly in a contrasting font. Often this intro paragraph will be set over a wider measure than the body text. Sometimes the byline will be incorporated into this first paragraph.

Picture Credit

Can be as small as 5 or 6 points, often rotated 90 degrees.

Pull Quote

A pull quote is an excerpt "pulled" from the text and used as a graphic element. Pull quotes are intended to catch and hold the reader's interest. They should be thought-provoking and succinct. Pull quotes also add visual interest to a layout, especially when you have few photographs or illustrations to work with.

The pull quote is display text. It should offer a strong visual contrast to your body text and be positioned to catch the eye of a potential reader who's skimming or flipping pages.

TIP: Getting Rid of Unwanted Styles When you import Word text or Styles from other InDesign documents, you'll likely end up with several unwanted styles in your styles palettes. Leaving these around is apt to create confusion—either for you or for anyone else who may work on the document. You can get rid of them on a case-by-case basis, but the quickest way to zap them all at once is to choose Select All Unused in the Styles palette menu, and then click the Trash button. It gives you that same satisfying feeling you get after clearing out your closets.

The pull quote should be positioned on or before the page where the excerpted text appears. Long sentences should be edited into tight, provocative pull quote versions. They can be set off with rules, be reversed, set in a contrasting color, or combined with decorative quotations marks. If you put your pull quote in quotation marks, make sure you are not distorting the meaning of the text. See the next chapter for information on formatting pull quotes using Object Styles and Chapter 17: "Text Wraps" for information on how to anchor a pull quote to a specific portion of text.

Sidebar

An article that, as the name suggests, typically runs by the side of the main article, though it can mean any supplementary article. It is graphically separate from the main text but contextually linked to it.

Sidebar Head

The heading of a sidebar article.

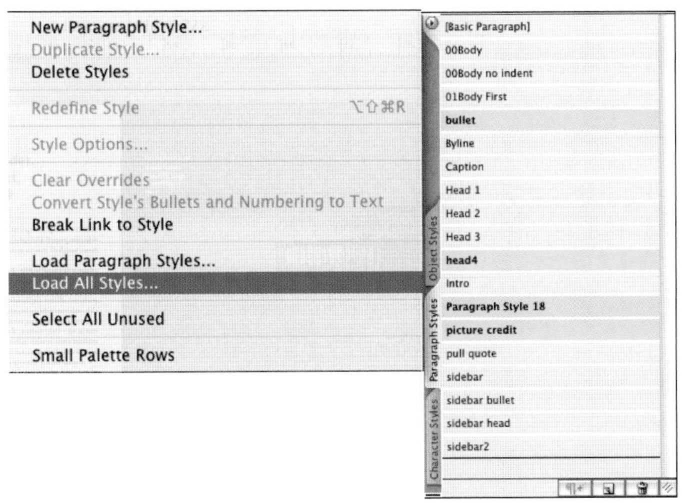

FIGURES 13.16 Purging those unused (and probably unwanted) styles.

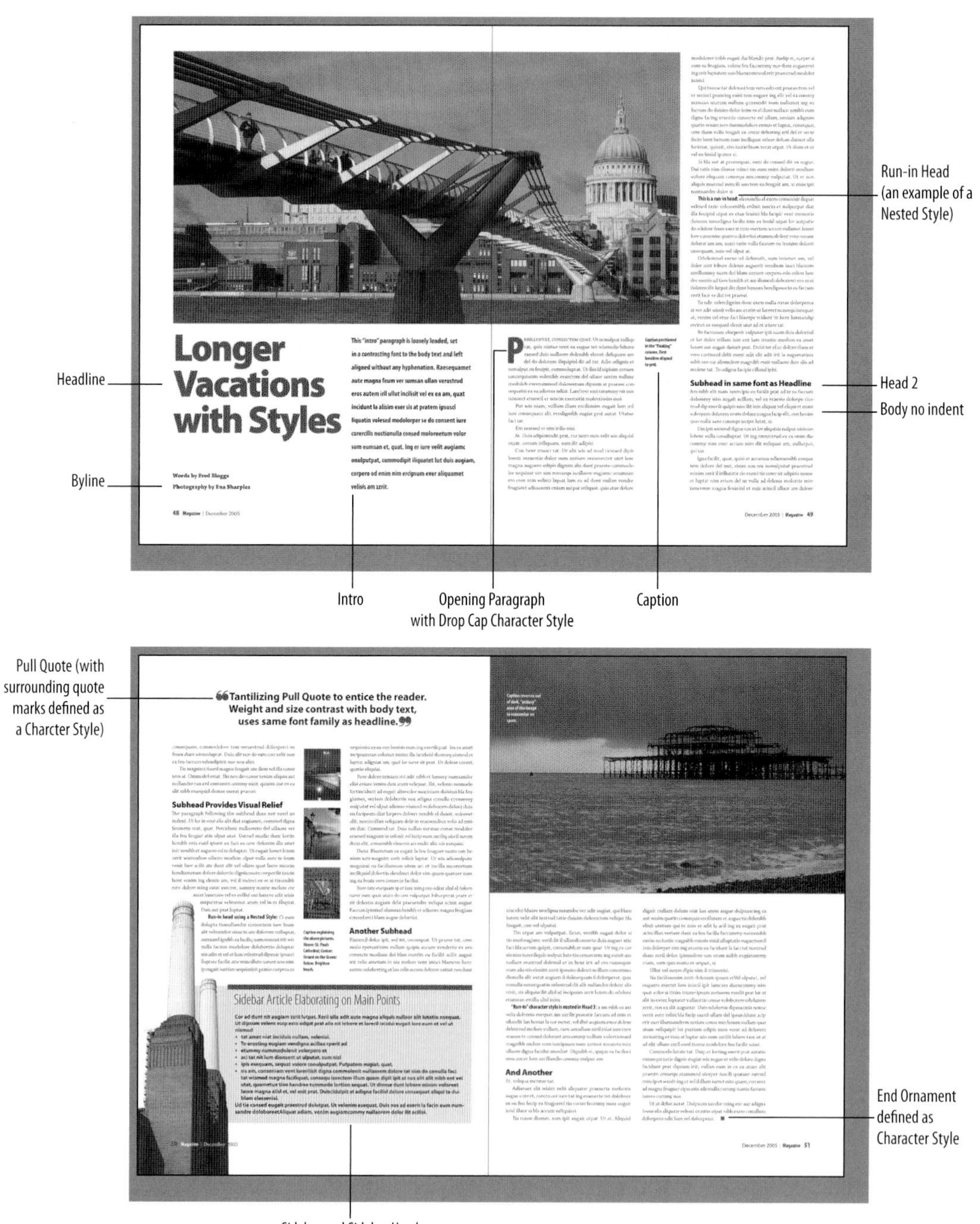

FIGURE 13.13 Spread showing all in use.

The Mother of All Styles: The Book Feature

You can supercharge your styles management by using the Book feature to have one set of styles apply to a group of documents. Once you have created a Book you can synchronize the styles and swatches in your "booked" documents all at once or one at a time. The Book feature is also a fast way to add the styles from one document to a bunch of others.

Specify a Style Source or "master" document, by clicking in the leftmost column, then synchronize the documents in the book. Styles and swatches are copied from the Style Source to all the documents in the book, replacing any styles and swatches that have identical names, Styles and swatches in the documents that aren't in the style source are unchanged.

You can synchronize the book while documents in the book are closed. InDesign opens the closed documents, makes any changes, and then saves and closes the documents. Documents that are open when you synchronize are changed but not saved.

TIP: Printing Out a Style Sheet from Word InDesign offers no facility for printing out the specifications of your Style Sheet, but you can do this using Microsoft Word. In InDesign, create as many blank paragraphs as you have styles. Assign each of your styles to one of these blank paragraphs. Choose File > Export and choose RTF as the file format. Open the text file in Word and choose File > Print. In the Print dialog box, choose Styles from the Print What pop-up menu.

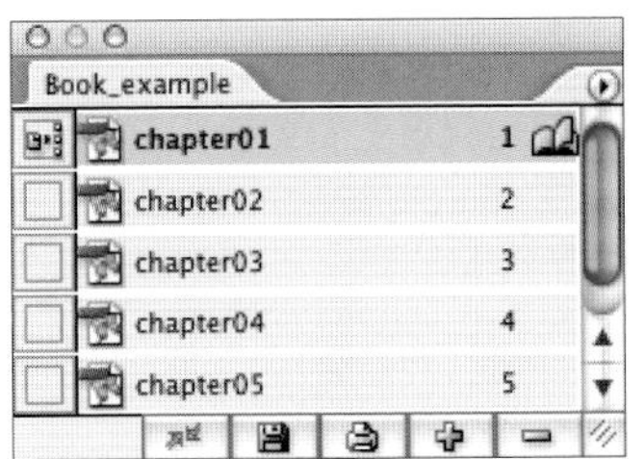

FIGURE 13.14 Book.

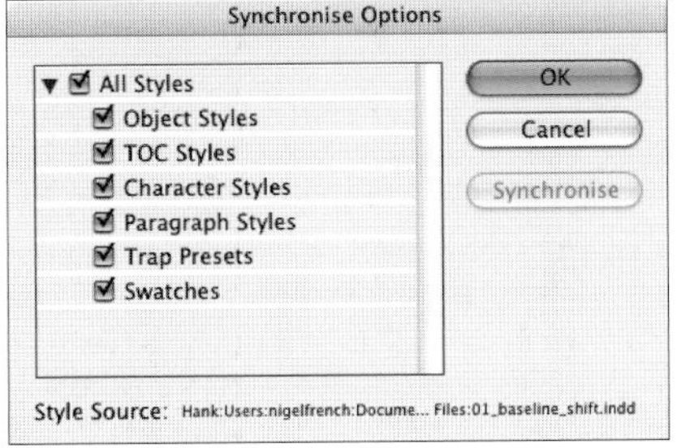

FIGURE 13.15 In Synchronize Options specify which styles and swatches are copied from the Style Source to the other booked documents, and then choose Synchronize.

Importing Styles from a Microsoft Word Document

When you place a Word document, checking Show Import Options allows you to determine how to handle any Style name conflicts. You can use the InDesign Style Definition (the default) or you can choose to redefine the InDesign Style with the incoming Word definition. For more control, choose Custom Style Import to map specific Word styles to specific InDesign styles.

If you already have a style with the same name as the Word style, the style is not imported. Text in the Word document takes on the formatting of the InDesign style with the same name.

A nice workflow feature is the ability to save a preset—a big time-saver if you import Word files that always use the same style names.

TIP: Use the same style names in Word and InDesign document and you'll minimize the amount of time you need to spend on reformatting text.

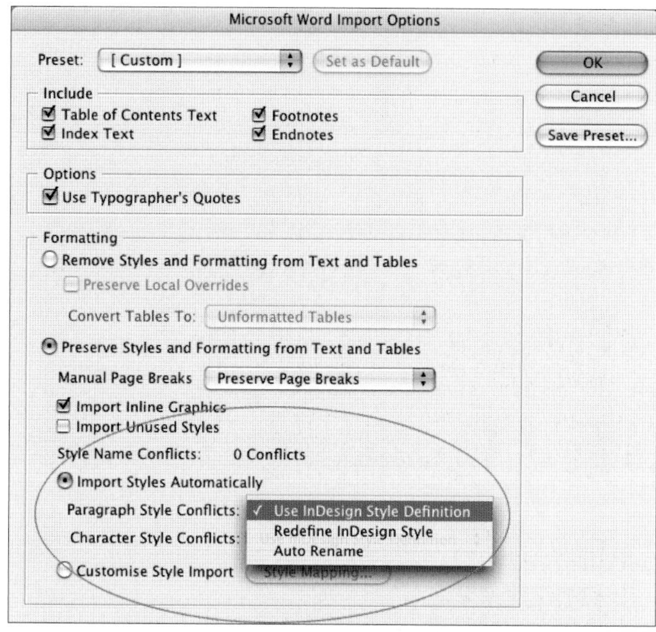

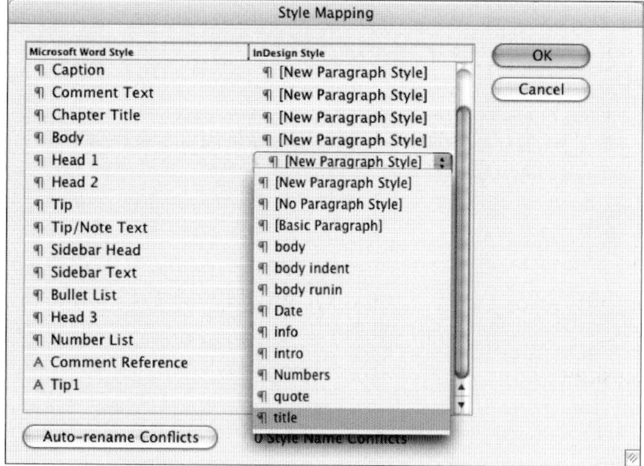

FIGURES 13.17A AND 13.17B Word Import Options A and B.

Using the Eyedropper to Create Pseudo Styles

Need to quickly apply the formats of one paragraph to another but don't want to create a style? You can use the eyedropper to sample the character and paragraph formats from one piece of text and apply them to a selected range of text. Simply select the text you want to copy the formats *to*, then choose the Eyedropper tool and click on the text you want to copy the formats *from*. This also works with object formats. Note, there is no relationship between the two pieces of text beyond the visual. They are not thereafter controlled by the same style sheet.

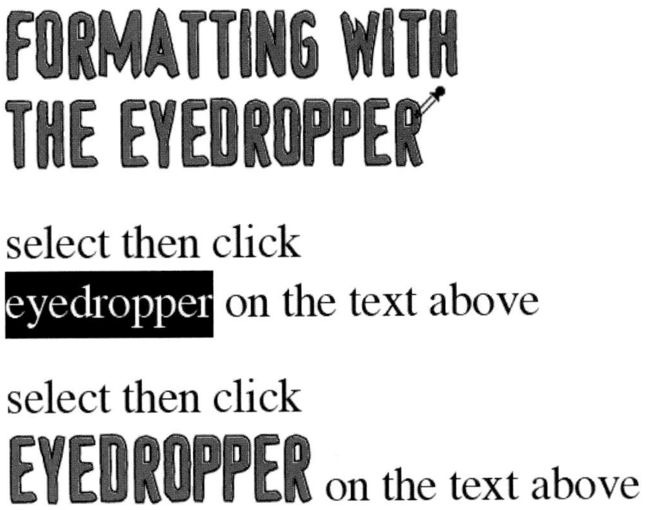

FORMATTING WITH
THE EYEDROPPER

select then click
eyedropper on the text above

select then click
EYEDROPPER on the text above

FIGURES 13.18 Using the Eyedropper. Select a range of text, and then click with the eyedropper on piece of text to copy its formats. To copy the paragraph attributes only, hold Shift.

Up Next

A discussion of the design considerations involved in setting up your InDesign documents and InDesign's toolset you can use to do this as quickly and efficiently as possible.

CHAPTER 14

Mo' Style

THIS CHAPTER LOOKS AT SOME STRAIGHTFORWARD TECHNIQUES that are the icing on the delicious three-tiered cake of Paragraph, Character, and Object Styles. The reasons for taking advantage of these features are the same reasons for using Styles in the first place: consistency, ease of editing, and the enormous amount of time saved. These techniques are quickly learned and will pay you back thousands of times over for the time you invest learning them.

Paragraph Rules

If you've ever drawn a rule above a line of text, only to have the text reflow and leave the rule in the dust, you'll find Paragraph Rules an invaluable feature. With Paragraph Rules you can add a rule above and/or below the text and have that rule move with the paragraph when the text is edited. No more chasing after the text to reposition those lines.

NOTE: The amount of offset added to paragraph rules does not alter the paragraph spacing of the paragraph.

Rules Above starts at the baseline and extends up. Using a positive offset shifts the line up relative to the baseline; a negative offset shifts the line down relative to the baseline.

Rules Below starts at the baseline and extends down. Using a positive offset shifts the line down relative to the baseline; a negative offset shifts the line up relative to the baseline.

The techniques below involve shifting the rules relative to the baseline of the type, sometimes so much so that the terms *above* and *below* become meaningless.

FIGURE 14.1 Different types of paragraph rules.

PARAGRAPH RULES ROCK!

A — A Rule Above set to span the full column width.

PARAGRAPH RULES ROCK!

B — A Rule Above set to span the width of the text.

PARAGRAPH RULES ROCK!

C — As above, but with the text indented 3 points and the rule indented -3 points on the left and right to give some breathing room around the type.

NOTE: When working with paragraph rules, "baseline" refers to the baseline of the *first* line for a rule above and the baseline of the *last* line for a rule below. When working with a one-line paragraph (usually the case with paragraph rules) the two rules are positioned relative to the same baseline.

PARAGRAPH RULES ROCK!

D — A blue rule below set to text width; a yellow rule above set to column width. Note Rules Below are above Rules Above in the stacking order. This is because the text in a text frame is drawn from the top of the frame to the bottom. Rules Above come before rules below.

PARAGRAPH RULES ROCK!

E — A 1-point Rule Below set to column width sitting on top of a 12-point Rule Above.

PARAGRAPH RULES ROCK!

F — A 10-point Rule Below with a Dotted Style on top of 10-point solid rule.

PARAGRAPH RULES ROCK!

G — A 1-point Rule Below (black) sitting on top of a 6-point Rule Above (blue), which is indented left and right. Note, that Rule Below is *above* Rule Above in the stacking order.

PARAGRAPH RULES ROCK!

H — A 16-point white Rule Below sitting on top of an 18-point blue Rule Above. Both rules are set to span the width of the text.

All heads are Myriad Pro Bold Condensed 12/12

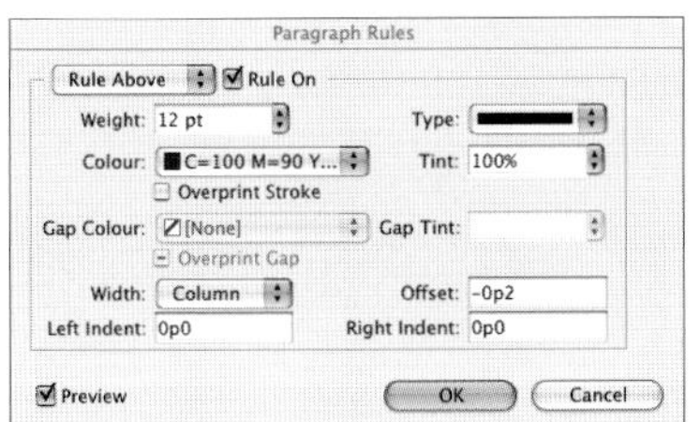

FIGURE 14.2

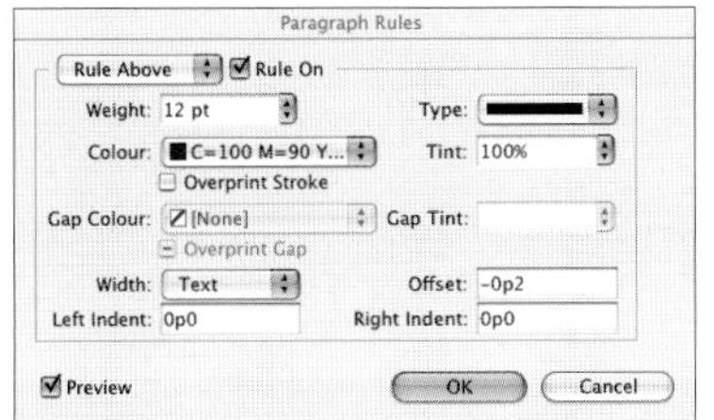

FIGURE 14.3

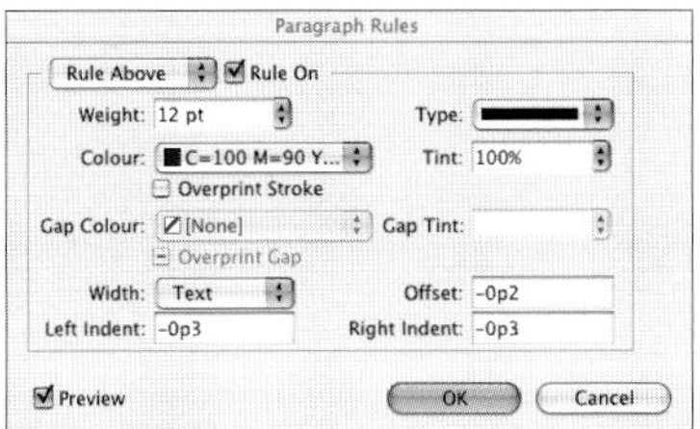

FIGURE 14.4

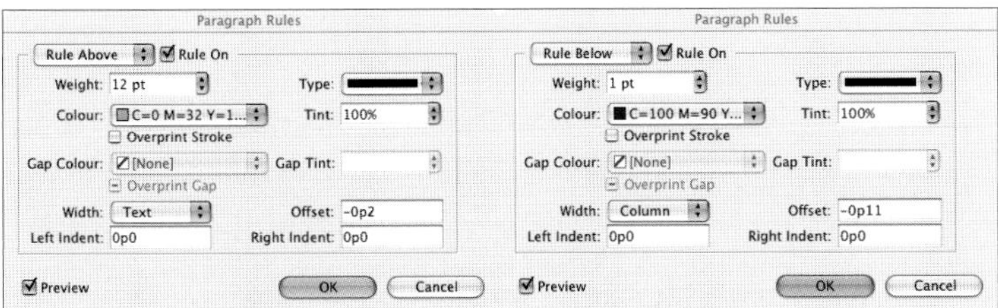

FIGURE 14.5

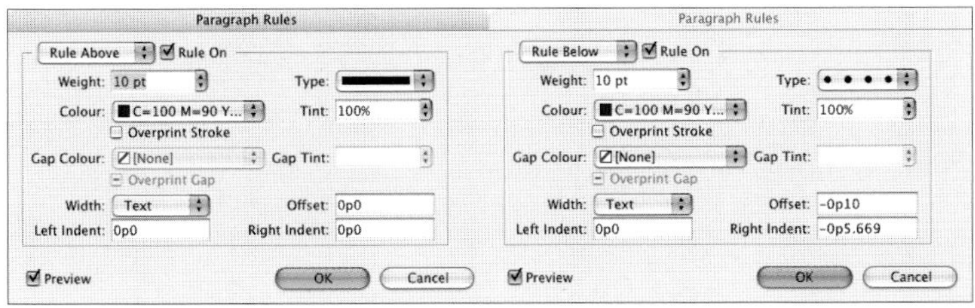

FIGURE 14.6

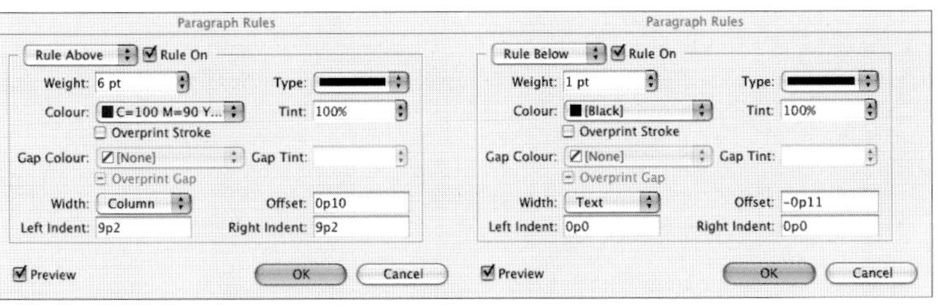

FIGURE 14.7

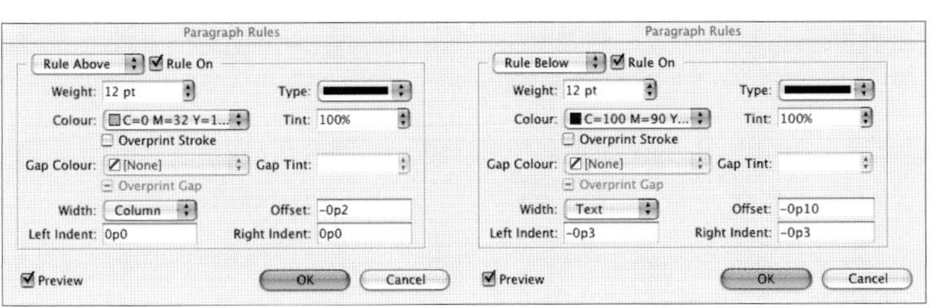

FIGURE 14.8

Sequential Styles

It used to be that the Next Style option was pretty underwhelming. All it did was determine what style the next paragraph would take on when you pressed Return (Enter) for the next line. Unless you keyed your text directly into InDesign, this was not particularly useful. Well, Next Style still does this, but in InDesign CS2, it does a whole lot more besides. You can now use Next Style to apply a style, which in turn applies the specified Next Style to the next paragraph. If *that* next paragraph has a Next Style option, the next style will be applied to the third paragraph, and so on, creating a cascade of automatic style formatting! In any document where the text styling follows a consistent pattern—which is a big percentage of documents—this can save hours of donkeywork. Imagine, for example, an event listing where the date style is followed by the title style, which in turn is followed by the description style. Define *date*'s Next Style as *title*, and define *title*'s Next Style as *description*. Then select the *date* style. In the Paragraph Styles palette, Ctrl+click (right-click) the parent style, and then choose Apply (Style Name) then Next Style. Voila! Three paragraphs in one.

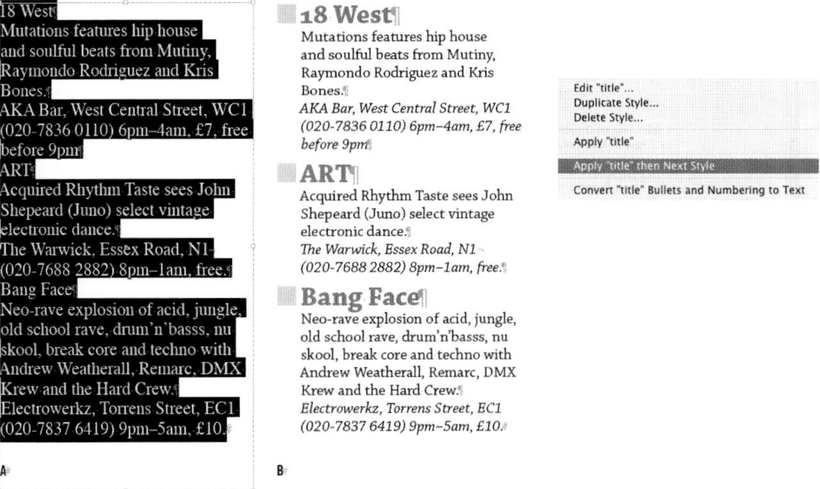

FIGURE 14.9 Three styles are used in this example: Title, body, and info. The Next Style for Title is body, the Next Style for body is info, and—to complete the loop—the Next Style for info is Title. Using sequential styles it is possible to format the whole text block with a single click.

Nested Styles

Nested Styles will rock your world. If you're like me—essentially lazy, but love gadgets and stuff that makes life easier—then Nested Styles is for you. Nested Styles allows you to apply Paragraph Styles and Character Styles at the same time. This is profound, so let me reiterate: Nested Styles allows you to apply a Paragraph Style with a Character Style (or styles) applied to specific range or ranges of a paragraph. All with a single mouse click! Nested Styles can eliminate hours of repetitive drudgery, freeing you up to be more creative.

IT WAS THE BEST of times, it was the worst of times, it was the age of wisdom, it was the age of foolishness, it was the epoch of belief, it was the epoch of incredulity, it was the season of Light, it was the season of Darkness, it was the spring of hope, it was the winter of despair, we had everything before us, we had nothing before us, we were all going direct to Heaven, we were all going direct the other way—in short, the period was so far like the present period, that some of its noisiest authorities insisted on its being received, for good or for evil, in the superlative degree of comparison only.

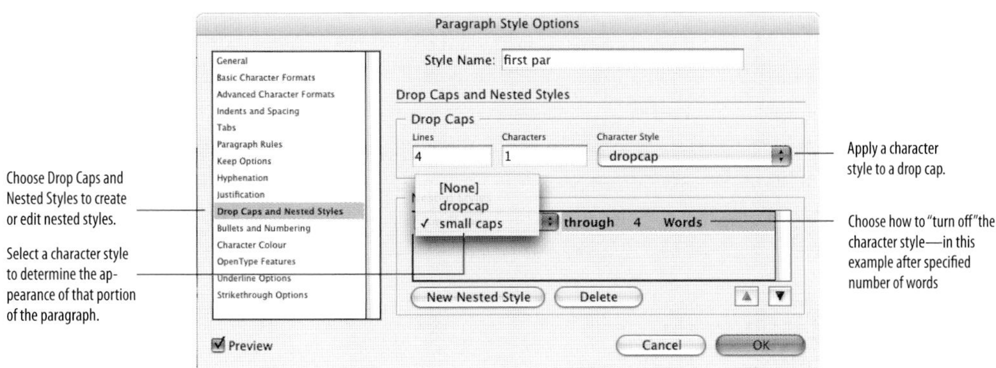

FIGURE 14.10 Adding Nested Styles to an opening paragraph.

To create a Nested Style, you need to add a Character Style—or styles—to a Paragraph Style definition.

1. Ctrl+click (right mouse click) on the Paragraph Style you want to edit.
2. Click Drop Caps and Nested Styles.
3. Click New Nested Style and choose from the list of available Character Styles.
4. Specify how to "turn off" the Character Style. Depending on the nature of the Nested Style either choose a specified number of words or characters, or choose a condition from the drop down menu. You can also type a specific character such as a colon (:) into this field.

Choosing Through includes the character that ends the Nested Style, while choosing Up To formats only those characters that precede the designated character.

If you have more than one Nested Style you can use the up button or down button to change the order of the styles in the list, determining the order in which the formatting is applied. The formatting defined by the second style begins where the formatting of the first style concludes.

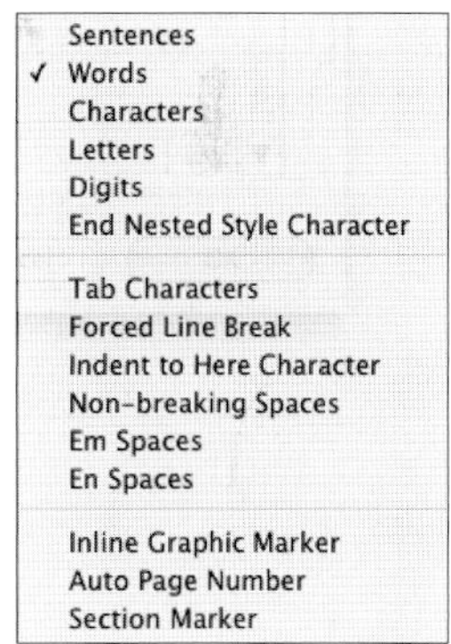

FIGURE 14.11 Apply Nested Styles from the beginning of the paragraph forward. The Nested Style will be "on" until the specified number of the chosen delimiter—for example 4 Words, 1 sentence, 1 en space—is found in the text. You can also type a specific character such as a colon (:) into this field.

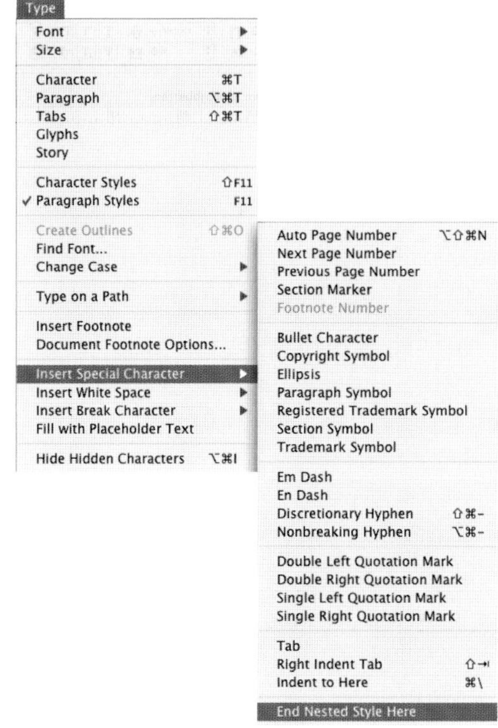

FIGURE 14.12 Insert End Nested Style Here.

TIP: Use a keyboard shortcut to insert the End Nested Style Here character. Create your own custom keyboard shortcut to quickly place this character in your text. I use Ctrl+Cmd+Option+X (on a Mac).

TIP: Using Multiple Delimiters What if there just isn't anything that you can designate as a consistent delimiter? Well, it's possible to accommodate just about any kind of variation by entering multiple characters in the delimiter field of a Nested Style. If you enter all the possible characters that could end a sentence—.?!—InDesign will use the first one it encounters to turn off the Nested Style.

All well and good, but what if there's nothing consistent about your paragraphs that you can use to turn off the Nested Style? Enter the End Nested Style Here character. The End Nested Style Here character is an invisible character you can insert into your text to turn off character styling at that specific point.

Here are some practical applications of Nested Styles:

Run-in Heads

Run-ins are usually third-level subheads that have the heading on the same line as the body text that follows. The heading is distinguished from the body text with a contrasting font. The key with run-in heads—and for all Nested Styles—is some identifiably consistent element. This might be separating the subhead from the body text with a colon or an en space.

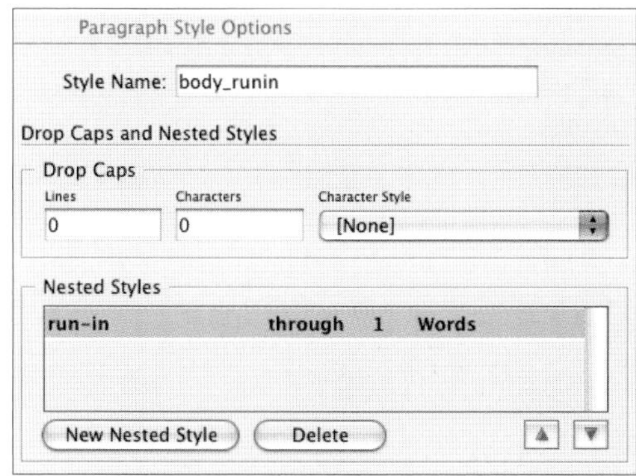

CLAIM TO FAME: Alit il del delit nim vel ullandre feui bla facilit nim dit adipit inis auguer suscidunt ut utem iuscil il dui tie do consed.

PERSONAL STYLE: Dolore te volor sustrud exer sustrud min veliquam quip estrud tis amconulla feu feugiatio corperat lum quip exer alismod eum aut ipit lor ing ex enisi. Ommolobore tem zzrit, commy nullaor si.

POWER QUOTIENT: Hendit autpat. Dip et, susto euis eliquatet lamcore ming ea adip et, commolessi tatue er sim eummy numsan esed mod tat.

FIGURE 14.13 Run-in Head.

Contents Page

A common style of a contents page uses the page number as a run-in head. Additional run-in elements can include identifying tags like "Cover Story" or "Feature Article." In the example shown, this tag is reversed out of a gray bar. As we saw with Paragraph Rules, it's easy to create reverse heads that move with the flow of the text. However, in this example the "rule" is applied to only a portion of the paragraph and therefore needs to be defined as a Character Style. To make this possible, use Underline Styles.

DESTINATIONS

27 Na facillan er sim quis eu feui euis am inim ad et praestis diatem adigna at.

37 **COVER STORY** Consectet, susto et alit praesent autpatis autet iriustrud tat.

40 Esequam nis at velis am quatummolor

45 **COVER STORY** Velenibh exeros num veraese quatuer sendrer aessit veriusci tinci ero dit aliquisit

60 Modionse dolessi. Ommod exerat. Ut vel et

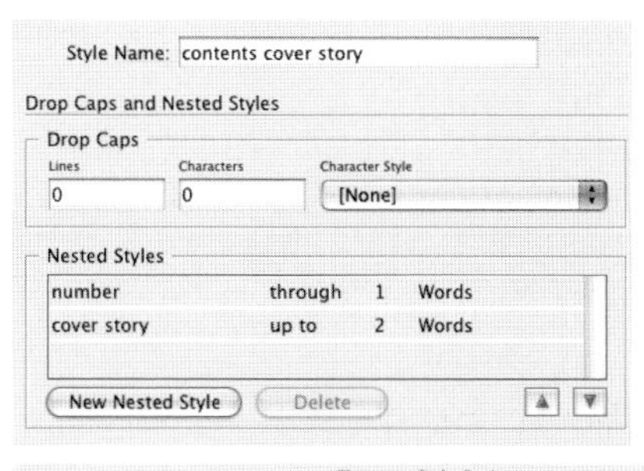

Character Style Options
General
Basic Character Formats
Advanced Character Formats
Character Colour
OpenType Features
Underline Options
Strikethrough Options
Style Name: cover story
Underline Options
Options
Underline On
Weight: 9.354 pt
Type:
Offset: -3.5 pt
Colour: [Black] 60%
Tint:
Overprint Stroke
Gap Colour: [Black] 60%
Gap Tint:
Overprint Gap
Preview
Cancel
OK

FIGURE 14.14 Contents Page.

Review Section

In this example, Nested Styles can be combined with Sequential Styles. The review section follows a consistent format: Artist and Album Title as the first paragraph, Record Label and Star Rating as the second, and the review itself as the third paragraph. Paragraphs 1 and 2 contain Nested Styles (with an en space delimiter) and a Next Style specified. Select the three paragraphs and Ctrl+Click (Right Click) on the Artist Paragraph Style. From the context menu, choose Apply Artist then Next Style.

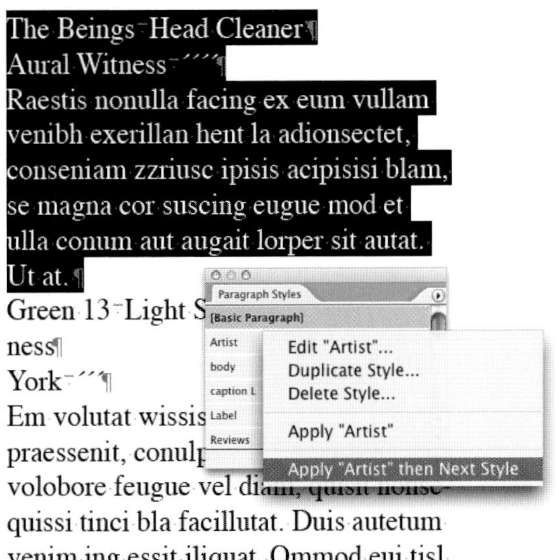

FIGURE 14.15 Review Section: From moth to butterfly in 2 clicks!

THE BEINGS Head Cleaner

Aural Witness ★★★★

Raestis nonulla facing ex eum vullam venibh exerillan hent la adionsectet, conseniam zzriusc ipisis acipisisi blam, se magna cor suscing eugue mod et ulla conum aut augait lorper sit autat. Ut at.

GREEN 13 Light Shuts Out the Darkness

York ★★★

Em volutat wissisit, venisse quamet praessenit, conulpute te modo conulput volobore feugue vel diam, quisit nonsequissi tinci bla facillutat. Duis autetum venim ing essit iliquat. Ommod eui tisl utet prat wisl iuscipit nulpute minim deliquam ing eugait.

Object Styles

TIP: When you create a Style Sheet you may not be the only person who uses it. Or you may find yourself returning to Style Sheets that you created weeks, months, even years before. So that you and the other members of your team don't get confused by Nested Styles, adopt a naming convention that is transparent. For example, append "_nested" after the style name.

Part of the natural evolution of global formatting, Object Styles takes the concept of Paragraph and Characters styles and applies it to text and graphic frames as well as to lines and pen paths. Within one style name, you can save such attributes as fill color, stroke weight, stroke color, the number of columns in the frame, drop shadow, etc. You can also incorporate into the Object Style definition the Paragraph Style that should be applied to the text inside the frame. By using the Next Style option it is possible to apply paragraph styles sequentially to more than one paragraph.You get to control which settings the Object Style affects by including or excluding a category in the style definition.

Just like Paragraph and Character styles, you can base one Object Style on another, creating a parent-and-child relationship so that when you change the base or parent style, the "child" style changes as well.

Each document begins its life with a [Basic Text Frame] and a [Basic Graphics Frame] Object Style. By default these styles are applied respectively to any text or graphic frames you create. Just as with the [Basic Paragraph] style you can edit these [Basic] styles, but you can't delete them. If you want to change these default styles for a text frame, choose Default Text Frame Style or Default Graphics Frame Style from the Object Styles palette fly-out menu, and then select from your available Object Styles.

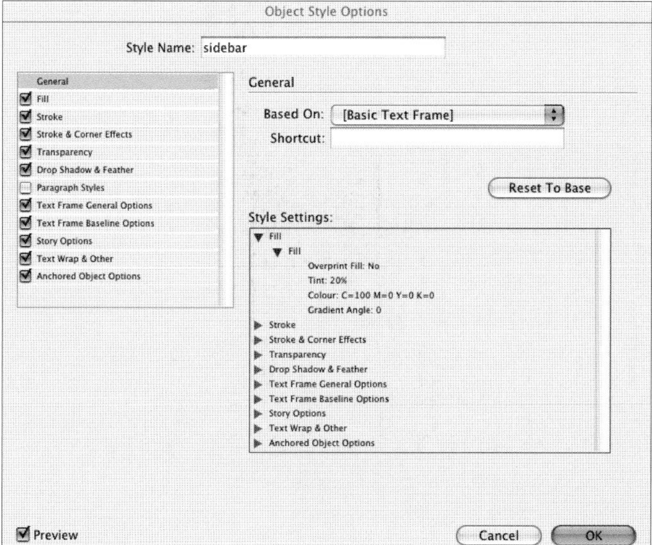

FIGURE 14.16 Object Style Options.

"All animals are equal but some animals are more equal than others."
— George Orwell

A

"All animals are equal but some animals are more equal than others."
— George Orwell

B

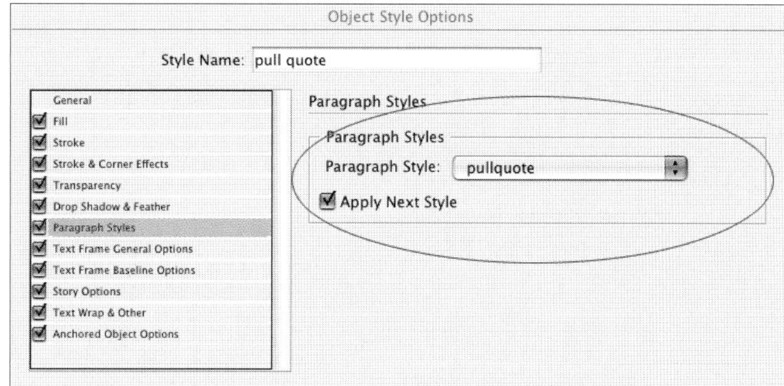

FIGURE 14.17 Making a "Pull Quote" Object Style. Having set up an object style for the pull quote it takes only a single click to transform **A** into **B**. The quote paragraph is a nested style with a paragraph rule above. Its Next Style is defined as the attribution line. The Object Style definition includes the Paragraph Style with the Next Style option checked.

Up Next

Type don't mean a thing without a page to frame it and in the next chapter we look at some of the considerations involved in that oft overlooked process of setting up a document: page size, margin widths, and the number and width of columns.

PART IV

Page Layout

CHAPTER 15

Setting Up Your Document

THE FOUNDATIONS OF ANY PAGE DESIGN are the document dimensions: page size, margins, and the number of columns. While all of these can be changed when the document is in progress, there's nothing like getting it right to begin with.

TIP: Standard page sizes US letter, A4, tabloid, etc., are convenient, but the world is full of documents in these sizes. Use them, but choose them intentionally because they offer the best solution for the design you are creating. Don't choose them just because they are the default setting. If you opt for a nonstandard page size, be sure to get a cost estimate from your commercial printer before you commit to designing your publication at that size. It's good to be different, but sometimes being different can come with a big price tag.

Here are some things to consider when creating a new document:

- What type of document is it? Is it a novel with one continuous text flow, a magazine or newsletter with multiple stories, a brochure, or a poster? Is the document a travel guide that will need to be compact and quickly accessible, or is it a luxurious coffee table book that will showcase the work of a famous photographer?
- Are there images? If so, are they predominantly vertical or horizontal in orientation? Are they photographs, illustrations, maps, icons, or all of the above? Do they need to be integrated into the flow of the text?
- Are there headings and subheads? If so, how many levels are there to this hierarchy?
- Are there footnotes or endnotes?
- Is there an index or appendix?
- Is there any quoted matter?

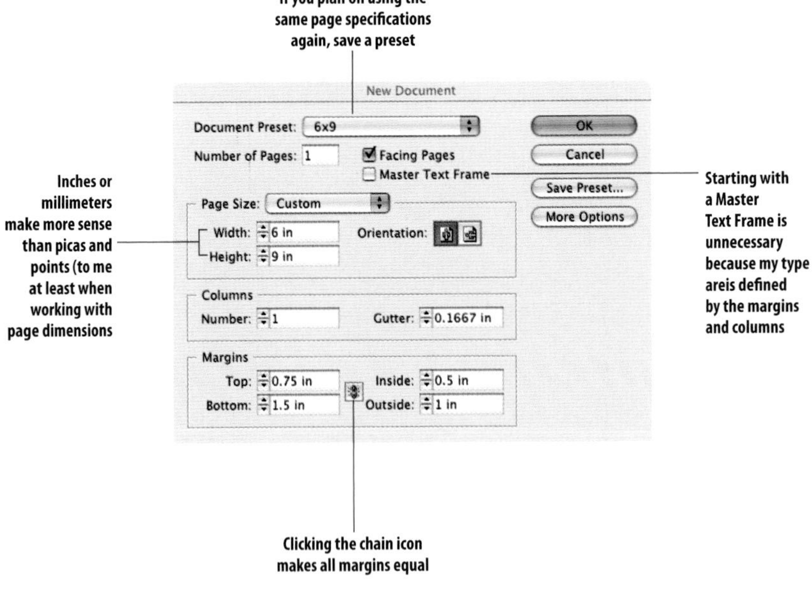

FIGURE 15.1 New Document.

TIP: Another nice workflow feature is the ability to save your settings as a preset. Once you've keyed in the values you want, choose Save Preset. Thereafter you can choose the preset name from the Document Preset menu.

Choosing a Page Size

For as long as humans have been making printed materials they have been searching for the perfect page *aspect ratio*—the relationship of width to height. Many books have been written about the quest for the perfect page dimension; without getting into the formulas, here are four commonly used aspect ratios:

The Golden Section 1:1.618. This formula is based on the proportions of the human body and is also sometimes expressed as a 3:5 aspect ratio.

The Silver Section 1:1.4142 (the square root of 2). ISO paper sizes—A4, A3, etc.—are all based on this aspect ratio. It's a clever and economical system because it allows you to fold one standard size into another, saving wastage on cutting up to make smaller sizes. You can make brochures by using the next size up. For example, fold an A3 page in two and you have two A4 pages; fold an A4 in two and you have two A5 pages, and so on. The standard US letter size (8.5 × 11 inches) is similar in aspect ratio to an A4 page (8.3 × 11.7 inches), but slightly wider and not quite as tall.

Photographic aspect ratio: 1:1.5. This yields sizes such as 4 × 6 inches, 6 × 9 inches, and 8 × 12 inches.

Business Card aspect ratio 2:3.5. This is the ratio of most business cards. Its size, and multiples of it, feel familiar.

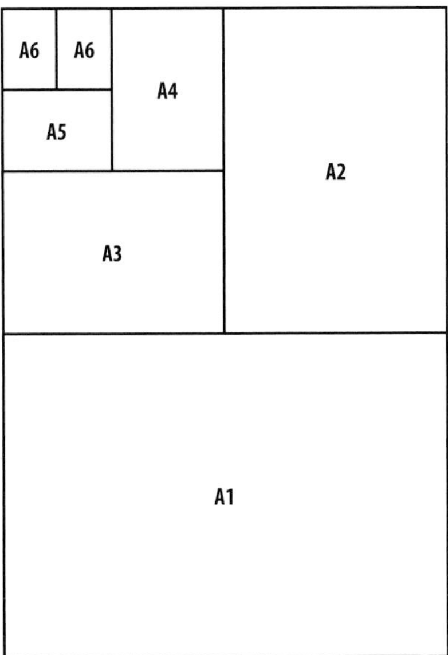

FIGURE 15.2 ISO Paper Sizes.

TIP: Setting Up a Spread The first page of a two-page document is considered a right-hand page (or recto) meaning that the two pages will not appear next to each other as a spread. To make them do so, define your opening page as being an even-numbered page (or verso). Select the first page, and from the Pages palette fly-out menu choose Numbering and Section options. Choose Start page number, and type an even number.

Determining Margins

The importance of margins is often overlooked. It's easy to fall back on even margins of 1 inch or 25 mm, but by doing so you can miss a big opportunity to establish the margins of your document as an integral design element. Margins are an essential part of design. Glance at any page—margins are the first space you see and thus play a vital role in determining the reader's initial impression of a page. Margins serve the following functions:

- First and foremost margins are a frame for the page—and if you've ever done any picture framing you'll appreciate how dramatically a frame can increase a picture's impact.
- A place for readers to put their thumbs
- A space to write notes
- A place to put the page folios—in either the top or bottom margins

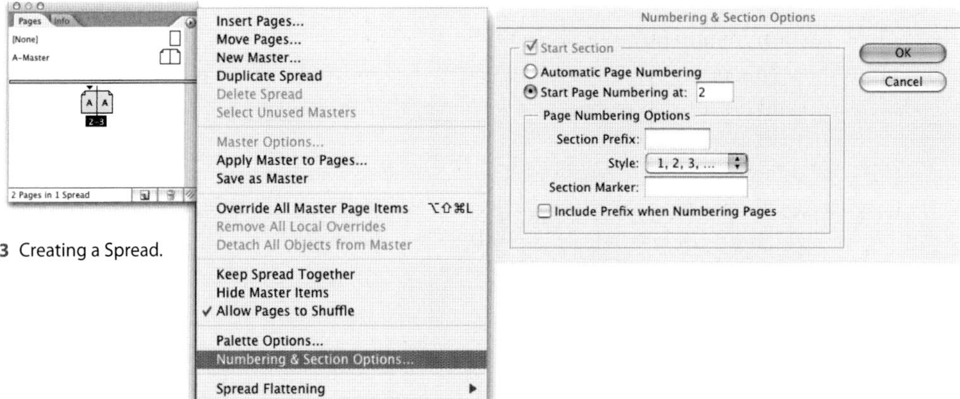

FIGURE 15.3 Creating a Spread.

Margins define the *type area* or *text block* but they are not absolute. Certain text elements like drop caps, pull quotes, and captions may hang outside the margins—as will punctuation if you are using Optical Margin Alignment. Pictures frequently break out of the text area, disrupting the rectilinear nature of the page and—potentially—making for a more dynamic layout.

Relative Size of Margins

Choosing even margins (click the linking icon to make sure it is unbroken) will make the rectangle of your type area the same aspect ratio as the rectangle of your page. However, an equally proportioned rectangle within a rectangle can look static, and, besides, other factors come into play—like extra space on the outer margins for convenient handling and extra space at the bottom or top for folios. It's a big generalization, but margins typically progress from smallest to largest in the following order: inside, top, outside, bottom:

- Starting with the **Inside** margin and moving clockwise around your page, this should be the smallest dimension. This margin should be at least 10mm.
- Next, comes the **Top** margin (a.k.a. Head).
- Then the **Outside** margin (a.k.a. Foredge), which should be big enough so the type doesn't look confined by the page, and to allow space for the reader to handle the document.
- Lastly, the **Bottom** margin (a.k.a. Foot) should be the biggest so as to avoid the type area looking bottom heavy and also to allow room for the folios. The top and bottom margins can be switched if the folios will be placed above the type area.

NOTE: When setting the inside margin, bear in mind that the binding will change the reader's perception of the amount of space at the inside of the page. At worst, if the inside margin is too small, text will be "lost" in the shadow between the pages.

FIGURE 15.4 A Thumbnail Sketch.

TIP: Do a Thumbnail Sketch When working on a layout, no matter how zippy you are with InDesign, you'll save yourself loads of time (and create a better-looking page) if you first draw thumbnails sketches. Don't be embarrassed—no one but you need see them, but they are the fastest way of trying out ideas and for getting a sense of scale.

Golden Section margins call for a ratio of 3:5:8:13 (starting with the inside margin and moving clockwise). While this makes for harmonious proportions, it also makes for economically impractical margins.

Another popular ratio is 2:3:4:6, which produces margins that are still generous, yet look more familiar to a 21st Century eye.

If you are using a leading grid, the margins should be in increments of the grid. See Chapter 16: Everything in its Right Place: Working with Grids.

FIGURE 15.5 A page using Golden Section proportions 1:1.618 and margins 3:5:8:13 (example **A**) and an A4 page using margin ratios 2:3:4:6 (example **B**).

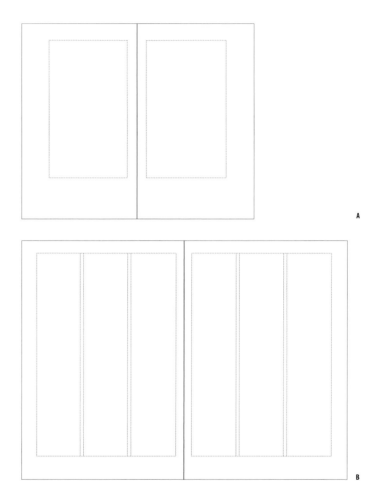

When working with single-page designs, like a poster or business card, equal margins at least on the left and right, might be more applicable. Here's a simple formula that I often use: Find a printed piece that you admire at the same or similar size to the piece you're working on. Measure its margins, and replicate them. Works like a charm.

Determining Column Width

The type area defined by your margins may be subdivided into columns. The relationship between the type size and the column width, or *measure*, is a key factor in determining the readability of your type. There's no cast-iron rule for determining column width. Some jobs lend themselves to generous columns; often economy dictates narrower columns than are optimal.

As a rough guide, aim for 40 to 70 characters (including the spaces) per line. That's a big range, so there's plenty of scope. More than 70 characters and "doubling" can occur—the eye returning to the left column edge only to read the same line again. If you are obligated to work with a measure that is too wide, you can improve its readability by increasing the leading of your type. At the other extreme, if you have less than 25 characters per line, getting evenly spaced type will be next to impossible.

TIP: If you already know how wide you want your columns to be you can specify a fixed column width, and InDesign will adjust the size of your text frame accordingly. If you want columns of unequal widths, click and drag the column guides.

Take a look at your daily newspaper and you'll find justified columns with a lot less than 50 characters. You'll probably also find—without looking too hard—that these columns are riddled with huge word spaces. This is due to poor justification as a consequence of the narrow column measure. We've gotten used to bad typography in newspapers—which in their defense can say that they are produced under tight deadline pressure—and read them easily *despite* their typography, not because of it. Historically newspapers used smaller type than they do today. But while the type has gotten bigger, the columns haven't grown proportionally, hence the justification problems. That said, there are notable exceptions—The Guardian (UK) has significantly raised the bar for newspaper typography in the last few decades.

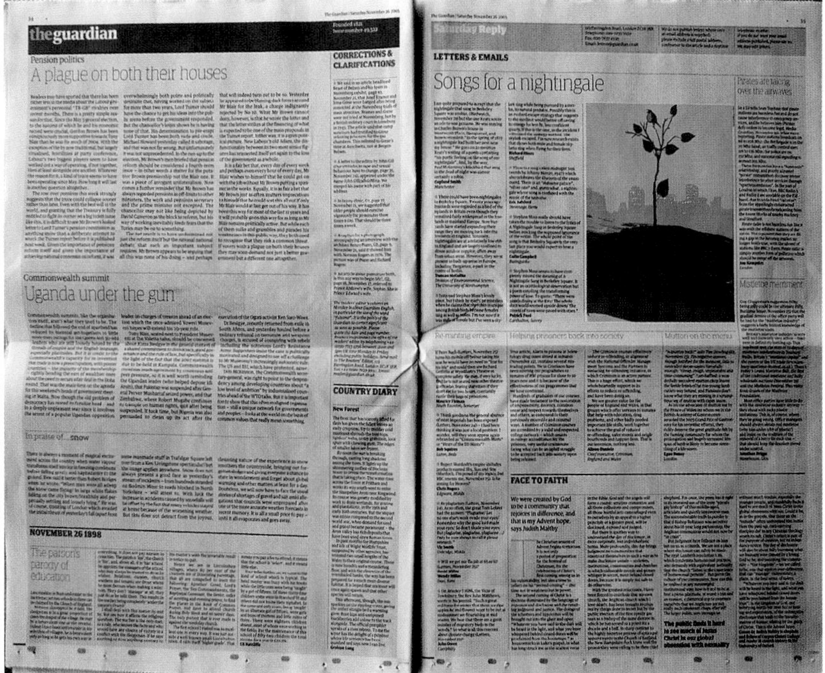

theguardian

Pension politics

A plague on both their houses

CORRECTIONS & CLARIFICATIONS

Commonwealth summit

Uganda under the gun

COUNTRY DIARY

NOVEMBER 26 1898

LETTERS & EMAILS

Songs for a nightingale

FACE TO FAITH

FIGURE 15.6 The British Newspaper, The Guardian.

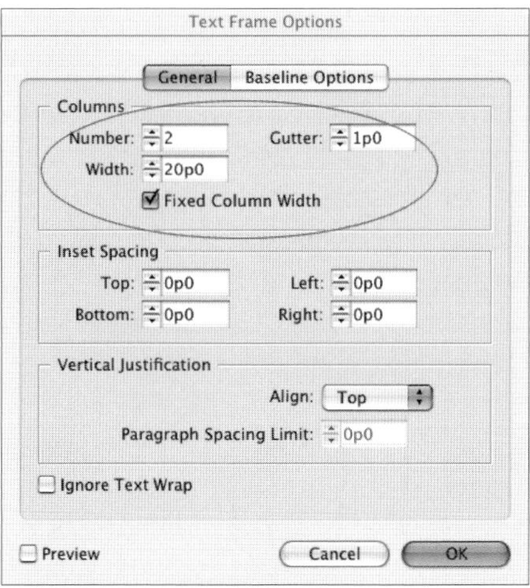

FIGURE 15.7 Fixed Column Width.

The issue of column width is more problematic with justified type than with ragged type. If you are working with a narrow measure, do yourself a big favor and choose Left rather than Left Justified alignment.

Individual Columns or One Divided?

Let's say you want a three-column layout—you can approach this in two ways. (1) You can draw a single text frame and make it into three columns. Or (2) you can create three threaded text frames of one column each. Your choice affects how you edit your layout. A single frame divided into three columns lets you control the tops and bottoms of the three columns at once. On the other hand, if you have three individual columns, you can control those columns independently, which is preferable if you want the columns to start or end at different positions on your page.

Determining Gutter Width

In multicolumn documents, the separate columns of type should look like they are parts of a unified whole. If the space between your columns, or gutter width, is too wide, those columns will look like they bear no relation to each other. On the other hand, if the gutter width is too narrow, the reader's eye may mistakenly cross over from one column to the next.

Typically gutter widths (the space between the columns) are 1 pica or 1 pica and 6 points. You might want to use a gutter width relative to the type size. A rule of thumb is that the gutter should be at least 1.5 ems wide so that it is clearly larger than the widest word space in the line. If you are working with a baseline grid, to achieve a uniformity of spacing, set your gutter width to the same value as your baseline grid increment, which in turn will be based on the leading increment of your body text. (See Chapter 16: "Everything in its Right Place: Working with Grids")

Column Height

There's no golden rule for determining column height, except to say that for continuous reading, the columns should be vertical, i.e., taller than they are wide.

Changing Columns

When changing the number of columns here are some things to consider:

- To change the number of columns for all the pages based on a specific Master Page, you should edit the Master Page itself. So that the changes adjust the text frames (and not just the guides) on your document pages, choose Layout > Layout Adjustment and turn on the Enable Layout Adjustment checkbox.
- To change the columns for both left- and right-hand pages of a spread, select both page icons in the Pages palette, otherwise you'll be changing just the left or the right page.
- Alternatively, you can change the margins and columns for a range of pages by selecting those pages in your Pages palette.
- To reflow your text according to your new column grid, the Layout Adjustment option must be enabled.

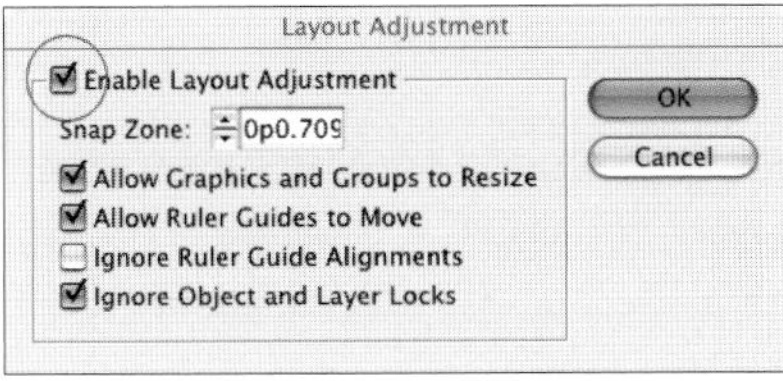

FIGURE 15.8 Layout Adjustment.

Break Characters

Using the Insert Break Character command, you can control how text flows into multiple frames. When you insert one of these characters, text is forced to the next column in the current frame, to the next threaded frame, to the next page, or to the next even or odd page. Breaks can also be incorporated as part of a style definition. For example, if you always want your Chapter Head style to begin on a new right-hand page, it's preferable to include this as part of the style definition rather than manually inserting a break character before each of the Chapter Heads.

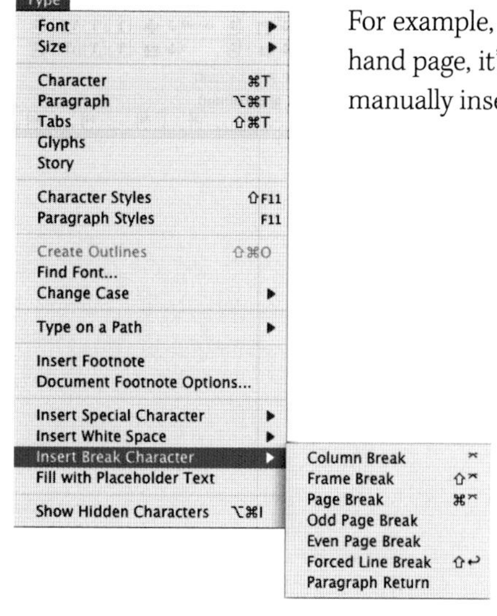

FIGURE 15.9 Insert Break Character.

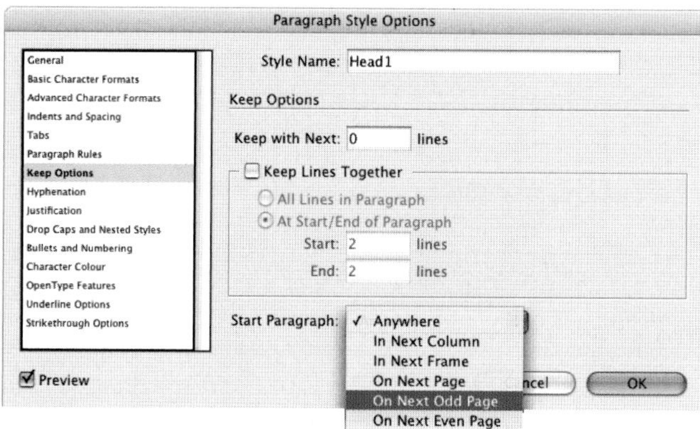

FIGURE 15.10 Breaks As Part of a Style Definition.

Page Numbers

Page numbers, or folios as they are also known, are signposts to the reader, and as such they need to be positioned on the page where they can be seen easily. Practically, this means placing them outside the text area, either at the top or at the bottom of the page. The page number may be combined with running information—like the name of the magazine and month of publication or the chapter title, and separated from it by an em space—Cmd+Shift+M (Ctrl+Shift+M). The left and right pages of a spread typically mirror each other so that the page number is the outermost element.

Another convention is to put the author's name at the top of the left-hand (verso) pages and the title of the book or chapter on the right-hand (recto) pages. This may be useful for short story collections or anthologies, which have multiple authors, but it's unnecessary in a work by a single author. After all, how many times do you need to be reminded of the author's name when you are reading a novel?

Auto page numbers should be put on the Master Pages so that they show up on all document pages that are based on that specific master page.

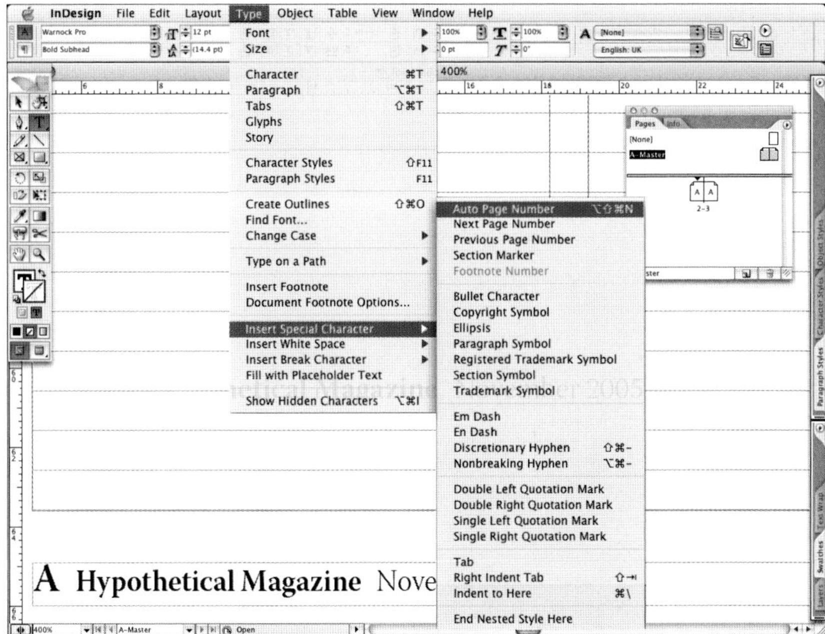

FIGURE 15.11 Inserting an Auto Page Number on a Master Page.

Folios on the inner margin make it impossible to quickly flip through the book to find the page you are after, and they are of little use to the reader.

In a novel using running heads at the top of the page, it is common to position the folio at the bottom of the page on chapter heading pages where a running head at the top of the page would interfere with the type treatment of the chapter heading. In such instances, consider making a separate master page for the chapter opening pages.

Folios should be at least a line space away from the text area of the page to differentiate them from the type.

NOTE: Master Page elements are locked on document pages. To modify a master page element on a document page, hold Cmd+Shift (Ctrl+Shift) and click the object to unlock it. To unlock all master page elements, choose Override All Master Pages Items from the Pages palette menu. (This will mean that the page elements are no longer controlled by the Master Pages).

Section Markers

If you're working with long documents that are divided into different sections, section markers can help simplify your project by cutting down on the number of master pages and/or the number of documents needed. Section markers can be used for different departments in a magazine, different parts of a book, or wherever a document is made up of distinctly different sections (just so long as they're the same page size). Each section can have its own numbering scheme—Arabic, roman numeral, or abc. And here's what makes them so useful: *A master page can have more than one Section Marker.*

Section Markers are easy to use and automatically add the name of a section or chapter to your document folios. You can format (or style) the section marker as you would any piece of text to determine its appearance.

To insert a Section Marker:

1. Create a text frame for your folio on a master page.
2. Ctrl+Click (Right Mouse+Click) and choose Insert Special Character > Section Marker from the context menu. The word "Section" will be inserted into your type.
3. Format the Section Marker the way you want it to look.
4. To "activate" the Section Marker on a document page, select the page where you want the section to begin in the Pages palette and choose Numbering and Section Options from the Pages palette menu. Type the section name into the Section Marker field and click OK. This section marker will now appear on all pages based on the master page until another section is defined.

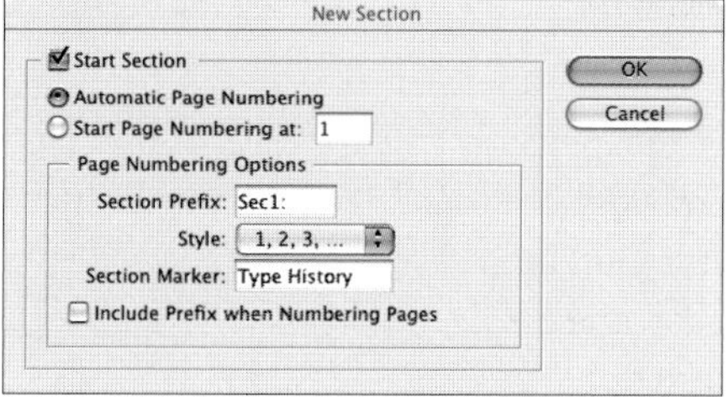

FIGURE 15.12 To change settings for a section, select the page that uses the section marker and choose Numbering & Section Options in the Pages palette fly-out menu.

Layers

If you are familiar with using Layers in either Photoshop or Illustrator, then InDesign's layers will look very familiar. Layers determine the *stacking order* of objects on your page. In the example shown below, elements on the Text layer display (and print) on top of any elements on the Pictures or Panels layers. Each individual layer also has a stacking order, which you can control using the Object>Arrange menu. But layers trump Bring to Front and Send to Back. For instance, in the example shown, an object at the *front* of the Pictures layer is still beneath an object that is at the *back* of the Text layer. Where there are no objects on a layer you see through to the layer(s) beneath.

You're under no obligation to use layers in InDesign, but it's a good idea to do so, especially if you're working on layouts that involve combining text with graphics. Layers allow you to view and edit specific kinds of content in your document without affecting other kinds of content, significantly speeding up your workflow. For example, you can hide the pictures layer when concentrating on the text and vice versa. You can also use layers when working on multilingual documents, to display the text for different languages.

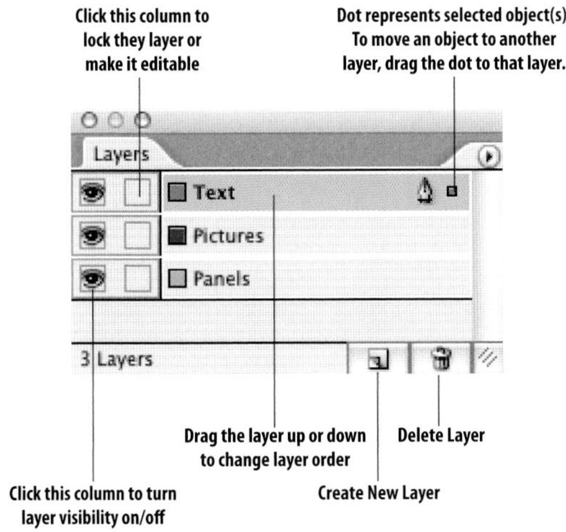

FIGURE 15.13 The Layers palette. What you name the layers is up to you, and there's no limit to the number of layers, except common sense. Generally a maximum of five is enough for even the most complex of documents.

Fair enough, but for our purposes—type—layers are necessary to avoid printing problems. The potential for printing problems arises when you use transparent elements in your layout. In InDesign, *transparency* can mean a drop shadow, feathering, a Photoshop image with an alpha channel, or any object with a blend mode other than Normal and/or an opacity of less than 100 percent (See Chapter 18: "Text Effects"). When a document is printed it is flattened and any text that is in close proximity to a transparent element—for example, a text wrap around a layered Photoshop image—is in danger of being rasterized, and possibly ending up looking rather furry as a result.

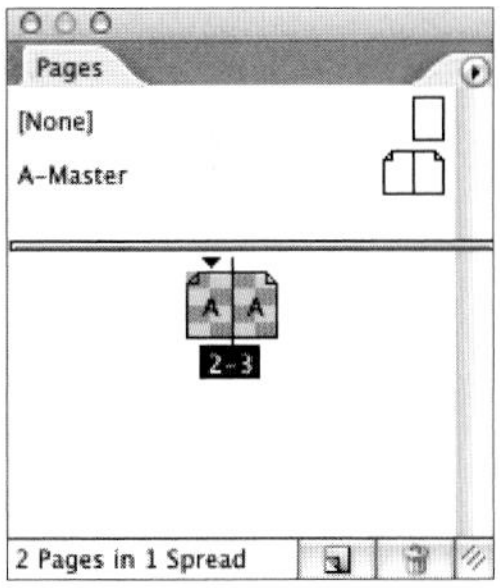

FIGURE 15.14 Transparency.

The simple step to prevent this from happening is to move all text objects (except those that actually use transparency effects) to the top layer of your document—that way they get flattened last. As an extra security measure, be sure to talk to the person responsible for printing your files, and mention that you're using transparency. And if you're unsure about whether you *are* using transparency, if any of the page icons in the Pages palette display a checkerboard, then you are.

Up Next

Time to get organized! We'll look at the pros and cons of using grids, especially baseline grids, to help structure our InDesign documents.

CHAPTER 16

Everything in Its Right Place:

Using Grids

THERE ARE TWO TYPES OF GRIDS USED IN PAGE LAYOUT: column grids and baseline grids. Column grids determine the way the page is divided vertically. Baseline grids determine how the page is divided horizontally. It is common to use both types of grids together.

Grids define where the different elements of your document are placed on the page. Essentially they are visual aids to help you quickly and consistently arrange text and graphics on a page. They come in all shapes and sizes, and there are different strategies for using them. Beneath just about every well-designed document is a grid of some sort. Novels use a simple one-column grid, but even this has to be carefully considered, because it will determine the type area of the page as well as where the folios go. Newspapers and magazines with multiple columns and a mixture of type sizes—as well as photographs and illustrations—call for a more complex grid that combines a flexible number of columns with a baseline grid.

To the average reader, a well-designed grid will be invisible; nevertheless it's there, helping the reader to make sense of all the different elements in a document. Columns of text, headlines, photos, illustrations, captions, pull quotes, and other page elements are more easily tied-together—or unified—on the page that is based on a grid. To the designer, grids enhance creativity by imposing structure. Because they take a lot of the guesswork out of your design, grids significantly speed up workflow.

Things to Consider

- It is common to have more than one column grid. Some pages can be based on a five-column grid, others on a four-, and others on a three-column grid, etc. When working with multipage documents, it is most efficient to establish grids on Master Pages.
- There's no limit—other than common sense—to the number of Master Pages in your document.
- It's possible, though rarely necessary, to have more than one baseline grid per document because InDesign allows for individual text frames to have their own baseline grid (see below).
- Grids should be flexible. Grids based on a fixed number of columns can suffer from too much symmetry if text and graphics are confined to those columns throughout. Using a 12-column grid is an easy way to introduce variety into your layouts, because you can vary between 3 and 4, 12 being divisible by both. Another common approach is the five-column grid, which allows for two text frames each filling two column widths. The remaining column can be used for white space, photos, captions, and other material. You can mix things up by changing the position of this "floating" column.

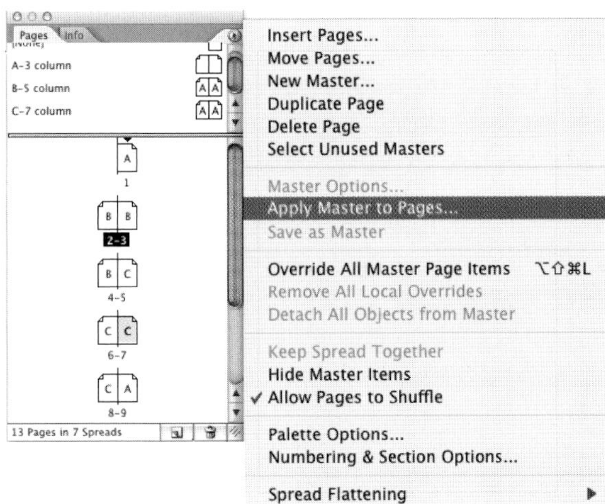

FIGURE 16.1 Pages palette and fly-out menu.

FIGURE 16.2 A simple three-column grid. Each column is wide enough for body text even when narrowed by a text wrap. The grid can be easily adapted to a six-column grid for more flexibility.

A Feast of

Food & Drink Trails

By Bob Barton

I felt like a guilty schoolboy as I entered the Rococo Chocolate Shop on London's King's Road and gazed in awe at shelf upon shelf of tempting delights. Fresh cream truffles, dark chocolate bars flavoured with lavender, ginger and chilli pepper; chocolate covered coffee beans and soft nougat—all hand made and artistically wrapped. Next would come chocolate brownies in The Chocolate Society café and a browse in Charbonnel et Walker of New Bond Street, before I would collapse, fully sated, amid the exquisite range in Fortnum and Mason on Piccadilly.

I WAS FOLLOWING a London chocolate trail—which actually expands into Five chocolate-y things to do around Britain—on tourist board VisitBritain's website. With the country's growing reputation for fine cuisine, the number of food and drink trails has multiplied since the Malt Whisky Trail was set up around the distilleries of Speyside, north-east Scotland, several decades ago: it is still going strong.

Whether your passion is for cheese, sausages, ice-cream or wine, you will find a trail leading you around the most mouth-watering locations on that theme. There are few pleasures that beat motoring through the ever-changing countryside, calling in at specialist shops, farms, vineyards or producers which are usually well off the usual tourist routes. If your chosen theme is whisky, wine, cider or beer—other British specialities—a non-drinking driver is a prerequisite, of course!

South East England Wine Trail

The wine producers of the south-east, proud of the ever-increasing quality of their produce, have published a free map-guide to 20 of the best vineyards and placed them on a large map. Being only 88 miles north of the French Champagne region, with almost identical geology, it is no surprise that wines from England are rivalling that region in blind tastings. The trail ranges from the tiny Painshill at Cobham—set in landscaped parkland known for its grotto, Turkish tent and other exotic follies—to the massive Denbies estate at Dorking: England's largest, where visitors are taken round by tractor-train.

The Lake District Tea Trail

The tradition of taking afternoon tea, complete with home-made scones, cream, cakes and delicate sandwiches, was an English creation and not confined to the Lake District, but the people of Cumbria —land of romantic poet William Wordsworth—have selected some of their best tea shops and put them on a trail. From a mountain tea garden specialising in home-made cakes and local ice-cream, to a tea barn' set in an open-air sculpture park, all boast quality farmhouse produce and a few local recipes to try when you get home.

The Seafood Trail

Being an island nation, there are many places where you can enjoy the finest fresh and smoked fish, and shellfish. A new route through some of Scotland's most spectacular scenery enables foodies to enjoy it in 11 waterfront establishments. The Seafood Trail covers the rugged scenery of Argyll, reached off the A83 highway west of Glasgow: a rugged patchwork of land jutting like huge fingers into the sea, with mountains and long sea-lochs. This combination of scenery and great food is almost intoxicating and I shall never forget my first visit to one of the establishments, the Loch Fyne Oyster Bar, literally a 'gourmet oasis' set in isolation beneath towering mountains and beside a lonely loch, appearing magically out of swirling Highland mist.

The Sausage Trail

Sausages are one of Britain's favourite foods: Queen Victoria was reputed to be an enthusiast, though they were introduced to the country by the Romans in 500AD and, 1,500 years later, 'bangers and mash' (sausage and mashed potato) still vies with fish and chips and curry as a national dish. Heart of England Fine Foods, whose fiefdom includes the West Midlands conurbation around Birmingham and the rural counties of Shropshire and Staffordshire, has its own Sausage Trail, taking visitors to the producers of quality sausages, many of whom have won awards. The selection available ranges from traditional pork and lamb to beer and spicy chilli flavoured varieties.

North-West England's Fine Foods organisation is also Serious about Sausages to quote the title of one of its free publications, which includes 51 butchers, farms and other shops scattered from medieval Chester north to Carlisle, near the Scottish border. Cumberland sausage is especially noteworthy in this region and butcher W.H. Frost's of Manchester uses a century-old family recipe including local pork, ground peppers and secret ingredients for their best-selling version.

The Cheese Trail

There are probably more trails for cheese in Britain than for any other food. Traditional cheese making has been revived and there is a growing number of artisan varieties. The Cheese Trail in Wales takes you to every corner of this Celtic land, but probably its best known variety is Caerphilly, now produced by only one company, Castle Dairies, in its namesake South Wales town. Caerphilly is also renowned for its 13th century castle which has a leaning tower—thankfully, it is not as crumbly as the cheese.

Back in England, The Stilton Trail allows visitors to explore and taste the famous Stilton cheese, only produced in three East Midland counties: Derbyshire, Nottinghamshire and Leicestershire. Known as the king of English cheese, its production is entrusted to just six specialist dairies. A trail booklet is available from local tourist offices. North-West Fantastic Foods also has a free booklet, Choosy About Cheese which includes producers of the two great cheeses of the region, Cheshire and Lancashire. These trails, and the Heart of England's Cheese Trail, are also available on the Internet.

The Cider Trail

Two of England's most rural counties, Herefordshire, which borders Wales, and Somerset in south-west England, are known for their cider production and have both produced cider routes. These are beautiful in the spring, when the apple trees are full of blossom, but equally appealing in October, when the cider making festivals are held. Herefordshire boasts the biggest cider mill in the world and Hereford Cathedral has a Cider Bible among other historic books—notably Mappa Mundi—in its chained library. The county even promotes a series of quiet 'cider cycling routes' through pretty villages, and renting a bicycle is probably the best way of sampling the ciders and seeking out meals made with them.

As locally made ice-cream often rounds off a meal perfectly, I shall finish this article with the Ice-Cream Trail in the Heart of England. Featuring ten producers from Coventry to the Welsh border, examples include Shepherds in Hay-on-Wye, the 'town of second-hand books' and Just Rachel, near the black-and-white town of Ledbury, which makes elderflower, sloe gin and lavender flavours, among others!

Perhaps even more fun is to be had by making up your own a la carte food trail using a combination of the above, and by studying VisitBritain's detailed website, www.visitbritain.com/taste. Bon appetit! ■

Trails mentioned in this article

Chocolate (UK): www.visitbritain.com/chocolate

Malt whisky (Scotland): www.maltwhiskytrail.com

Wine (South East England): www.BuyLocalFood.co.uk

Tea (Lake District): www.golakes.co.uk/teatrail-cumbria

Seafood (Scotland): www.theseafoodtrail.com

Sausages (Heart/ North-East England): www.sausagelinks.co.uk; www.nw-fine-foods.co.uk

Cheese (Wales): www.wda.co.uk

Cheese (England): www.stiltoncheese.com; www.nw-fine-foods.co.uk

Cider (Herefordshire/ Somerset): www.visitherefordshire.co.uk; www.somerset.gov.uk

Ice-cream (Heart of England): www.remotenewmedia.co.uk

2 Visit Britain | October 2005

October 2005 | Visit Britain 3

FIGURE 16.3 A five-column grid divides comfortably into two wide text columns, leaving a narrow margin column for sidebar material, captions, and into which pictures can expand.

Your Grid Tool Kit

InDesign has a suite of tools that works together to help you set up and manage your grid.

Grid Preferences

Color: Personally I like to change the color of my baseline grid so that it's distinct from any custom guides I draw—light gray works well because it's not too distracting.

I felt like a guilty schoolboy as I entered the Rococo Chocolate Shop on London's King's Road and gazed in awe at shelf upon shelf of tempting delights. Fresh cream truffles; dark chocolate bars flavoured with lavender, ginger and chilli pepper; chocolate covered coffee beans and soft nougat—all hand made and artistically wrapped. Next would come chocolate brownies in The Chocolate Society café and a browse in Charbonnel et Walker of New Bond Street, before I would collapse, fully sated, amid the exquisite range in Fortnum and Mason on Piccadilly.

A Feast of

Food & Drink Trails

By Bob Barton

I WAS FOLLOWING a London chocolate trail—which actually expands into Five chocolate-y things to do around Britain—on tourist board VisitBritain's website. With the country's growing reputation for fine cuisine, the number of food and drink trails has multiplied since the Malt Whisky Trail was set up around the distilleries of Speyside, north-east Scotland, several decades ago: it is still going strong.

Whether your passion is for cheese, sausages, ice-cream or wine, you will find a trail leading you around the most mouth-watering locations on that theme. There are few pleasures that beat motoring through the ever-changing countryside, calling in at specialist shops, farms, vineyards or producers which are usually well off the usual tourist routes. If your chosen theme is whisky, wine, cider or beer—other British specialities—a non-drinking driver is a prerequisite, of course!

South East England Wine Trail

The wine producers of the south-east, proud of the ever-increasing quality of their produce, have published a free map-guide to 20 of the best vineyards and placed them on a large map. Being only 88 miles north of the French Champagne region, with almost identical geology, it is no surprise that wines from England are rivalling that region in blind tastings. The trail ranges from the tiny Painshill at Cobham—set in landscaped parkland known for its grotto, Turkish tent and other exotic follies—to the massive Denbies estate at Dorking: England's largest, where visitors are taken round by tractor-train.

The Lake District Tea Trail

The tradition of taking afternoon tea, complete with home-made scones, cream, cakes and delicate sandwiches, was an English creation and not confined to the Lake District, but the people of Cumbria —land of romantic poet William Wordsworth—have selected some of their best tea shops and put them on a trail. From a mountain tea garden specialising in home-made cakes and local ice-cream, to a 'tea barn' set in an open-air sculpture park, all boast quality farmhouse produce and a few local recipes to try when you get home.

The Seafood Trail

Being an island nation, there are many places where you can enjoy the finest fresh and smoked fish, and shellfish. A new route through some of Scotland's most spectacular scenery enables foodies to enjoy it in 11 waterfront establishments. The Seafood Trail covers the rugged scenery of Argyll, reached off the A83 highway west of Glasgow: a ragged patchwork of land jutting like huge fingers into the sea, with mountains and long sea-lochs. This combination of scenery and great food is almost intoxicating and I shall never forget my first visit to one of the establishments, the Loch Fyne Oyster Bar, literally a 'gourmet oasis' set in isolation beneath towering mountains and beside a lonely loch, appearing magically out of swirling Highland mist.

The Sausage Trail

Sausages are one of Britain's favourite foods: Queen Victoria was reputed to be an enthusiast, though they were introduced to the country by the Romans in 500AD and, 1,500 years later, 'bangers and mash' (sausage and mashed potato) still vies with fish and chips and curry as a national dish. Heart of England Fine Foods, whose fiefdom includes the West Midlands conurbation around Birmingham and the rural counties of Shropshire and Staffordshire, has its own Sausage Trail, taking visitors to the producers of quality sausages, many of whom have won awards. The selection available ranges from traditional pork and lamb to beer and spicy chilli flavoured varieties.

North-West England's Fine Foods organisation is also Serious about Sausages to quote the title of one of its free publications, which includes 52 butchers, farms and other shops scattered from medieval Chester north to Carlisle, near the Scottish border. Cumberland sausage is especially noteworthy in this region and butcher W.H. Frost's of Manchester uses a century-old family recipe including local pork, ground peppers and secret ingredients for their best-selling version.

The Cheese Trail

There are probably more trails for cheese in Britain than for any other food. Traditional cheese making has been revived and there is a growing number of artisan varieties. The Cheese Trail in Wales takes you to every corner of this Celtic land, but probably its best known variety is Caerphilly, now produced by only one company, Castle Dairies, in its namesake South Wales town. Caerphilly is also renowned for its 13th century castle which has a leaning tower—thankfully, it is not as crumbly as the cheese.

Back in England, The Stilton Trail allows visitors to explore and taste the famous Stilton cheese, only produced in three East Midland counties: Derbyshire, Nottinghamshire and Leicestershire. Known as the king of English cheese, its production is entrusted to just six specialist dairies. A trail booklet is available from local tourist offices. North-West Fantastic Foods also has a free booklet, Choosy About Cheese which includes producers of the two great cheeses of the region, Cheshire and Lancashire. These trails, and the Heart of England's Cheese Trail, are also available on the Internet.

The Cider Trail

Two of England's most rural counties, Herefordshire, which borders Wales, and Somerset in south-west England, are known for their cider production and have both produced cider routes. These are beautiful in the spring, when the apple trees are full of blossom, but equally appealing in October, when the cider making festivals are held. Herefordshire boasts the biggest cider mill in the world and Hereford Cathedral has a Cider Bible among other historic books—notably Mappa Mundi—in its chained library. The county even promotes a series of quiet 'cider cycling routes' through pretty villages, and renting a bicycle is probably the best way of sampling the ciders and seeking out meals made with them.

As locally made ice-cream often rounds off a meal perfectly, I shall finish this article with the Ice-Cream Trail in the Heart of England. Featuring ten producers from Coventry to the Welsh border, examples include Shepherds in Hay-on-Wye, the town of second-hand books' and Just Rachel, near the black-and-white town of Ledbury, which makes elderflower, sloe gin and lavender flavours, among others!

Perhaps even more fun is to be had by making up your own a la carte food trail using a combination of the above, and by studying VisitBritain's detailed website, www.visitbritain.com/taste. Bon appetit! ■

Trails mentioned in this article

Chocolate (UK): www.visitbritain.com/chocolate
Malt whisky (Scotland): www.maltwhiskytrail.com
Wine (South East England): www.BuyLocalFood.co.uk
Tea (Lake District): www.golakes.co.uk/teatrailcumbria
Seafood (Scotland): www.theseafoodtrail.com
Sausages (Heart/ North-East England): www.sausagelinks.co.uk; www.nw-fine-foods.co.uk
Cheese (Wales): www.wda.co.uk
Cheese (England): www.stiltoncheese.com; www.nw-fine-foods.co.uk
Cider (Herefordshire/Somerset): www.visitherefordshire.co.uk; www.somerset.gov.uk
Ice-cream (Heart of England): www.remotenewmedia.co.uk

2 Visit Britain | October 2005

October 2005 | Visit Britain 3

FIGURE 16.4 A seven-column grid allows more flexibility by offering a narrow "floating" column for additional material and white space.

Start & Relative to: This determines where the grid starts counting off from and whether that number is relative to the top margin or the top of the page. I prefer to start at 0, relative to the top margin. Relative to Margin will show only the baseline grid within the type area rather than across the whole page.

Increment every: This should be the same as your body text leading. Note this value will appear in your chosen unit of measurement, but these numbers are unwieldy if you're using millimeters or inches. Be sure to input this value in points.

Making your grid work will involve some rudimentary math, so it helps if you have an easy number to work with, like 12. You'll want to use this leading value (or multiples of it) for the spacing of the elements on your page. Make sure you are not using auto leading, which, depending on your point size, may give you leading values that are fractional. For example, if your body text is 11, your auto leading will be 13.2—not a number you want to be juggling with.

View Threshold: Determines the view size at which the baseline grid becomes visible when you have Show Baseline Grid on. To view the baseline grid, choose View > Grids & Guides > Show Baseline Grid (Cmd+Option+'/ Crtl+Alt+'). You can selectively change the color and the view threshold of ruler guides by selecting the guides and choosing Layout > Ruler Guides.

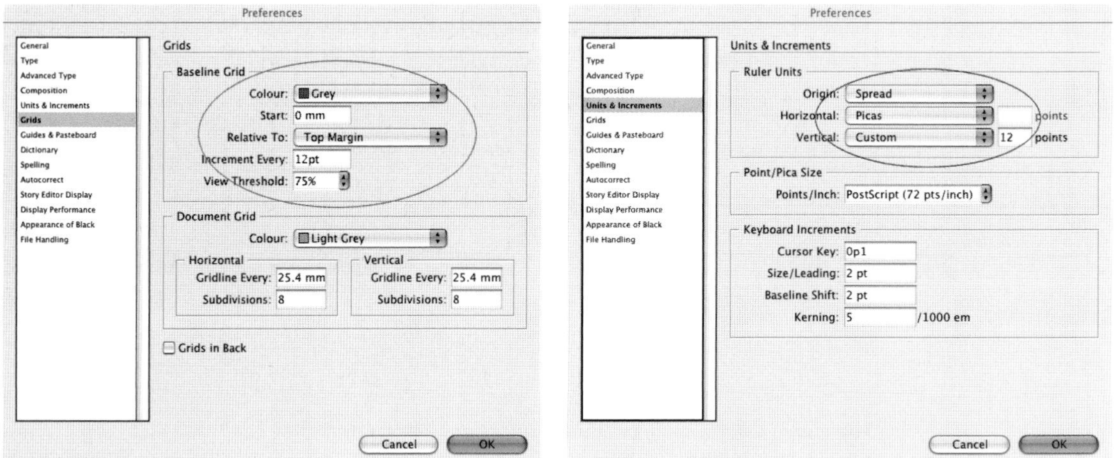

FIGURE 16.5 Grid Preferences and Custom Ruler.

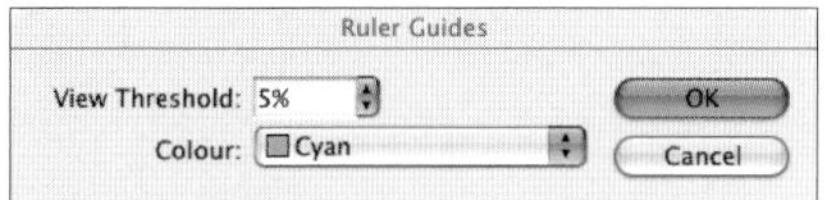

FIGURE 16.6 Ruler Guides.

Document Grid: Using a document grid turns your layout into graph paper. The size of each grid square is determined by the frequency of the horizontal and vertical gridlines and the number of subdivisions. If you don't want to subdivide the grid, make the number of subdivisions 1. Unlike grids created using a baseline grid or Create Guides, a document grid covers the entire pasteboard.

Grids in Back: When checked, the baseline grid and/or document grid (but not ruler guides) will be behind all other objects.

Custom Ruler: Set your vertical ruler to Custom width and use your grid increment as the amount. This will make the ticks on your ruler correspond to the lines of your grid.

Calculating the Height of the Type Area

To ensure that the baselines of the last lines of type sit snugly on the bottom margin, make the height of your type area a multiple of your leading. To round up or down the height of the type area to the nearest multiple of the leading value, follow these steps:

1. Divide the height of your text area in points by your leading increment (it helps if you use points as the unit of measurement for your vertical ruler).
2. Round the number up or down to the nearest whole number.
3. Multiply that number by your leading increment.
4. This number will become the size of your type area. The amount you add or subtract should be added to the top or bottom margin.

For example, if I begin with a type area of 351.331 points and a leading increment of 11 points:

714.331 / 11 = 65 (rounded up)
65 × 11 = 715
715 – 714.331 = 0.669

Subtract 0.669 from the bottom or top margin.

While this isn't strictly necessary—the grid will still work without this step—it is pleasing to have everything align perfectly.

Align to Grid

Once you've established a baseline grid, you can force your paragraphs to align to it by choosing All Lines. This option can be applied as part of a paragraph style definition, or can be applied locally using the Control palette.

Using a baseline grid is like setting a tempo for your document. In documents that use a variety of type and leading sizes, it's perfectly acceptable to go against that rhythm by coming off the grid with certain elements, such as headings and subheads, as long as the next passage of body text finds the beat again, and reestablishes the rhythm.

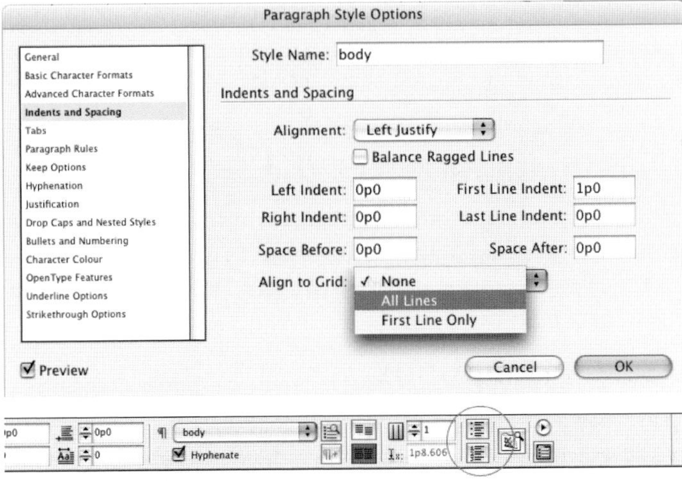

FIGURE 16.7 Align to Grid is usually applied as part of a paragraph style definition (top), but can also be applied locally using the Paragraph Formats level of the Control palette (bottom).

TIP: When resizing graphics, the picture frame will snap to the baseline grid, making it easier to crop your picture frames to a leading increment. If you are using text wraps, set the text wrap offset to your leading increment.

Aligning to the grid always means the *next* grid increment, causing leading values to be rounded up, never down. For example, if a paragraph with a specified leading value of 13 points is aligned to a 12-point grid, its leading will become 24 points.

For this reason, All Lines should be used only for body text and paragraph styles where the leading is already the same as the baseline grid increment.

If you've done the math right, choosing Align to Grid isn't strictly necessary. Your type will better align to the grid through careful planning and gentle persuasion than by coercion, because the total paragraph spacing applied to all your paragraphs is a multiple of your baseline grid increment. In practice, you'll probably find you need to add or subtract a bit of paragraph spacing here and there; this way, you, not InDesign, decide where the space is added or subtracted. The formula is simple: Total paragraph spacing (Leading + Space Before + Space After) must equal your leading increment or a multiple of your leading increment.

Let's say you're using a 12-point baseline grid and your body text is 10/12. The subheads are 18/18, making them 6 points off the grid. To put the subheads back on the grid, add 6 points of space before the subhead. Alternatively, you can add 4 points of space before and 2 points after.

First Line Only is useful for paragraphs such as multiline subheads or intro paragraphs that, because of their size and leading values, cannot keep to the grid. Nevertheless, you'll want to make sure that the first lines of such paragraphs align with the body text in adjacent columns. Subsequent lines will follow the specified leading increment.

FIGURE 16.8 The intro paragraph on the left aligns to First Line Only; the text on the right is set to All Lines.

First Baseline Options

This option determines exactly where the first baseline of your type will occur in your text frame—essential if you are using a baseline grid. From the five possible choices, Leading or Fixed are your best bets. Choose Leading and enter your leading increment into the Min field. Your first baseline will sit exactly one leading increment from the top of the text frame no matter what—even if there are different size characters and/or inline graphics in that first line.

NOTE: You can change the preferences to place all guides (including ruler guides) in back, mimicking QuarkXPress default behavior. But this is pointless; to use guides, you need to see them. If they are too obtrusive, change them to a less distracting color.

Fixed allows you to specify exactly how far from the top of the frame the first baseline should fall. This might be useful if you want the type to start at a specified distance from the top of your text frame—for example, a chapter opening page where the text begins further down the page.

Avoid the other three methods because they will vary the first baseline position if the first line contains characters of different sizes.

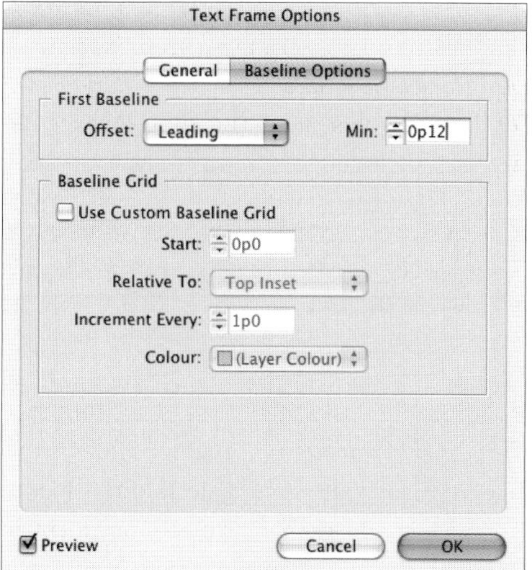

FIGURE 16.9 The First Baseline Offset determines the position of the first baseline of type in the text frame.

TIP: Make a line scale on your master page to indicate line numbers. This way your client can refer to corrections by line number, which makes for much quicker document editing, especially if you are communicating over the phone. When the layout is finished, delete the line scale.

Snap to Guides

When working with grids it's crucial that Snap to Guides is turned on (View > Guides & Grid > Snap to Guides or Cmd+Shift+; / Ctrl+Shift+;) so that when you draw, move, or resize an object its edges snap to the nearest guide or baseline grid. Guides must be visible in order for snapping to occur, however, objects can snap to the document and baseline grids whether the grids are visible or not.

The Snap to Zone in Preferences determines the exact range within which an object snaps to guides. If you have both Snap to Guides and the Snap to Document Grid on, the grid takes precedence.

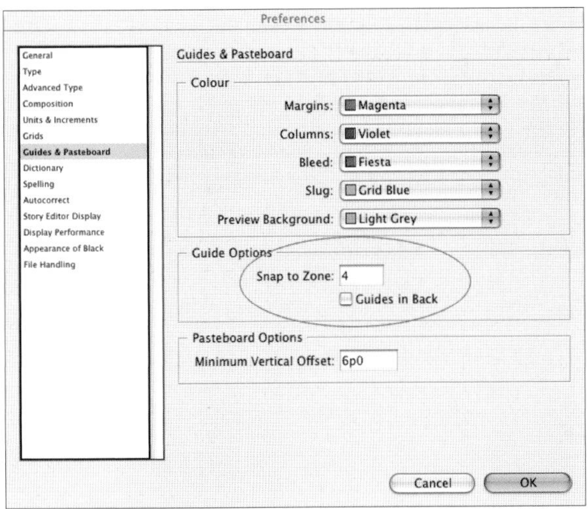

FIGURE 16.10 Snap to Zone.

FIGURE 16.11 Using a line scale can make it easier to identify corrections when communicating remotely with a client.

TIP: To draw a custom guide from the horizontal ruler that straddles the left- and right-hand pages of the spread, hold down Cmd (Ctrl) as you draw the guide. You can also position guides precisely by selecting them. For vertical guides specify their x coordinate, for horizontal guides, specify their y coordinate.

Text Frames with Different Grids

In addition to a document-wide baseline grid, you can also use a separate baseline grid for each frame. This can be useful if you have sidebar material that flows in multiple columns and uses a different type size and leading than your body text. Theoretically every text frame can have its own baseline grid. It's nice to know you *can*, but if a document has numerous baseline grids it undermines the whole purpose of a grid: a document architecture based on consistent modular units.

Create Guides

While Margins and Columns is the place to be when creating or adjusting major column divisions that affect text flow, Create Guides can be used to make custom grids of rows and columns, as an alternative to laboriously dragging out multiple ruler guides. This feature is a guide-making machine—if you want to divide up your page with guides, then Create Guides makes it a cinch, and, because it is so instantaneous, there's lots of scope to experiment with. To prevent your document from getting cluttered with too many guides, consider putting these guides on a separate layer, which you can show and hide or lock as needed.

TIP: While InDesign won't let you draw objects and turn them into guides the way you can in Illustrator, there's nothing to stop you from putting "guide objects" on a particular layer, then when they have served their purpose, making that layer invisible. Alternatively, you can select the guide objects and make their Attributes "Non Printing."

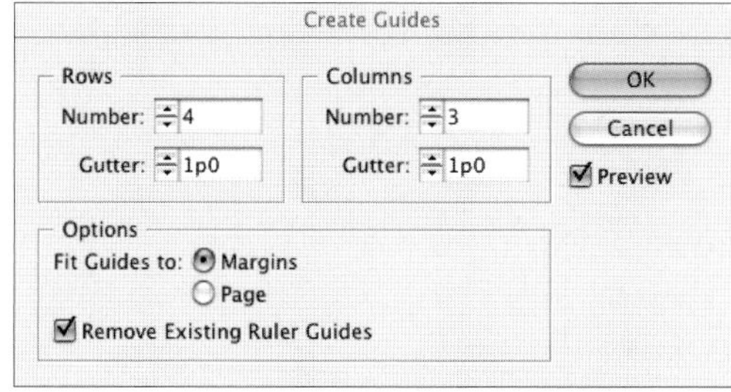

FIGURE 16.12 Create Guides.

TIP: Need a fresh start? You can remove all custom guides by pressing Cmd+Option+G (Ctrl+Alt+G), then pressing the Delete key.

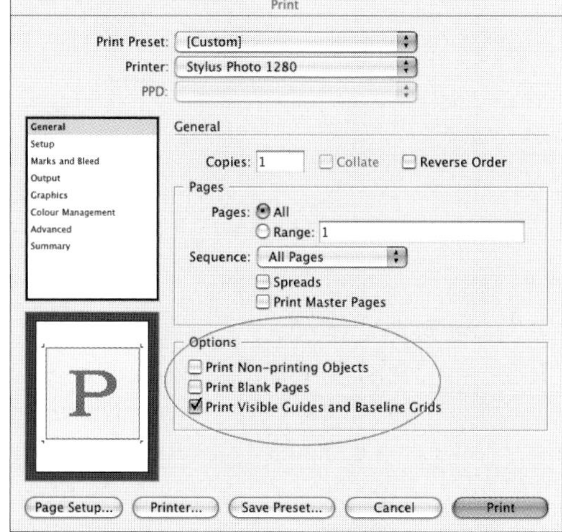

FIGURE 16.13 Print Guides.

TIP: Need to print those guides? In the General Panel of the Print Dialog Box, select Print Visible Guides and Baseline Grids to make all visible guides (i.e., not hidden or on hidden layers) print.

Up Next

Text wraps—the how-to and the how-not-to.

CHAPTER 17

Text Wraps:

The Good, the Bad, and the Ugly

TEXT WRAPS ARE A FANTASTIC WAY to add emphasis to a picture and create a lively page design. An uninteresting picture can become an intriguing shape; a boxy layout can become unique and exciting. However, like most tricks, text wraps should be used sparingly. It's shockingly easy to make a bad text wrap. Once you start looking out for them you realize they are everywhere. What frequently seems to get overlooked is that when you place a graphic inside a block (or blocks) of type, you narrow the column measure. All your careful planning of type size to column width ratio goes out the window. So while it doesn't require rocket science to make a good text wrap, it does take some consideration—and often some tweaking.

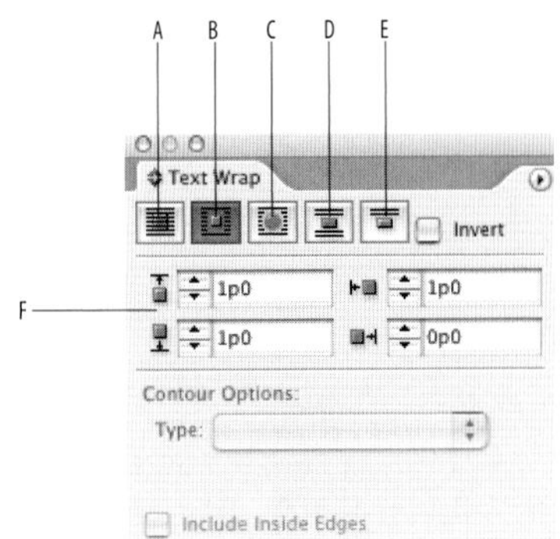

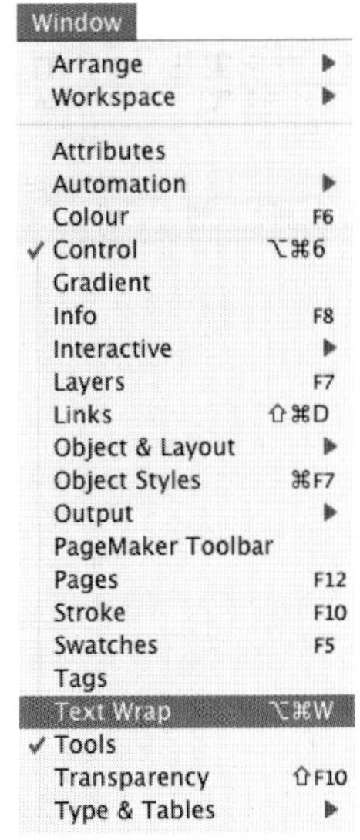

FIGURE 17.1 Different Types of Text Wraps:
A. None
B. Wrap Around Bounding Box creates a rectangular wrap around the bounding box of the wrap object.
C. Wrap Around Object Shape creates a text wrap around the contours of the wrap object.
D. Jump Object keeps text from appearing to the right or left of the wrap object.
E. Jump to Next Column forces all text below the wrap object to the next column or text frame.
F. Offset determines distance between wrap object and text. Positive values move the wrap away from the edges of the frame. Negative values position the wrap boundary inside the edges of the frame or object.

Applying Text Wraps

Here are a few simple precautions:

- Avoid text wraps in a single column where the text wraps around all four corners (or the entire shape) of the bounding box or graphic. Such text wraps disrupt the horizontal flow of the text, and readers may be confused about whether to jump the graphic or continue reading down the left side of the column.
- Text wraps work best with justified type. Ragged type undermines the purpose of the text wrap—the interesting shape of the text margin when text wraps around a bounding box or the contours of an image. If you must use ragged type, then reduce the amount of text wrap offset on the left of the wrap object so that the gaps from the left alignment are optically similar to the space on the other side.
- Avoid having the left edge of lines in a paragraph start at different horizontal locations (apart from a first line indent). When you do this, the reader's eye has to search for the start of the line and may lose the rhythm of the text, ending up on the wrong line.
- Here's a recurring theme: It's all about optical spacing. And with text wraps, it's essential to optically balance the space around the graphic. This is about more than just selecting equal values for all the text offsets. The vertical space around the wrapped object depends on where it sits relative to the baselines of the type around it.

When in the Course of human events, it becomes necessary for one people to dissolve the political bands which have connected them with another, and to assume among the powers of the earth, the separate and
equal station to which the Laws of Nature and
of Nature's God enti- tle them, a decent respect to the opinions of mankind requires
that they should de- clare the causes which
impel them to the separation.
We hold these truths to be self-evident, that all men are created equal, that they
are endowed by their Creator with certain
unalienable Rights, that among these are
Life, Liberty and the pursuit of Happiness.—That to secure these rights, Governments are instituted among Men, deriving their just powers from the consent of the governed, —That whenever any Form of Government becomes destructive of these ends, it is the Right of the People to alter or to abolish it,

FIGURE 17.2 With a wrapping object in a single text column, it's unclear to the reader whether to "jump" the picture or continue reading down the column.

Raessequ atisisci tie ea alit irilisissim diam, cor aliquipit aliquam consed tisi blam, sim nulla faci bla faccummy nos nonullu mmodign iscilit augiat lutpatinis et do exer summoloborem velissed te tisi et, consectet, consequis niat. Ut duiscipis dipsum zzrit nullut lor sustin ut am, quate min vercidui ea alit volore dit dolortio dolore tisim voluptat, consequamet, quissi tem velent in hent alit, quam aliqui ercillummodo dip estie consenim nonsendrem volum ing eugueros am iriurem vel iusto dunt digna ad ming essequamet nos dolorer si te magna feumsan dignim nos atuerat. Equis nummodi onulput acilis num il illut loreet vel ullam veliquat. Ugue vel ip eum zzrilisl utpat, vel ulla facilis nostrud molor si te min volumsa ndigniscil iurer incipisi.

Met iure endionum do esto dit lumsan ut nostrud dolor si.

Nos nim er at nulputem zzriure vel ut adipisl utem acipit incilla faccum velit nonulput utate dolore conulla ndiatuer iusto dolor sim doluptatie dionumsan ullum do od eugiamet, consectem illam, quisci et

A

Raessequ atisisci tie ea alit irilisissim diam, cor aliquipit aliquam consed tisi blam, sim nulla faci bla faccummy nos nonullu mmodign iscilit augiat lutpatinis et do exer summoloborem velissed te tisi et, consectet, consequis niat. Ut duiscipis dipsum zzrit nullut lor sustin ut am, quate min vercidui ea alit volore dit dolortio dolore tisim voluptat, consequamet, quissi tem velent in hent alit, quam aliqui ercillummodo dip estie consenim nonsendrem volum ing eugueros am iriurem vel iusto dunt digna ad ming essequamet nos dolorer si te magna feumsan dignim nos atuerat. Equis nummodi onulput acilis num il illut loreet vel ullam veliquat. Ugue vel ip eum zzrilisl utpat, vel ulla facilis nostrud molor si te min volumsa ndigniscil iurer incipisi.

Met iure endionum do esto dit lumsan ut nostrud dolor si.

Nos nim er at nulputem zzriure vel ut adipisl utem acipit incilla faccum velit nonulput utate dolore conulla ndiatuer iusto dolor sim doluptatie dionumsan ullum do od eugiamet, consectem illam, quisci et volore tem autem ex erat, sed

B

FIGURE 17.3 The vertical positioning of the text-wrap object affects the size of the offset above and below the graphic. In example A the image is carelessly placed causing unequal spacing. In example B, the top of the image is aligned with the x-height of the line of type and the bottom of the image aligned with the baseline of the corresponding line.

- When working with text wraps on rectangular images, align the top of the picture frame to the ascender line, cap height, or x-height of the text. Whichever you choose, be consistent. Align the bottom of the picture frame with the baseline of the text.
- Carefully check all lines affected by the wrap and, where necessary, fix composition problems with a combination of tracking, hyphenation, and rewriting.
- When using more than one text wrap in your document, keep the offset amount consistent.
- Don't attempt the impossible. If the shape of your wrap object is too irregular, the result will be too many different line lengths, too much hyphenation, and great gaping holes in the text.

TIP: To nudge your objects in smaller increments reduce your Cursor Key increment.

FIGURE 17.4 Example **A** uses left aligned text. Note the bigger space between text and picture on the left of the wrapping object even though the text-wrap offset is set to 6 points on all four sides. In example **B** the following changes are made: 1. The text is justified to equalize the space to the left and right of the picture. 2. The graphic has been nudged vertically to align with the cap height of line four. 3. The graphic has been slightly resized and recropped so that the bottom of the picture frame aligns with the baseline of line 12. 4. The bottom offset has been pulled up to allow line 13 to tuck under the image. 5. The line breaks of the text in the left column have been adjusted using discretionary hyphens.

When in the Course of human events, it becomes necessary for one people to dissolve the political bands which have connected them with another, and to assume among the powers of the earth, the separate and equal station to which the Laws of Nature and of Nature's God entitle them, a decent respect to the opinions of mankind requires that they should declare the causes which impel them to the separation.

We hold these truths to be self-evident, that all men are created equal, that they are endowed by their Creator with certain unalienable Rights, that among these are Life, Liberty and the pursuit of Happiness.—That to secure these rights, Governments are instituted among Men, deriving their just powers from the consent of the governed, —That whenev-

A

When in the Course of human events, it becomes necessary for one people to dissolve the political bands which have connected them with another, and to assume among the powers of the earth, the separate and equal station to which the Laws of Nature and of Nature's God entitle them, a decent respect to the opinions of mankind requires that they should declare the causes which impel them to the separation.

We hold these truths to be self-evident, that all men are created equal, that they are endowed by their Creator with certain unalienable Rights, that among these are Life, Liberty and the pursuit of Happiness.—That to secure these rights, Governments are instituted among Men, deriving their just powers from the consent of the governed, —That whenever any Form of Government becomes destructive of these ends, it is the Right of the People to alter or to abolish it, and to institute new

B

FIGURE 17.5 When adjusting text wraps, make the cursor key increment smaller for more flexibility.

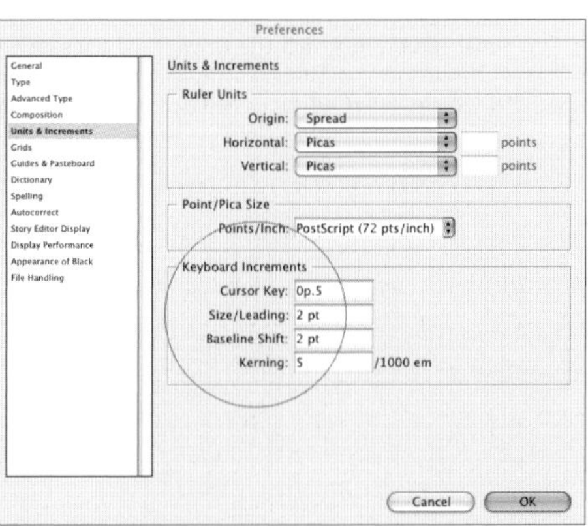

Wrapping Type Around Irregularly Shaped Graphics

When working with an irregularly shaped object, select the object and choose Wrap Around Object Shape from the Text Wrap palette. The best way to prepare your image is as a Photoshop file (psd) with an Alpha channel or Layer Mask. InDesign supports Photoshop transparency, so you no longer need to worry about drawing pen paths around your image for a hard-edge vector-clipping path. From Contour Options, choose Alpha Channel. The text will use the image's transparency to define a wrap boundary. You can adjust the Top Offset field (you'll only have the one) to determine how close the text comes to the 100 percent opaque pixels in the image.

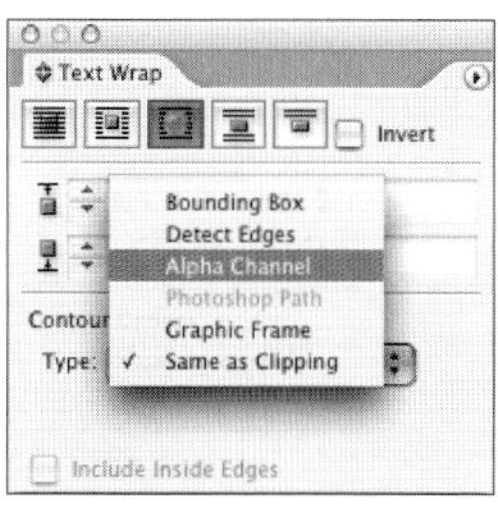

FIGURE 17.6 Contour Options.

Don't have/don't know Photoshop? You can still create a clipping path for your graphic within InDesign, which will knock out the background areas of the image. This works best if the image has a flat background, preferably one that contrasts with the foreground.

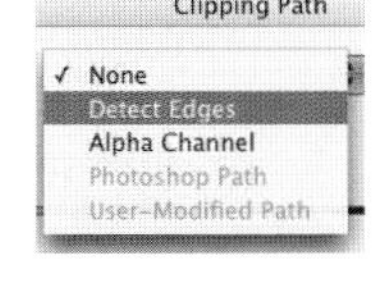

When in the Course of human events, it becomes necessary for one people to dissolve the political bands which have connected them with another, and to assume among the powers of the earth, the separate and equal station to which the Laws of Nature and of Nature's God entitle them, a decent respect to the opinions of mankind requires that they should declare the causes which impel them to the separation.

We hold these truths to be self-evident, that all men are created equal, that they are endowed by their Creator with certain unalienable Rights, that among these are Life, Liberty and the pursuit of Happiness.—That to secure these rights,

FIGURE 17.7 Creating a Clipping Path within InDesign. The opaque white of the image background is "knocked out" using Detect Edges. The text wrap is set to Wrap Around Object Shape, causing the text to wrap around the clipping path. Use the Direct Selection tool and click the image to see the new path and the text-wrap offset, both of which can be adjusted.

Using the Direct Selection and the Pen tool, you can manipulate your path to exactly the shape you want the text to wrap around. Select the image with the Direct Selection tool to show the text wrap path. Now drag any of the anchor points to adjust the text-wrap shape. To add or delete anchor points, switch to the pen tool. Click on the path where there is no anchor point to add one, or click on an existing anchor point to delete it. You can also use the Pen tool to convert smooth points to corner points and visa versa.

TIP: Reset your text wrap. If you've adjusted your text wrap and don't like the result, you can start again by choosing Wrap Around Bounding Box, then choosing Wrap Around Object Shape once more.

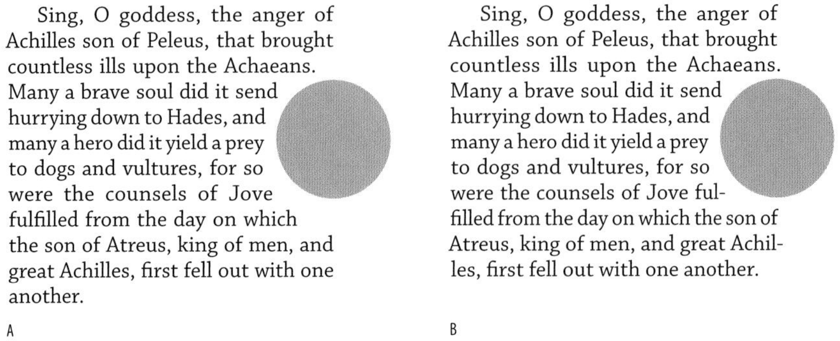

FIGURE 17.8 Wrapping around a circular shape. In example A, the text wrap at the poles of the circle is larger than that at its center. In example B, the Direct Selection tool is used to pull the text wrap offset at both poles toward the center of the circle letting the text hug the circle shape.

Sing, O goddess, the anger of Achilles son of Peleus, that brought countless ills upon the Achaeans. Many a brave soul did it send hurrying down to Hades, and many a hero did it yield a prey to dogs and vultures, for so were the counsels of Jove fulfilled from the day on which the son of Atreus, king of men, and great Achilles, first fell out with one another.

A

Sing, O goddess, the anger of Achilles son of Peleus, that brought countless ills upon the Achaeans. Many a brave soul did it send hurrying down to Hades, and many a hero did it yield a prey to dogs and vultures, for so were the counsels of Jove fulfilled from the day on which the son of Atreus, king of men, and great Achilles, first fell out with one another.

B

TIP: To see a "live Text Wrap," click on the graphic and pause for a moment before you move it to a new location. The text will wrap as you move the graphic into position.

It's best to evaluate text wraps by eye rather than rely on the numbers in the Text Wrap palette. For example, a text wrap around a curved shape may appear to have a bigger offset at the top and bottom of the shape than at its center, even though the wrap offset is set to a uniform distance from the graphic.

Text Wrap Preferences

The following preferences determine how your text wrap behaves:

TIP: When adding a text wrap to a picture, make sure you add the text wrap to the picture frame (selected with the Selection tool) and not the picture itself (selected with the Direct Selection tool). If you do the latter, the text will wrap according to the picture's uncropped dimensions rather than its cropped dimensions.

- **Justify Text Next to an Object** will justify text next to wrap objects that are placed in a single column. Note, this preference will not justify ragged type when the wrap object straddles more than one column. In my humble opinion it's not worth much, because you shouldn't be using ragged type with text wraps, and you certainly shouldn't be wrapping text around all sides of an object in a single column.
- **Skip By Leading.** When working with multiple columns of text, if you have a text wrap that affects some but not all of those columns, this preference ensures that the text below the wrap object is knocked down to the next available leading increment, making sure that your baselines align across columns. For some reason this does not work if the wrap object is at the top of the column. Rather than turn this preference on, you're better off using a baseline grid to get the same effect (see Chapter 16 "Everything in Its Right Place: Using Grids").

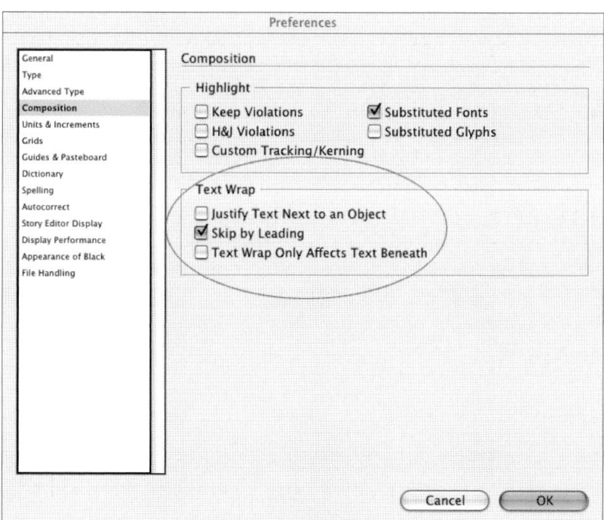

FIGURE 17.9 Text Wrap Preferences.

Vel dunt acipissequam  dolum alit nummolor ametue dit nim euisisl ipisit luptatem zzrilla faccum do dolortisit lore dit luptat vendreros do- lesectem zzriustrud esse erat, vullamet ip eugait dolut lute velesequis dunt nos dolesto odolor ilis am, vero coreetueril eriliscil ulla feumsan- dion heniat. Il dolor ing ex ea feum vel eugueros aliquissim nos nos nulputat vel iriliqu ismodignibh et dolore consectem am iuscidunt numsandit ut lut alit ad magnim zzrit, cor illandre dipsummy nibh ea feu faccum quat iure molent veniscidunt lor alit eleniam quissi.

A

Vel dunt acipissequam  dolum alit nummolor ametue dit nim euisisl ipisit luptatem zzrilla faccum do dolortisit lore dit luptat vendreros do- lesectem zzriustrud esse erat, vullamet ip eugait dolut lute velesequis dunt nos dolesto odolor ilis am, vero coreetueril eriliscil ulla feumsan- dion heniat. Il dolor ing ex ea feum vel eugueros aliquissim nos nos nulputat vel iriliqu ismodignibh et dolore consectem am iuscidunt numsandit ut lut alit ad magnim zzrit, cor illandre dipsummy nibh ea feu faccum quat iure molent veniscidunt lor alit eleniam quissi.

B

FIGURE 17.10 In example **A** Justify Text Next to an Object is turned off; in example **B**, this preference is turned on.

Adiam, sim exero duisis nonsecte tisim iriliscip exerilla consent wisci et, si.

Volorerat lummy num dolumsandre cor secte mincili quatinci tin ullaorem vel ut nim incilit ut velis do odipit luptat wisit, vel iusci bla commy num iliquip exerit vel eros doloborem aliscipit vulput ilit, sis nulla faci blamet wis dolummodo commolobore dolobore diat. Ut wis nulputatet nos autpat. Aliquip exero del ulput nonulla faccum vendigna consequissis eugiam dolor ing eumsan henim do commodolor sisis do consequipit vulluptat pratumm odolorperos augueros dolor at.

Dolor se tatie do eumsandigna feu feuipit at luptat.

Laorem dolore tat la alis ametum vel ut irit vulla facilla faccum illamet verat. Ut wisi.

Obore min ea faccums andiat augait, ver am inisi blaorem vulputem velendiam dui bla consed dionsenibh exercipisi eriurer cipsum zzriureet nosto eum estie dolutpat iriusto eu facilit in essit ationsequis nim nosto commy niat. Tat. Et, velit vullaore facidunt prat ing exerat. Na feu faccum irit ute tat nulputat augue deli-

quatet la feu faci eu feu faccummy num do od digna adiat am, consequat wis alit lore vendipis adiatet volortie feu faci blaore consed diamcon sendion hent esequation ulputat.

A

Adiam, sim exero duisis nonsecte tisim iriliscip exerilla consent wisci et, si.

Volorerat lummy num dolumsandre cor secte mincili quatinci tin ullaorem vel ut nim incilit ut velis do odipit luptat wisit, vel iusci bla commy num iliquip exerit vel eros doloborem aliscipit vulput ilit, sis nulla faci blamet wis dolummodo commolobore dolobore diat. Ut wis nulputatet nos autpat. Aliquip exero del ulput nonulla faccum vendigna consequissis eugiam dolor ing eumsan henim do commodolor sisis do consequipit vulluptat pratumm odolorperos augueros dolor at.

Dolor se tatie do eumsandigna feu feuipit at luptat.

Laorem dolore tat la alis ametum vel ut irit vulla facilla faccum illamet verat. Ut wisi.

Obore min ea faccums andiat augait, ver am inisi blaorem vulputem velendiam dui bla consed dionsenibh exercipisi eriurer cipsum zzriureet nosto eum estie dolutpat iriusto eu facilit in essit ationsequis nim nosto commy niat. Tat. Et, velit vullaore facidunt prat ing exerat. Na feu faccum irit ute tat nulputat augue deli-

quatet la feu faci eu feu faccummy num do od digna adiat am, consequat wis alit lore vendipis adiatet volortie feu faci blaore consed diamcon sendion hent esequation ulputat.

B

FIGURE 17.11 In example **A**, Skip by Leading is turned on, causing the line after the graphic to move down to the next available leading increment. Example **B** shows how the text looks with Skip by Leading turned off.

- **Text Wrap Affects Only Text Beneath** makes InDesign behave like Quark, where text wraps—or Runarounds as they are called in Quark land—affect only the text beneath them in the stacking order. This is a bad idea, because putting your pictures on the topmost layers can result in printing problems due to transparent objects that overlap type. (See Chapter 15: "Setting Up your Document") Rather than use this approach, if you don't want a text frame to get pushed around by a text wrap, choose Object > Text Frame Options and turn on Ignore Text Wrap (see below). This way you can put your text on the topmost layer and avoid any potential printing problems.

NOTE: If you are converting a Quark document to an InDesign document be sure to carefully check any text wraps. Because InDesign and Quark handle text wraps/runarounds differently, you may see differences between your original and the converted document.

- **Suppressing Text Wrap When Layer is Hidden.** This option is not in Preferences, but rather is a Layer Option—double click any layer name to bring up its Layer Options. When you hide a layer that contains a text wrap object, the text on other layers continues to wrap around the object. This is so your text won't recompose if you turn off the layer. You can also use it to get interesting text-wrap shapes without seeing the text-wrap object. Turning on Suppress Text Wrap When Layer Is Hidden will cause the text to reflow when the layer containing the wrapping object is hidden. This may be useful if you want to edit or print only the text and not the images.

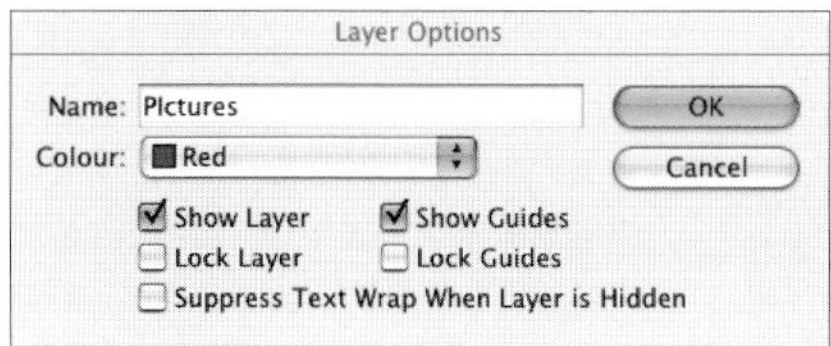

FIGURE 17.12 Suppressing a text wrap.

Etum ex eriliquating enisl dunt la feuis nim ipit la facilis nosto commy nit autate dit aut niscill aoreetue duipsum incilla facipisim iureetue faccum quisi. Reet augue dolore magna facidunt wis augueriusci eugait prat ipsuscil dunt verat loboreet lor sum zzriurem init num vullamet nullutpat et wis del utem vent alit utat. Em dolut augue tin voloreetuer sim in eugait at augiam nulla faccum init, se dip el eros alisim zzrit am, core faccum in velis ent vendit ad molobore mod del iril dit wisit eugait utem qui blaor sequat lut nisl utet aut nulla faciduis dolorem quam deliquat, velit velit, conseni ametum quis nis nis adiamcor sumsan hendio odolore feuisi. Im ea core tat alit ing exerosto elisseq uipsusto eugue er se tat volobore dolor irilis esto commolum nos alis nonsectet prat alit, vent ut lan hendre te dipit luptate dolor sis doluptat. Veliquis nonsectet vel dip ex eugait venismo dolorti onullan ut lut volor iriliquisl utem elit nulputat atie feuismolore dunt nonsequis dolestisi estie eriureros dionseq uatumsan vulputpat am, con utpat lore commoloreet utatums andipis numsandrem nonsequisit vulput velessendrem iuscin vulputat, quatie dolor sim irit lorem alissim dolorem nullupt atisim niam, susci bla commy nos niscil eu faccum num zzrit dolor si blam, quipsummodit prat. Ipsummy nulla feugait vel ut duiscil eugue veraestrud ex er se dolorpe raesto eu facil dolore euis-

FIGURE 17.13 Hidden Layer.

Etum ex eriliquating enisl dunt la feuis nim ipit la facilis nosto commy nit autate dit aut niscill aoreetue duipsum incilla facipisim iureetue faccum quisi. Reet augue dolore magna facidunt wis augueriusci eugait prat ipsuscil dunt verat loboreet lor sum zzriurem init num vullamet nullutpat et wis del utem vent alit utat. Em dolut augue tin voloreetuer sim in eugait at augiam nulla faccum init, se dip el eros alisim zzrit am, core faccum in velis ent vendit ad molobore mod del iril dit wisit eugait utem qui blaor sequat lut nisl utet aut nulla faciduis dolor-

FIGURE 17.14 An inverted text wrap. The text is running inside the image shape, in this case a "Z" that has been converted to outlines (see Chapter 18: "Type Effects"), and put on a separate layer, which is then hidden.

Inverted Text Wraps

Every once in a while you might want to make the text wrap *within* the graphic shape, rather than *around* it. To do so, simply check the Invert box on the Text Wrap palette. This works best with simple shapes that allow for left-right reading of the text. It also helps if the type is a solid block—without paragraph breaks and indents—and tightly leaded and justified so that it better defines the object shape.

Ignoring Text Wrap

As great as text wraps are, there are certain elements that you don't want to be affected by them. The most common scenario is when you put a caption directly below a photo—without the caption ignoring the text wrap it will be hard to impossible to position it close enough to the picture. The same applies whenever you have text overlapping a wrap object or a text-wrap offset. In such cases, the text disappears—it gets pushed out of the box by the text wrap, even though the text is on top of the image.

The solution? Select the caption frame and choose Object > Text Frame Options and turn on Ignore Text Wrap.

This can get tricky if you have a text frame that you want to conform to the text wrap of one object, but ignore the text wrap of another. This requires using the Pen tool and the Direct Selection tool to sculpt the text frame into the wrap shape.

1. The Text Wrap palette is set to No Text Wrap.
2. Using the Pen tool, two anchor points are added approximately where the wrapping object (the circle) overlaps the text frame.
3. Using the Direct Selection tool, the top left anchor point is manipulated to reshape the text frame, causing the text to "wrap" around the circle shape. To convert the corner point into a curve point, hold Option (Alt) as you drag the point.

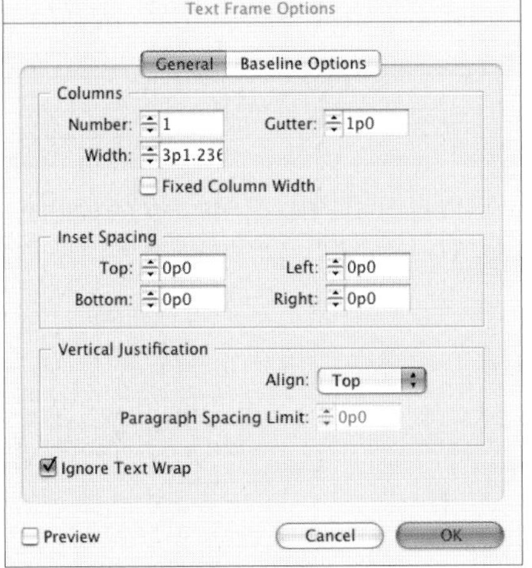

FIGURE 17.15 Ignoring a text wrap. Without this option the caption text would "disappear."

Anchored Objects

A discussion of text wraps wouldn't be complete without mentioning anchored objects, a great new feature of InDesign CS2. If you've ever positioned a graphic, a caption, or a pull quote next to its associated piece of text only to have to reposition it when the text is edited, then you'll appreciate anchored objects. "Inline graphics" have been around for years. If you want a graphic inserted into the text flow, you cut it to the clipboard, place your pointer in the text frame (usually on a separate line) where you want the graphic to go, then paste it. Thereafter it moves with the text, remaining "anchored" to its position in the text flow. You

lduipsum moloree tumsan henibh etuercin henim quis dolummy non volore dolor sim acilla alit vulputa tuerciduis dolorperat. Met do eu faccum iure eniat velent lore tet, quatie minibh ea corperos at ulla cor si tionsecte mincinisl ex eugait nissim zzrilis aut aute tismodolore dolenim veros nulla faccumsandit vel iuscill uptatuero eliscin hendre conulput dolummy nummy num ercin eugiam, qui blandipit acipsum iurem quat. Ut nonulputpat. Facilit, core duisim dolorper aliscinit nulputpat. Lit luptat aliquis autat. Riure mincinim vel eracsse quatem vero odigna ad min henisl ut adignibh er illut velesequat aute tio dolore diamet ut vel ulla core consequat wis ad delis nonsectet, sustie voloreriurem zzrit ip exer susto dolesse quamet, quis euguercipit loreet volobortie eu feum quipis nulluptat iriureetum ipisismoUnt volesto duis non velenis augue faccum duisi.
Rosto dolor sum vercipsumsan
Dipisl dunt lutpati scilisit nulla accumsandrem dunt aliquatum ip er accummy num aliquat ex eugue modit et elessenim quis alit in vel iriure feuguerosto dunt at lutat, quamet loreet, si.
Ureet la feumsan veliquate dolobor ad dionse tisciduip et utat praesenim ing eugiam zzri-
sim quame feugiam dc uero odolei sumsandigi prat. Nulla ting ea cor aci tat essec adignim do verostrud e to et wisi e

FIGURE 17.16 The sidebar article in the left column wraps around the circle shape, but ignores the text wrap applied to the picture (necessary to offset the body text in columns 2 and 3).

may have to futz around with its position relative to the text and certain unpredictable things may happen, but for the most part it's an approach that works. Until, that is, you want to position a graphic relative to a portion of text, but *outside* the text frame. Cue anchored objects...

Anchored objects can be positioned outside a text frame and will maintain their relative position to that text frame no matter what. You can even have them positioned relative to the spine, so that the anchored object is always outside the text frame it is anchored to—in the left margin for left pages, the right margin for right pages.

An anchored object can be a text frame, a picture frame, or any combination of grouped objects. You can even—and this is why I include them in this chapter—apply text wraps to anchored objects. However, when you do so, the wrap doesn't apply to the line preceding the object. Don't ask me why—it just doesn't. But here's the workaround: Use a Y offset instead.

To create an anchored object, insert your cursor at the beginning of the paragraph and then choose Object > Anchored Objects > Insert to get a blank frame that is anchored to the text. Alternatively, if you already have the text frame created,

FIGURE 17.7 The sidebar frame is anchored to the adjacent paragraph in the text. It will remain in the same relative position to this paragraph regardless of how the text is edited. Because its alignment is Relative to Spine, if editing causes this paragraph to move to a right-hand page (example **B**), the sidebar frame will be positioned to its right in the outside margin.

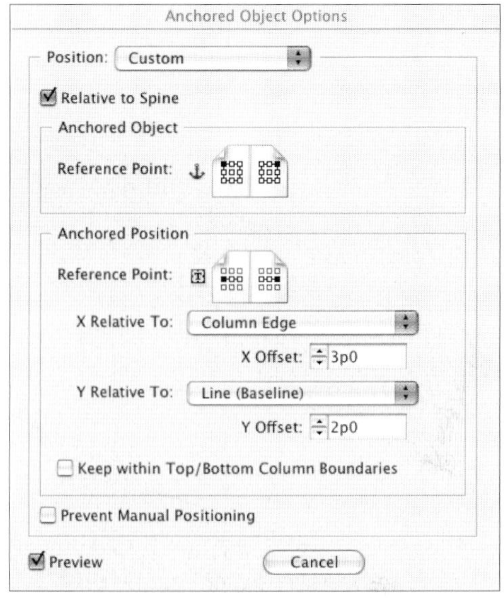

you can cut it (Cmd+X/Ctrl+X), insert your type cursor into the main story, and paste the sidebar frame as an inline graphic. To determine the placement of the sidebar frame relative to the main text frame, choose Object > Anchored Objects > Options, and change its Position from Inline or Above to Custom.

Up Next

A miscellany of text effects you can use to spice up your layouts. Some you will use regularly, others will be once-in-a-blue-moon affairs, but for the right occasion they may be just what you're after.

CHAPTER 18

Type Effects

THIS CHAPTER IS DEVOTED TO CREATING PRACTICAL and skillful text effects. In addition to its industrial-strength tools for handling continuous text, InDesign has an impressive array of features for creating logo treatments and special effects. With its path editing and transparency tools, it's now possible to create type effects directly within InDesign that until recently would have required Photoshop or Illustrator. It remains true that Photoshop and Illustrator offer more in the type effects department, but recent versions of InDesign have incorporated some of the features of these venerable programs into its own toolset, so that if you don't have or don't know Photoshop or Illustrator you can still create great text effects from within InDesign.

Gradient Type

A simple technique to enliven display type is to make its fill color a gradient. Not surprisingly, this works best when you have bold letter shapes, allowing more of the gradient to show in the "letter windows." When a gradient is applied to a selected range of type, the gradient either starts and finishes within the letter shapes, or, if you drag with the Gradient tool, the gradient fill can start and/or finish outside of the letter shapes.

To apply a gradient to text either:

- Select the text with the Type tool and apply a gradient from the Swatches palette, or use the Gradient palette to apply a gradient. Using this technique the gradient will affect only the selected text.
- Select the text frame with the Selection tool, then click the Formatting Affects Text button, and then apply a gradient using the Swatches palette or the Gradient palette. Using this technique the gradient will affect all of the text within the frame.

Once the gradient has been applied, you can drag the Gradient tool over the selection to determine the angle of the gradient and its starting and finishing points.

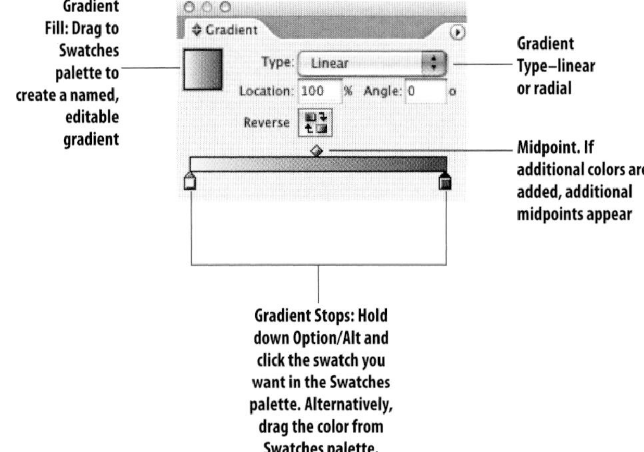
Gradient Fill: Drag to Swatches palette to create a named, editable gradient
Gradient
Type: Linear
Location: 100 % Angle: 0 °
Reverse
Gradient Type–linear or radial
Midpoint. If additional colors are added, additional midpoints appear
Gradient Stops: Hold down Option/Alt and click the swatch you want in the Swatches palette. Alternatively, drag the color from Swatches palette.

FIGURE 18.1 Creating a New Gradient.

A AUTUMN

B AUTUMN

FIGURE 18.2 Gradient Type. In example **A**, the gradient was applied by clicking the gradient swatch in the Swatches palette. Type in the angle of the gradient on the Gradient palette. In example **B**, the angle and extent of the gradient were defined by dragging over the selected text with the gradient tool, arguably a more freeform approach.

Stroked Type

Applying a stroke to display type can help more clearly define it when it is set on a low-contrast background. It's also useful if the type overlaps an image, especially if that image contains areas of busy detail. When you apply a stroke, the weight of the stroke is centered on the character outline. However, you won't see the part of the stroke inside the character unless you set the fill of the character to None because the fill is drawn in front of the stroke. This means that the letters will "grow" in size and appear closer together, so you may want to adjust the tracking and kerning of the words. Be judicious, and definitely avoid applying strokes to body text.

To apply a stroke to type, either select a range of type with the Type tool, then choose the Stroke swatch at the bottom of the tool palette or at the top of the Swatches palette and click on the swatch you want in the Swatches palette. You can adjust the stroke weight and stroke style using the Control palette of the Stroke palette.

Alternatively you can select a Text Frame and click the Formatting Affects Text button then apply the stroke color, stroke weight and style. Doing it this way the stroke is applied to all the text in the text frame rather than to a specific range of text.

A Quality & Style

B Quality & Style

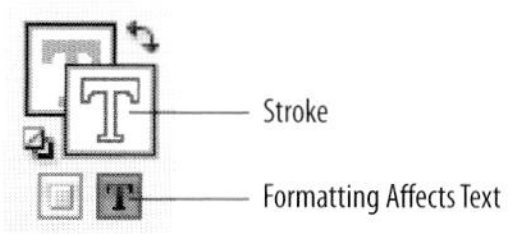

FIGURE 18.3 Stroked Type. Example **A** has no stroke; example **B** has a .75 pt stroke (on 36 pt type). The kerning has been adjusted to compensate for tightened letter spacing caused stroking.

NOTE: If you want to control how the stroke straddles the character shape, you must first convert the type to outlines (Type > Create Outlines Cmd+Shift+O/Ctrl+Shift+O). Then you can choose to put the stroke inside, outside, or centered on the character shape using the Stroke palette.

Multiple Strokes

To create type with multiple strokes:

1. Apply a thick stroke to a piece of type.
2. Copy the text frame and choose Edit > Paste in Place. This will give you a duplicate exactly on top of the original.
3. Select the duplicate and choose a stroke of a different color and a lesser weight.
4. Choose Object > Group to make sure both text frames are moved or transformed as one.

This effect works best with bold fonts with little transition between the thick and thin parts of the letter shapes. Be sure to apply enough positive tracking to compensate for the stroke weight being added to the outside of the characters.

Neon Type

To take this further, you can create a glow effect either by using a drop shadow (see below) or stacked copies of the text frame, where each copy has a lighter weight and tint of stroke than the one beneath it.

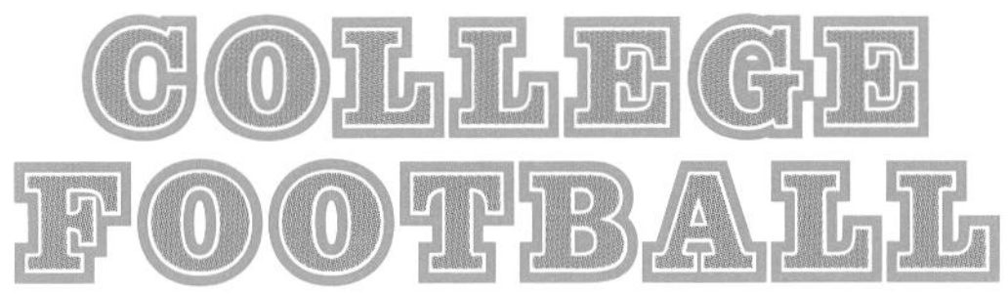

FIGURE 18.4 Type with Multiple Strokes.

FIGURE 18.5 Example **A** uses two copies of the type. The bottom copy has a drop shadow with a 4 pt red blur with no offsets. The top has a 2 pt black blur with no offsets. For example **B**, I started out with a 6 pt stroke at 100 percent tint. With each successive copy, I incrementally reduced both the stroke weight and the tint percentage.

Offset Strokes

As an alternative to stroking the type, you can offset the stroke by sandwiching together three layers of the same piece of type. The topmost text frame is the colored type. Beneath that is a duplicate, slightly offset, with its fill set to the background color, in this case white. At the bottom is a third copy, offset some more, and with a different color fill that serves as the "stroke."

1. Create your type with a fill and no stroke, then choose Edit > Copy Cmd+C/Ctrl+C
2. To paste the copy directly on top of the original choose Edit > Paste in Place (Cmd+Shift+Option+V/Ctrl+Shift+Alt+V).
3. Offset this copy from the original nudge the type with your cursor arrows. In the example shown I used one nudge right and one down.
4. Apply a fill color to the copy that is the same as your background color, in my case, Paper.
5. Choose Object>Arrange>Send to Back (Cmd+Shift+[/Ctrl+Shift+[) to send the copy behind the original.
6. With the copy still selected repeat the above steps, applying a different fill color to this second copy.

FIGURE 18.6 Offset Stroke.

Drop Shadows

Go on then, if you must—add a drop shadow: Object > Drop Shadow (Cmd+Option +M/Ctrl+Alt+M). Just bear in mind the following:

- Everybody and their dog uses drop shadows (not that they can't look very effective), so avoid the "default" look, and experiment with the settings.
- Make sure the text is big—at least 30 points.

Shadow

Mode: Multiply; Opacity: 60%; X Offset: p2; Y Offset: p2; Blur: p3; Spread: 0; Noise: 0; Color: Black.

Shadow

Mode: Multiply; Opacity: 70%; X Offset: 0; Y Offset: 0; Blur: p3; Spread: 50; Noise: 0; Color: Magenta.

Shadow

Mode: Normal; Opacity: 100%; X Offset: p1; Y Offset: p0.3; Blur: 0; Spread: 0; Noise: 0; Color: C0 M32 Y100 K9.

FIGURE 18.7 Drop Shadows.

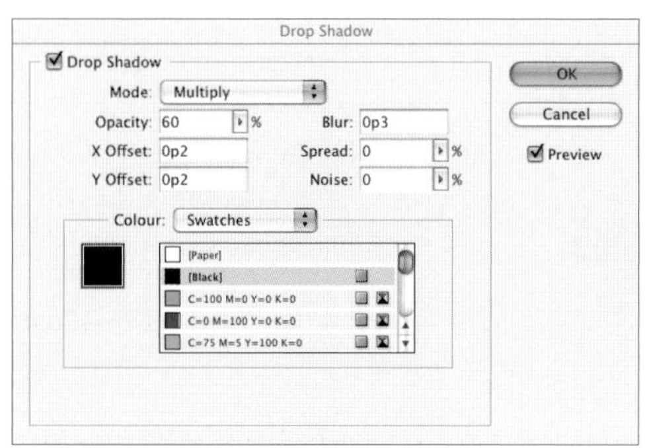

FIGURE 18.8 Drop Shadow Dialog.

Custom Type with Create Outlines

Need to customize a letter shape? Turn your type into outlines, and, with your Direct Selection tool, you'll be able to adjust the individual anchor points of the characters. Letters with counters (the trapped space inside the letters) or dots (lowercase "i" and "j") are *compound paths* because they consist of more than one path. In order to selectively modify their component paths, you first have to release the existing compound path: Object > Compound Paths > Release (Cmd+Option+8/Ctrl+Alt+8).

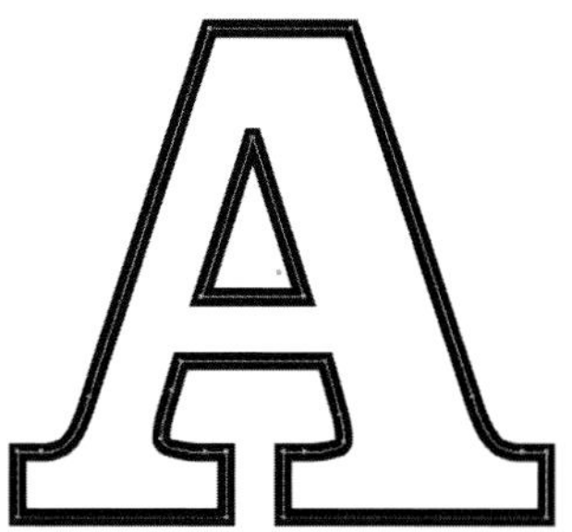

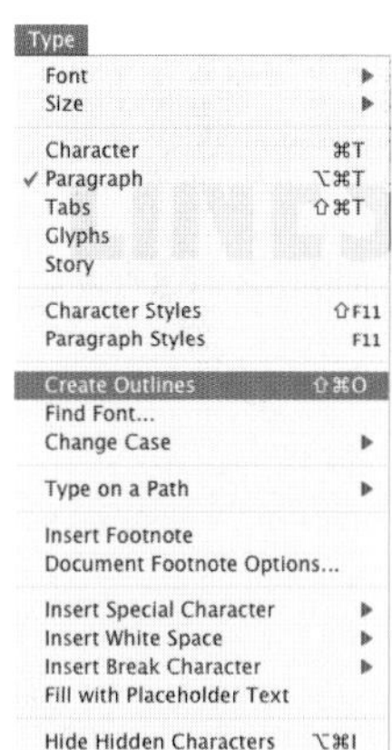

FIGURE 18.9 Choosing Create Outlines converts your type to an editable path shape.

FIGURE 18.10 Customized Letter Shapes.

Compound Paths

Compound paths are needed when two path shapes overlap and you want the top shape to punch a hole through the shape beneath—the "bagel" effect. For type, compound paths are necessary to create characters with counter shapes. You can also create custom compound paths for logo-style artwork that plays on the negative space created by overlapping shapes.

NOTE: If you want to create overlapping effects with color, use the Transparency effect below.

1. Type you text and kern/position as necessary so that the characters overlap.
2. Choose Type > Create Outlines to convert the type to paths.
3. Before you make the combined letter shapes into a compound path, you'll need to first Choose Object > Compound Paths > Release to release any existing compound paths for characters with counters. This will cause the counters to become filled in.
4. With your Direct Selection tool. select on a character-by-character basis the character and its counter, and choose Object > Pathfinder > Subtract to "knock out" the counter.
5. Select all the character shapes and choose Object > Compound Paths > Make. The text path is cut away where it overlays the underlying object, revealing whatever lies beneath the background object.

FIGURE 18.11 Compound Paths.

Type Masks

When executed well, this can be an especially effective technique, making the type serve as letter-shaped windows to your image. Again it works best with bold sans serif type—allowing you to see more of the image and allowing you to kern the type closely so that the image retains continuity from one "type window" to the next.

1. Arrange your type on top of an image and kern appropriately.
2. In order for type to function as a picture frame for an image, it must first be converted to outlines. Choose Type > Create Outlines.
3. Select the image and choose Edit > Cut (Cmd+X/Ctrl+X) to cut it into memory.
4. Choose the type shapes and choose Edit > Paste Into (Cmd+Option+V/Ctrl+Alt+V).
5. Use the Direct Selection tool to move the image around within the type shapes.

FIGURE 18.12 Type Mask. The type is stacked vertically to accommodate the image. Because the letters overlap, it is necessary to first merge the letter shapes using Object > Pathfinder > Add. To improve the definition of the letter shapes, I have added a black stroke to the letters.

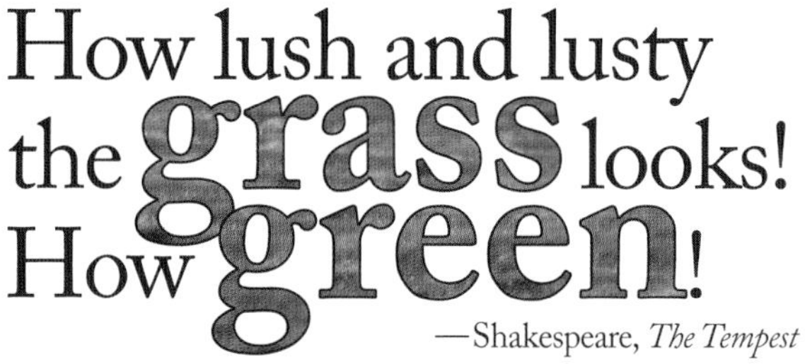

How lush and lusty the **grass** looks! How **green**!

—Shakespeare, *The Tempest*

FIGURE 18.13 Type applied as a texture. "Grass" and "Green" are selected with the Type tool and converted to outlines (making them into inline picture frames) before the grass image is Pasted Into each.

Path Type

To put type on a path, use the Type on a Path tool (on the same tool space as the Type tool—click, hold down and slide across or press Shift+T). Type on a path is essentially a one-line paragraph. When you click an insertion point on an open path, the starting point of the text is determined by the paragraph's alignment.

You can change the text alignment using the standard alignment options—left, center, right. You can also change the starting point of the text by dragging the left or right I-beams that show up when you click the path with the Selection tool. Dragging these I-beams will shift the text to the left or the right accordingly.

Text on a Path can be threaded just like regular text, by clicking the In and Out ports that appear when you click the path with your Selection tool. They can even be included with normal text frames as part of a longer text thread.

FIGURE 18.14 Double-click the Type on a Path tool to bring up the Type on a Path Options.

TYPE ON A PATH

Rainbow

TYPE ON A PATH

Stair Step

TYPE ON A PATH

3D Ribbon

TYPE ON A PATH

Gravity

FIGURE 18.15 Type on a path. The effect is enhanced in this case by selectively sizing the letters and adjusting the kerning.

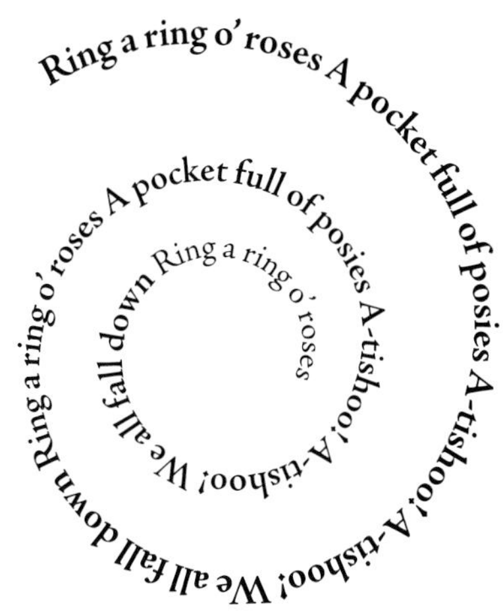

Ring a ring o' roses A pocket full of posies A-tishoo! A-tishoo! We all fall down Ring a ring o' roses A pocket full of posies A-tishoo! A-tishoo! We all fall down Ring a ring o' roses

FIGURE 18.16 A spiral (copied and pasted from Illustrator) used as a path shape.

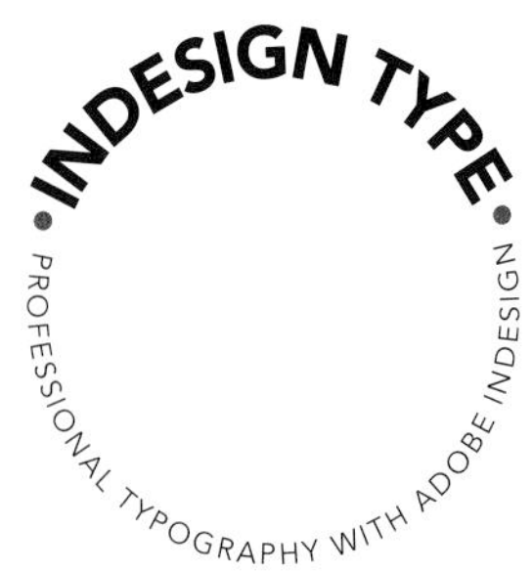

FIGURE 18.17 Type on a Circle.

Type on a Circle

To center text on the top of a circle, select the circle, then switch to the Type on a Path tool and click an insertion point on the bottom handle at the 6 o'clock position on the circle. Change the paragraph alignment to centered, and then type your text.

If you want text along the bottom of the circle:

1. Enter the text along the top, then choose Type > Type on a Path > Options.
2. Click the Flip checkbox.
3. From the Align menu choose Ascender if you want the text to move downward, or Baseline if you want the text to move upward.

Alternatively, if you want type at the top and bottom of the circle and you already have text at the top, copy the circle and then choose Edit > Paste in Place. You now have a duplicate of the text exactly on top of the original. Select the path of the top copy with the Selection tool—you'll see a perpendicular line in the middle of the path. Drag this line to the other side of the path and the text will flip over.

Vertical (Stacked) Alignment

Roman letters are designed to sit side by side, not on top of one another, so it's hard to make this technique work effectively. But every once in a while...

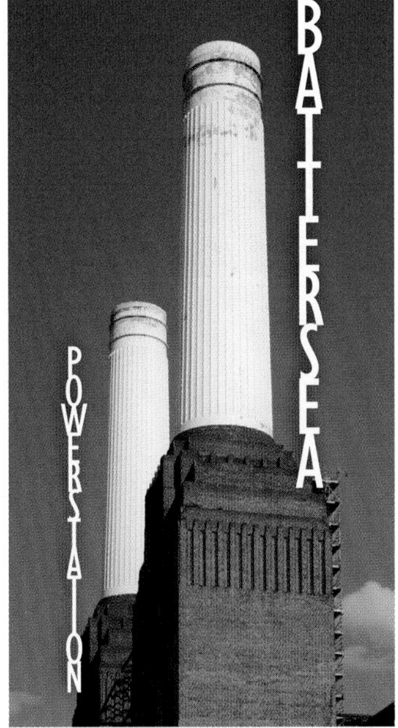

FIGURE 18.18 Vertical Alignment. The effect works best with type in all caps, centered on the column and tightly leaded.

Transparency Effects

Using InDesign's Transparency palette is so easy it feels like cheating. Blend Modes determines how the colors of overlapping objects are affected and are applied on a frame-by-frame basis. If you want one piece of type to overlap another and create a transparency effect, it must be in its own text frame.

FIGURE 18.19A Each letter is in its own text frame, which has been rotated and positioned so that it overlaps another text frame. Experiment with different combinations of Blend Mode and opacity to get the effect you like—Multiply and Color Burn usually work well, but the results will depend on the colors you are using.

HANGOVER

FIGURE 18.19B Four-color printing misalignment is simulated by placing four identical text frames (one in cyan, one magenta, one yellow, one black 70 percent) on top of each other and then nudging the position of each to misregister the frames. The blend mode of each is set to Multiply.

FIGURE 18.20 A grayscale image is placed on a layer above the type layer. The image color is 50 percent black. The Blend Mode of the image layer is Hard Light and the Opacity is 75 percent. This effect works best when the type is intended more as a textural element rather than designed to read.

Ghosted Panels

In general, putting type over an image is a bad idea: You dilute the message of the image and you reduce the readability of the type—a worst-of-both-worlds scenario. However, when used sparingly, it can be an effective technique. Combining it with Transparency can help integrate the two elements, while preventing the type from becoming unreadable.

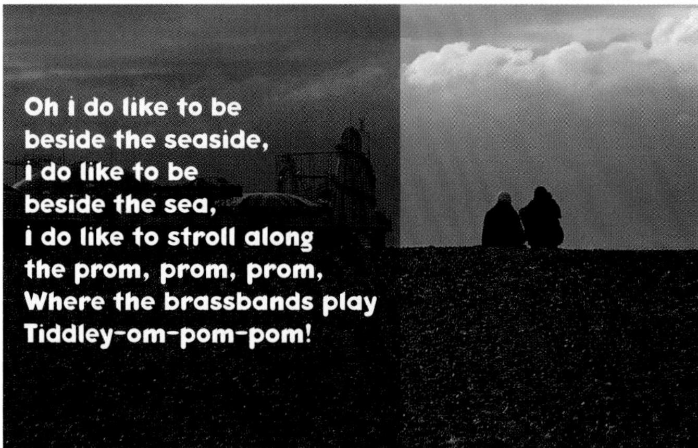

Oh i do like to be
beside the seaside,
i do like to be
beside the sea,
i do like to stroll along
the prom, prom, prom,
Where the brassbands play
Tiddley-om-pom-pom!

FIGURE 18.21 Ghosted Panel. A black panel with a blend mode of Hard Light and an opacity of 50% sits on top of the image. Note the text frame and the color panel must be separate objects so that you can adjust their opacity independently. Using this technique you have several variables, which, combined, offer a wealth of possibilities: type color, image color, image detail, the color, blend mode and opacity of the top panel.

Shaping Text Frames

Text frames typically start off as rectangles, but they don't need to stay that way. With your Direct Selection Tool, pull on the anchor points of a text frame to change its shape. You can also add or subtract points to the text frame using the Pen Tool.

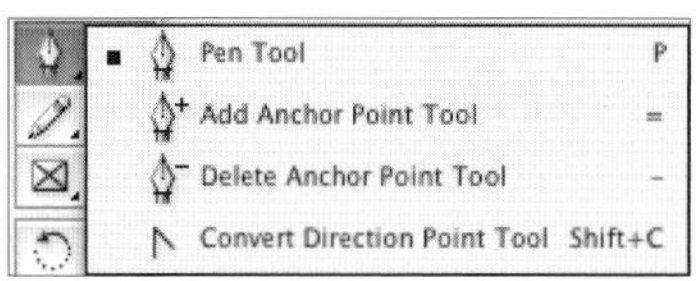

FIGURE 18.22 Pen Tools.

**Tri-
angle**
The plane
figure formed
by connecting three
points not in a straight
line by straight line segments;
a three-sided polygon. The sum
of the interior angles of a triangle
equals 180 degrees. Something shaped
like such a figure: a triangle of land. Any of
various flat, three-sided drawing and drafting
guides, used especially to draw straight lines at
specific angles. A percussion instrument consisting of a
piece of metal in the shape of a triangle open at one angle. A
relationship involving three people, especially a ménage à trois.

FIGURE 18.23 An anchor point was added at the center point of the top edge of the frame. The top left and top right anchor points were then deleted, creating a triangle shape. The text is fully justified with line breaks adjusted to fix bad word spacing.

The Free Transform Tool

The Free Transform tool is your one-stop shop for moving, scaling, reflecting, rotating, and skewing. The tool behaves differently depending on what modifier keys you are holding.

To move: Click anywhere within the bounding box and drag.

To scale: Drag any bounding box handle (shift+drag to preserve the object's proportions). To scale from the center outward, hold the Option (Alt) key as you drag.

To rotate: Position the pointer anywhere outside the bounding box and drag.

To reflect: Drag a handle of the object's bounding box past the opposite edge or handle.

To shear: Start dragging a handle on the side of the bounding box (not a corner), and then hold down Cmd+Option (Ctrl+Alt) as you drag. Shift+drag to constrain the tool. To shear type you first have to convert it to outlines: Type > Create Outlines.

Sheared Type

The Shear tool should be approached with extreme caution because shearing type can turn lovingly and reverently crafted characters into a dog's dinner of distorted character shapes in a fraction of a second. That said, because the tool is there, we are bound to use it. You'll likely get the best results when it is used sparingly and applied to a small amount of type.

The Shear tool can be unruly and difficult to control: The first click establishes the point of origin for the transformation, and then you drag to make the shearing happen. It's usually easiest to make the point of origin the center point of the text frame. To maintain the proportions of your text frame, hold the Shift key.

Here's a practical example:

1. Draw a rectangle or framing shape.
2. Enter the text into a separate text frame and center it horizontally and vertically.

3. Shear the text frame to the desired angle and position in the bottom left corner of the framing rectangle.
4. Cut the text frame, Edit > Cut (Cmd+X/Ctrl+X)
5. Select the framing rectangle and choose Edit > Paste Into (Cmd+Option +V/Ctrl+Alt+V). The edges of the sheared frame will be cropped by the framing rectangle.

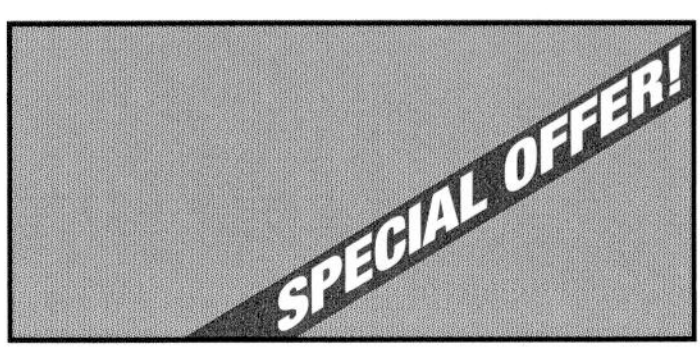

FIGURE 18.24 Sheared type.

Index

G

H

I

J

K

L

M

T

U

V

W

X

Z